THE CANNED FOODS STORE
Tacoma: 11011 Pacific Hwy. SW (581-5333)
Hours: M-Sat. 9-6; Sun. 11-5

Canned and packaged groceries are cheaper to stock than perishables—by far—and that is how this unusual outlet in an old Fred Meyer market cuts their operating costs and passes the savings on to the consumer. They also specialize in buying closeouts from manufacturers all over the United States, so you will see some labels you won't recognize unless you've lived in other parts of the country. A whole section is devoted to the big #10 cans which generally represent the biggest dollar savings. Store policy is to stay 25-40% below standard retail. **Local checks only**

CROZIER FINE FOODS, INC.
Seattle: 938 N. 200th (546-5178)
Hours: M-F 8:30-4:30

This is an outlet for a limited audience, which is just as well because Crozier is in the gourmet restaurant supply business—not the gourmet retail trade. However, if your gourmet club is considering ordering a case of truffles and 24 tins of snails, give them a call. Other savory selections include pâtés, Dijon mustard and French gherkins plus a full line of dehydrated soups and sauces. Items are fairly expensive and appeal primarily to the gourmet. You will, however, discover a few shortcuts used by restaurants among their products. It helps if you can knowledgeably discuss fine foods and will not faint—as we nearly did—at the price of a bag of dried morel mushrooms. For free delivery, there is a $50 minimum. A product list is available if you stop by the office. **Checks**

DUTTON'S
Seattle: 302 S. Spokane (622-8078)
Hours: M-Th 9-4:30; F 9-5; Sat. 10-1 (mid-June through Aug.)

Frozen fruit is available all year at Dutton's, either in individually-quick-frozen or in solid-pack cartons. Fresh fruit and some vegetables can also be purchased in season. Minimum quantity on the frozen items is 5 lbs. Only a limited selection of frozen vegetables is available. Their policy is to keep prices comparable to or below the markets, and they welcome retail trade. Savings on 5-lb. quantities of very basic items is minimal. Savings increase with larger quantities and with the more exotic items. Frozen vegetables were priced well under name brands, but not quite as low as the lowest competitive brands. A price list will be mailed to you, and orders can be placed over the phone. Prices fluctuate; check them if your list is a few months old. **Checks**

36 Food

ENER-G FOODS
Seattle: 6901 Fox S. (767-6660)
Hours: M-F 8:30-5 (call ahead)

Ener-G is in the Sam Wylde office, although their sign is on the warehouse door. If you know anyone on a special diet due to food allergies or celiac-sprue disease, this is the place to shop. Ener-G is a manufacturer of specialty foods for people who must substitute for wheat, gluten, eggs and milk. They also bake a low-protein bread which has a mere .3 grams per 2 slices. Their main products are mixes (rice mix, low-sodium mix, potato mix, etc.), but they also make pizza shells, hamburger buns, cinnamon buns and other delicacies that those of us fortunate enough to be free of food allergies take for granted. Please call for their product list. Plan to order in advance and either pick up at their office or have the items mailed. There is no minimum order. Ener-G is becoming known internationally for its products. **Checks**

GOLDEN AMERICAN
Seattle: 2142 8th N., Suite 205 (284-1139; 1-800-562-2112)

This discount program is for persons 55 years and older who can dine out between 4 and 6 p.m. Mon.-Fri. You avoid the crowds and you can save 20%. In some restaurants you will be able to order petite portions of selected entrees at a lower cost and still receive the 20% discount. The holder of the Golden American card may take up to 3 guests (if they are also over 55) and receive the discount for all of them. Write or call the above location for a pamphlet describing this program. There is a one-time-only charge of $8 for membership. A monthly bulletin updates the growing number of participating Puget Sound restaurateurs. At this printing there are 97 participating restaurants. If you have a special spot you'd love to see on that list, give the restaurant manager Golden American's phone number. They also offer discounts on travel packages, pharmaceuticals, eyewear, home repairs and auto repairs. **Checks**

HARLAN-FAIRBANKS CO.
Seattle: 1405 Elliott (284-7420)
Hours: M-F 8-5

Giving a large party? Harlan-Fairbanks will sell you 5 lbs. of pre-popped popcorn for about $5 ($1/lb.). Given the weight of popcorn, that's a lot of popcorn. They also sell a variety of items found in your theater's snack bar or vending machines. No minimum purchase requirements prevail, but you save money if you can use or share quantities of these specialty items. They also sell hot dogs and Karmel Korn. A product list is available.

Note to charity groups: You may be able to obtain large quantities of popcorn from your local theater if they pop their own. Prices generally are comparable to Harlan-Fairbanks *if* they will agree to sell in quantity. **Checks**

MARKET SPICE
Federal Way: 1937 Sea-Tac Mall (839-0922)
Seattle: Pike Place Market (622-6340)
Tacoma: Tacoma Mall (474-7524)
Hours: *Federal Way, Tacoma* **M-F 10-9; Sat. 10-6; Sun. 12-5;** *Seattle* **M-Sat. 9-6**

Shelves of large jars holding spices of all sorts fill these shops. Many of them we had never dreamed of: rosehips, licorice root—even powdered vanilla. Prices are good because everything is in bulk. The more you buy, the greater your savings will be. When we compared our purchases to the grocery store, we found we had done quite well. They also carry many different types of teas, selling $5.50-$6/lb. One lb. will make at least 200 cups. **Checks, M/C, VISA**

MOLIN AND OFFER
Seattle: 1770 4th S. (682-6740)
Hours: M-Sat. 9-6

If you know your food prices, you can really save money buying freight-damaged goods. Even if you're not that clever, you won't lose any. Sugar and bulk dog and cat foods are big items with Molin and Offer regulars, although stock varies according to what was in recent damaged shipments. Toilet tissue and paper towels are always available in bulk quantities. Despite the small area and jumbled aisles, you'll find an astounding variety. Watch for the damaged or slightly damaged items, especially those which have only soiled lables from a broken jar in the case. Other good buys are repackaged bulk items like dates. We consider Molin and Offer an adventure because you never know what you are going to run into. Take time to explore when you go. **Checks (charge cards not accepted for food purchases)**

POPCORN PLUS
Seattle: 1954 1st S. (622-5301)
Hours: M-F 8:30-5

Five lbs. of popped popcorn are $5. We were intrigued by the fact that $20 will rent a popcorn, sno-cone or cotton candy machine (they also sell the ingredients). Fund raisers should know that there is an 80% profit on these items! **Checks**

PUGET SOUND PRETZEL CO. (ALLIED FOOD SERVICE)
Seattle: 617 NW Bright (784-4199)
Hours: M-F 8-4; Sat. 8-3

Got a pretzel craving? Order a case (100 pretzels) and bake your own ($21—they do not split cases). They also sell pretzel salt. Pretzels do not have preservatives, so they come frozen and need to be kept refrigerated, or they will mold just like bread. It's possible to refreeze them, but the more you do this, the more you risk losing quality. You must call in advance to order and arrange a pick-up time. **Checks**

SAFEWAY STORES

We happily take advantage of the following budget-saving policies at Safeway: Fresh meats are reduced on a daily basis, and everything offered to a customer is guaranteed to be safely edible. Reduced meats go quickly, so they never have any left past their final pull dates. Day-old breads are sold for one day only. Supplies unsold after one day are donated to charity organizations. Dairy products are guaranteed for 10 days past the stamped pull date but are reduced for quick sale on that date anyway. Safeway will graciously return your money if you find even a reduced-price item to be unsatisfactory.

STONEFELT AND CO.
Kent: 20241 East Valley Rd. (872-7216)
Hours: M-Th 8:30-4:30; F 8:30-3

Stonefelt's cheese prices are excellent, especially in the larger sizes (2-6 lbs.). The very best buys are the 5-6 lb. sacks of trim cuts—one variety per bag. These occur when cheese is packaged into the 2-lb. loaves. Standard cheeses plus many specialty cheeses (jalapeño, low-salt, color-free cheddar, etc.) are distributed by this company. We strongly advise that you call ahead to check prices and place your order. Be sure to have cash in hand. It is difficult to locate consistently good cheese prices without a minimum dollar requirement, so your cooperation in using this special outlet will be appreciated. **Cash preferred**

TOTEM FOOD PRODUCTS, INC.
Kent: 6203 S. 194th (872-9200)
Hours: Call first to place an order

Totem sells snack foods and sandwiches in individual packages to schools, bars and convenience-type grocery stores. They also sell nuts in bulk (5-lb. minimum). Their minimum order amount is $25, so if you need sandwiches for a crowd (or burritos, or submarines, etc.) you will save around 40%. Nut prices were nearly half the cost of retail packages in the grocery stores. Snack items varied, but still represented savings, especially if you can use the bulk sizes. The sandwiches will keep 10-14 days in the refrigerator. You must call at least one day ahead to place your order. *Nuts note:* So far, the POST OFFICE GROCERY (at 216 Union in Seattle) has managed to beat every bulk nut price on selected popular nuts. They do not quote prices over the phone. There is no minimum, and you can buy 1 lb. and get the same savings. **Cash only**

SEAFOODS

CIRCLE SEA SEAFOODS
Woodinville: 13001 NE 177th Pl. (483-1177)
Hours: M-F 9:30-6:30; Sat. 9:30-5:30

The specialty of this fish market is smoked salmon, which they process themselves and which can be purchased in a variety of styles from lox to whole fillets. This item priced out well below the 5 other retail stores we sampled (savings ranged from over $1 to $5). Their other seafood items we checked were generally as good as, but not significantly below, the going market prices.
Checks, M/C, VISA

COAST OYSTER CO.
Poulsbo: Lamola Shore Dr. (779-4529)
Hours: M-F 8-5

Prove you're a local by identifying the name given to the "seconds" sold here. Oyster cuts. These are oysters which were sliced during shucking and are therefore rated imperfects. They are sold in ½-gal. containers for $7.35. The cheapest ½ gal. of perfect small oysters goes for $11.25 at Coast Oyster Co. Mediums cost $10.05; extra small are $11.97. Pint sizes are available. **Checks**

F. AND L. FOODS, INC.
Seattle: 801 2nd (682-7422)
Hours: Call ahead

F. and L. is a wholesale seafood company that specializes in crab, salmon and shrimp. They will sell *case* lots retail, and the savings can be impressive. If you can split up a case (six 5-lb. cans of crab meat or frozen whole crab, shrimp, prawns, salmon and others), give them a call. Orders must be placed in advance.
Checks

GLACIER BAY FOODS
Kent: 22409 72nd S. (621-8816; 872-7243)
Hours: M-F 8:30-5

40   Food

This is a great spot unearthed for us by our friendly fellow super shopper, Buffy McCune. Glacier Bay distributes seafood products and will happily sell to individuals—saving you at least 20-35%. They stock nearly 200 items ranging from the gourmet (lobster tails) to the basic (sole fillets and clam strips). Everything comes from the water except a few chicken items. There are no dollar minimums, but you must buy in 1-, 2-, 5-, or 10-lb. lots depending on the item and how it is packaged. They break cases but not containers. Everything is frozen unless you special order 48 hours in advance. Call in orders to save time. The friendly, helpful service from the Glacier Bay staff and a mailing list that will tell you what's on special (at below wholesale prices saving you 50% or more) make up one super seafood savings spot. Thanks, Buffy! **Checks**

KIRKLAND CUSTOM CANNERY
Kirkland: 640 8th (828-4521)
Hours: M-F 8-5; Sat. 9-4 (summer-Christmas); M-F 9-5 (winter)

In case you haven't discovered the Kirkland Custom Cannery, it's a *find* for two reasons. (1) It sells seafood gift packs for less than department stores. You can order all one kind or a variety. Smoked salmon, smoked sturgeon, crab, shrimp, albacore, tuna and fancy hand-packed salmon are available. Kirkland Cannery also sells by the case, and they will ship for you. How perfect for those out-of-town gifts! You'll also find refrigerated items like lox, kippered salmon, Indian-style smoked salmon, smoked cheese and cheese balls. Fresh and frozen salmon are also in stock. (2) The Kirkland Cannery custom cans seafood for individuals. **Checks, M/C, VISA**

NORTHERN FISH PRODUCTS CO.
Tacoma: 3911 S. 56th (838-1220)
Hours: M-F 5 a.m.-3:30

Buying selected fish and shellfish from this wholesaler will net you impressive savings. Their popular natural smoked kippered fish is $3.50/lb. (in the 5-lb. box). IQF (individually quick frozen) scallops and shrimp are also good buys and easy to store and use. They are not geared up for retail trade, so please respect their 5-lb. minimums/product which are set up so that the staff won't have to spend time weighing or cutting up product. **Checks**

PORT CHATHAM PACKING CO.
Seattle: 632 NW 46th (783-8200)
Hours: M-F 8-5:30; Sat. 9-5

This custom cannery processes seafood catches and packs their own canned seafood. Their smoked salmon products have a well-earned gourmet reputation and are very popular gift items. Port Chatham offers an excellent array of gift packs during the holiday season. "Factory" prices are worth the extra mileage to stock up for company and for gifts, year-round. **Checks**

SHIP AHOY SEAFOOD
Redmond: 17028 Avondale Way (881-2333)
Hours: M-F 9-7; Sat. 10-6

An excellent spot for fish lovers. We found prices very good on the day we visited. Salmon steaks $1.50/lb., pink salmon sides $1.25/lb., petrale sole fillets $3.49/lb. These prices may change, but we feel you'll find good prices when compared to your local grocery store. **Checks**

STEUART SEAFOODS MARKET
Everett: 1520 Norton (258-3344)
Hours: M-F 10-5:30; Sat. 9-4

YE OLDE FISH MARKETS
Everett: 1014 California (259-9110)
Hours: M-Sat. 10-6

It is worth a Bellevue fish lover's while to travel to either of these wholesale/retail fish markets at the Everett docks. Fresh red snapper was a full $1/lb. less than in Eastside markets. Scallops were nearly $2 less. Different specials at the 2 markets were as much as $4 below the Seattle and Bellevue grocers and fish markets that we checked for price comparison. **Checks**

WASHINGTON KING CLAM
Tacoma: 2304 Jefferson S. (838-1322 or 627-3101)
Hours: M-Sat. 7-4:30

If you're not a clam freak, forget this geoduck factory above the old Heidelberg Brewery. You can purchase whole or chopped geoducks and frozen geoduck steaks. We have included King Clam because finding geoduck locally at their prices is most unlikely. Many fish markets don't even carry the steaks. Savings can be as much as 40%. You can get an even bigger bargain by asking for the pieces that have been cut from the uniformly sized restaurant steaks. Call first about availability. **Checks**

WESTERN FISH & OYSTER CO., INC.
Tacoma: 1137 Dock St. (383-1668)
Hours: M-F 8:30-5:45; Sat. 8:30-5:30

If you call Phil in the morning, he can tell you what price breaks you can get by ordering seafood in full lots, i.e., 25 lbs. of fresh red snapper or a whole halibut which runs 20 to 40 lbs. When you figure 25¢-30¢/lb. savings on a 30-lb. fish, that's approximately $9. Shrimp Scatter comes in 5-lb. minimums. You must call ahead to place your order and there is absolutely *no* wrapping or cutting on special price orders. **Checks**

STOREFRONT CO-OPS

Four storefront co-ops operate in the Seattle area. Members buy goods at low prices in exchange for a slight monthly fee or labor. These stores will also sell to nonmembers but at higher prices. If you belong to one co-op, the others will usually sell to you at member prices. Monthly fees furnish the capital for keeping the shelves full and buying needed equipment for the stores. If you resign, most of the co-ops refund your working capital. All the co-ops are nonprofit organizations.

The majority of the co-ops concentrate on carrying natural and organic foods of all sorts. If you are really into health and natural foods, you will find a large and varied selection in the co-ops. However, know your prices! Some cost comparisons that we made on organic produce and raw milk showed that Nature's Pantry in Bellevue charged prices similar to those of one co-op's member prices. If you did all your shopping at the co-op, you would probably save overall.

CENTRAL CO-OP
Seattle: 1835 12th (329-1545)
Hours: M-F 10-7; Sat. 10-6; Sun. 12-5

Central Co-op carries a variety of everything: grains, dairy products, nuts, a few canned goods, staples, vitamins. To join, you pay a $5 nonrefundable joining fee and make your first $2 investment. You then invest $2 monthly until a total amount of $60 has been paid. This is refundable if you withdraw your membership. You must attend a one-hour orientation within 2 weeks of joining.

Prices marked are member prices; nonmembers pay 15% above the cash register's total. The co-op runs "vital foods specials" each month to help compensate for inflation and to aid members in stocking up on basic items. **Checks**

THE FOOD BAG CO-OP
Tacoma: 2601 6th Ave. (272-8110)
Hours: M-F 9:30-7; Sat. 9:30-6; Sun. 12-5

This co-op health food store can save you plenty whether you are a natural food fanatic or just a borderline case. There's a $5 joining fee plus $2 every month you shop. Working members and senior citizens get additional discounts. Nonmembers pay

10% of the shelf price additional. We were impressed with the fact that you pay pretty much the same for fresh, *organic* fruits and vegetables here as at the supermarket—in some cases, less. Bulk honey, spices, herbs, nuts, seeds, flours, cereals, etc. are good budget savers. Cheese prices were well below the markets, and they carry some gourmet varieties. The atmosphere isn't "upscale," but you can buy all the popular and some of the more unique health food store items here without paying for fancy overhead costs. **Checks**

PHINNEY STREET CO-OP
Seattle: 400 N. 43rd (633-2354)
Hours: M-F 11-7; Sat. 10-6; Sun. 12-5

This co-op aims to distribute nutritious foods at low prices. You'll find organic, natural foods, produce, dairy products, grains and canned goods on the shelves. Monthly members loan the co-op $3 each month or have worked 4 hours the previous month. Weekly workers commit to work two 3-hour shifts/week and attend 2 weekly meetings/month. Partial weekly workers work one 3-hour shift/week.

Nonmembers pay 30% above marked prices, monthly workers pay 10% over, paying members pay 16% over, partial weekly workers pay 3% over marked prices, and weekly workers pay 5% under wholesale prices. **Checks**

PUGET CONSUMERS CO-OP (EASTSIDE)
Kirkland: 10718 NE 68th (828-4621)
Hours: M-Sat. 9-9; Sun. 10-7

This is a good-sized co-op store (8,000 sq. ft.), specializing in all kinds of organic and natural foods: raw cow's milk, carob milk, vitamins, produce, dairy products, staples, grains and canned goods. You'll find a large and varied selection. We counted 110 large jars of different dried herbs and spices, including such unusual things as lavender, kelp, goldenseed and dandelion leaf. Bulk buying of many food items is available at this co-op store. PCC also sells books, clothes, pots, pans, paper products, hardware, yard goods, gift items and organic garden supplies. Different blends of coffee (Columbian, Viennese, French roast, etc.) sell for less here than most places. Another feature is the 24-hour recycling center for aluminum, tin, glass and newspapers.

Since the co-op opened, the membership has expanded rapidly. To join, you pay an initial $8, plus an additional $2/month to renew your membership. If you don't shop for a month, you don't pay the $2. A total of $6 from the initial joining fee plus each subsequent $2 payment are accumulated in your account. When it reaches $60, your membership is considered paid in full, and no more dues are required.

The prices on the shelves are membership prices. Nonmembers pay an additional 13.8% mark-up over listed prices. Child care is available Friday and Saturday mornings. **Checks**

PUGET CONSUMERS CO-OP
Seattle: 6504 20th NE (525-1450)
Hours: M-F 10-8; Sat. 10-6; Sun. 12-6

This is the original PCC, which stocks the same sort of merchandise as the Eastside store. Its popularity in the Seattle area has spread to such an extent that it has had to restrict its new members to those living in the NE quadrant of Seattle. **Checks**

PUGET CONSUMERS CO-OP (GREENLAKE)
Seattle: 6522 Fremont N. (789-7144)
Hours: M-F 10-8:30; Sat. 10-7; Sun. 11-7

This PCC store features natural foods, organic meat (fresh, nonnitrate), and deli items. It also sells beer and wine. **Checks**

CLOTHING

Each type of shop where clothing is sold for less than retail retains its own peculiarities. Each type exhibits characteristics that are important to you for shopping efficiency.

The following listings are organized according to their type and characteristics. Obviously, some shops are standouts in each category. If you are not already a regular off-beat shopper, you may never pay full price for any clothing again.

CHARITY RESALE THRIFT SHOPS

Used clothing sold at the numerous charity resale shops around the city has been donated. The contributor gets no cash but does receive an appraisal slip justifying the donation as an income tax deduction. Goods in resale shops will be worn, some more than others. Prices will reflect both wear and dated characteristics. Some of the best buys at resale shops are in children's dress-up clothing because they are outgrown before they are worn out. Stock changes regularly with the best items picked off quickly. Seasonal sales dispose of remainders at give-away prices.

ASLAN'S
Issaquah: 705 NW Gilman Blvd. (392-4500)
Hours: M-Sat. 10-5

This thrift shop, run by Bellevue Christian School, houses mostly clothing, shoes and accessories. **Checks**

ASSISTANCE LEAGUE THRIFT SHOP
Everett: 1916 Hewitt (252-3011)
Hours: M-F 10-4; Sat. 12-4

Volunteers staff this thrift shop which sells mostly clothing and knickknacks, along with some furniture. The proceeds go to "operation school bell," a program which helps clothe needy children and provides some basic dental care for them. All sales final. **Checks**

46   Clothing

BARGAIN BOUTIQUE
Bainbridge Island: 590 Winslow Way E. (842-5567)
Hours: T-Sat. 10-2; W 10-4

Volunteers from the Lenora Ostrander Children's Orthopedic Guild staff this charity resale shop. You'll find clothing, knickknacks, furniture and housewares. Both consignments and donations are accepted. Donations are welcome any time, and you will receive a tax credit receipt. In 1980, this guild shop donated almost $30,000 to the Children's Orthopedic Hospital and Medical Center, indicating that they do a brisk business here. All sales final. Consignments taken only during the first 7 days of each month.   **Checks**

BARGAIN FAIR
Seattle: 12304 Lake City Way NE (362-7022)
Hours: T-F 10-4 (Sat. in winter)

Note the new location for the Assistance League of Seattle's thrift shop. You will find a bit of everything and especially women's, children's and men's clothing and shoes. We found a long Gunne Sax dress for $8 and a unique designer top for $3. The prices are right! All sales final.   **Cash only**

BARGAIN LAND
Lynnwood: 3801 196th SW (771-1927)
Hours: M-Sat. 9-7; Sun. 10-6 (summer hours: M-Sat. 9-9)

Bargain Land's proceeds go to the Resource Foundation, which helps support programs for mentally handicapped children and young adults. This large, generously stocked thrift store carries just about everything a family can use—mostly used, some new. There's a good line of baby items and a special vintage and costume rack. Dressing rooms are available. Sunday is 30% off all *used* items day, and senior citizens receive 20% off every day. Note the colored tags: every week one color will be offered at half-price. On Mondays 2 colors are offered at half-price.

Special Note: Bargain Land keeps a stock of *new* mattresses and box springs on the floor at very good prices. Check them when you are comparison shopping for new bedding.

Checks, M/C, VISA

BURIEN THRIFT CENTER
Burien: 16035 1st S. (244-7397)
Hours: M-Sun. 9-7

A very large thrift store stocking a generous selection of appliances, shoes, clothes, knickknacks, books, furniture, toys—

Clothing 47

literally everything! Items are donated to the store, and a percentage of sales goes to benefit cerebral palsy. Everything is sold "as is," and you'll find everything marked down 30% every single Sat. **Checks, M/C, VISA**

THE BUTTERFLY
Bothell: 10216 NE 183rd (486-3552)
Hours: T-F 10-4; Sat. 11-2

The Butterfly fills a void in the Bothell area for quality second-hand merchandise. The store, manned by volunteers from the Episcopal Church of the Redeemer, carries clothing and household items. Donations and consignments are accepted. Receipts are given for all donated items, and all profits are recycled into the community. All sales final. **Checks**

CAMELOT THRIFT CENTER
Seattle: 7321 Greenwood N. (784-0332)
Hours: T-Sat. 9-4

A smaller-sized store selling family clothing, bric-a-brac, books, household items and jewelry with a few old items of vintage variety. It is run 100% by volunteers, and profits benefit 6 different group homes for the retarded. All sales are final except on electrical equipment. **Checks**

CHILDREN'S ORTHOPEDIC CORNER CUPBOARD
Seattle: 4560 University Village Plaza NE (634-5400)
Hours: M, T, F, Sat. 10-6; Th, F 10-9; Sun. 12-5

An unusual shop, the Corner Cupboard sells specialty antiques as well as new items, which have been donated to the Children's Orthopedic Hospital. Proceeds go to the Children's Orthopedic Hospital Medical Center. Exchanges and refunds gladly accepted. **Checks, M/C, VISA**

CHILDREN'S ORTHOPEDIC THRIFT SHOP
Seattle: 2026 3rd (622-7609)
Hours: M-F 9:30-4:55; Sat. 10-4:55

You'll find a bit of everything here: men's, women's and children's clothing, bric-a-brac, furniture, household items, jewelry and books. All merchandise is donated and the proceeds go into the Free and Part-Pay Care Program for the Children's Orthopedic Hospital and Medical Center. **Checks**

CITY OF HOPE SECONDHAND ROSE THRIFT SHOP
Seattle: 6421 32nd NW (784-0298)
Hours: M-Sat. 10-5

A very unique "Brand X" sale is held once a year. First quality merchandise is donated by a famous maker and sold at wholesale prices. Check to see when it takes place. Notification of the sale is published in the chapter bulletin. Only City of Hope members can shop the first day, then the sale is open to the public. After the sale, any leftover "Brand X" merchandise goes on the racks at the thrift shop. Stock from other manufacturer's sales representatives is also available. To become a member, send your name, address and phone number along with $10 to: City of Hope, 8852 SE 29th, Mercer Island, WA 98040.

CLOUD 9
Seattle: 6518 Roosevelt Way NE (525-4440)
Hours: M-F 10-4 (winter); T-Th 10-4 (summer)

Operated by St. Stephen's Episcopal Church, Cloud 9 stocks a large variety of clothes, furniture, knickknacks, housewares, sporting goods and antiques. The shop accepts public donations with all proceeds going to charitable organizations. No refunds or exchanges. The shop receives consignment merchandise on M-W, from 10-12, or from the first 45 customers—whichever comes first. **Checks**

COUNCIL THRIFT SHOP
Seattle: 1501 Pike Place (Market No. 301) (682-2697)
Hours: M-Sat. 9:30-4:30

A remarkable thrift shop run by the Seattle Section, National Council of Jewish Women. The store stocks everything: men's, women's, children's clothing (some new) and accessories; small appliances; jewelry; some furniture; and knickknacks of all sorts. An added boutique carries more expensive, high quality name-brand clothes. If you're interested in seeing these, inquire first, as they are not kept with the regular stock. Dressing rooms. No cash refunds. Layaway plan available. **Cash only**

E.C.A. THRIFT SHOP
Redmond: 16150 N. 87th (881-6100)
Hours: M-Sat. 10-4

This thrift shop sells a little bit of everything: books, clothes, knickknacks, jewelry—you name it. All items are donated, and you can receive a tax deductible slip for your donations. Volunteers (no paid help) run the shop. All sales benefit various Eastside community groups. The E.C.A. board decides who will receive funds. In the past they've helped the library, fire department, food banks, Custom Industries, just to mention a few. All sales final. **Checks**

Clothing 49

EMMY'S ATTIC
Mercer Island: 7418 SE 24th (232-6561)
Hours: T-Sat. 11-3

Sponsored by Emmanuel Episcopal Church, Emmy's Attic sells antiques, clothing (men's, women's, children's), collectibles, books, knickknacks and jewelry. Donations are welcome, and consignments are taken on Tues. Look upstairs for antiques, downstairs for thrift shop items. No refunds or exchanges on antiques. Exchange of thrift items downstairs permitted within 24 hours with sales receipt. **Checks**

FRUGALLILY'S
Seattle: 2215 E. Madison (447-2360)
Hours: M-F 10-6; Sat. 10-5

If you're going to donate or if you're going to shop, try to hit their first-of-the-month sales which occur for 3 days and consist half of generic super slashers such as "all shoes, jeans and pants half price." All proceeds from this full-line thrift store go to Planned Parenthood, and they will happily keep a record of your donations and send it to you in time to let the IRS know about your philanthropy. Aside from benefiting their parent agency, Frugallily's policy is to aid the community by keeping the prices on children's clothing, games and toys very low. T-shirts for kids under 6 run 25¢, for example. The shop is relatively new and therefore needs your donations as well as your purchasing dollars. Layaways are welcome with 10% down and 60 days to pay the balance. Each August and December there is a 50% off sale on all items. **Checks**

GRANNY'S ATTIC
Vashon: Sunrise Ridge Community Park
Hours: Th-Sat. 10-4:30

We found exceptional bargains at Granny's. The receipts and volunteers support the Health Center on Vashon. Since it is the only operation of its kind on the island, it is a choice spot for uncovering unusual and exciting finds. Nearly every category is represented. No returns. And since you are on the island, why not visit the Wax Orchards (131st Ave. SW and SW 232nd) to pick up some icy cold fresh cider. **Checks**

HADASSAH NEARLY NEW STORE
Seattle: 515 Harvard E. (325-4974)
Hours: M-F 10-5:45

Extremely low prices on clothing, shoes, purses, jewelry, books and bric-a-brac. All sales final. **Checks**

Clothing

HIGH HOPES THRIFT SHOP
Seattle: 6814 Roosevelt Way NE (524-3399)
Hours: M-F 10-4; Sat. 11-4

HIGH HOPES TWO
Auburn: 227 Auburn (939-5544)
Hours: T-F 10-4; Sat. 11-4

Practically everything (jewelry, clothing, small furniture, etc.) sold here. Receipts are given for donations (tax deductible). All proceeds benefit the King County unit of the American Cancer Society. Exchanges allowed for something of equal value.
Cash only

THE JFK ATTIC
Burien: 1st S. & 140th S. (243-3667)
Hours: Th-Sat. 10-4 (closed July)

Located in an old house next to JFK School, proceeds from this thrift shop support the school library. The readerboard outside the shop announces special bargains. With no storage space, periodic clean-out sales are necessary. The house is full of assorted donated items from small appliances to shoes. Toys are sold only in November. All sales final.
Checks

ODDS AND ENDS OF FRIENDS
Renton: 214 William S. (255-3777)
Hours: T-Sat. 10-4

Operated by Friends of Youth volunteers, this Renton thrift shop carries a little bit of everything. Furniture, antiques or household items in stock will be in good condition. Takes antiques and collectibles on consignment, Tues. only. All proceeds from sales benefit the Griffin Home for Boys in Renton. All sales final.
Checks

OVERLAKE SERVICE LEAGUE THRIFT SHOP
Bellevue: 167 Bellevue Mall (454-6424)
Hours: M-F 9:30-9; Sat. 9:30-6; Sun. 11-6

This charity resale thrift shop accepts donations only—no consignments. It offers good variety, and most things are in good shape for being secondhand. You'll find clothing, shoes, accessories, jewelry, wigs, books, *National Geographic* magazines, toys, records, linens and knickknacks. All sales final.
Checks

RAGS 'N RICHES
Seattle: 8018 15th NE (no phone)
Hours: W-Sat. 10-4

Have an urge to care for every stray cat or dog that comes your way? Then frequent this thrift store! It supports PAWS (Progressive Animal Welfare Society), which houses and feeds unwanted animals. The shop sells a little bit of everything, a lot of clothing—all donated items. **Checks**

R SHOPPE
Seattle: 5435 Ballard (783-4230)
Hours: M-F 10-4 (open every other Sat. 11-3)

The Ryther Guilds of the Ryther Child Center operate the R Shoppe and sell clothing, linen, housewares, knickknacks—donations by members. The children's clothes sell fast, and the stock changes rapidly. All sales final. **Cash only**

SAINTS ALIVE
Kirkland: 117 Central Way (822-8567)
Hours: M-F 10:30-4

Saints Alive is run by the Women of St. John's Episcopal Church with stocks of men's, women's and children's clothing of all sorts, toys, books, furniture, small appliances and knickknacks. A consignment section offers new and used items. The store keeps a third of the selling price on consigned goods. All proceeds are funneled to various charities. Dressing room available. No cash refunds. **Checks**

SECOND CLOSET
Tacoma: 3730 S. G (472-1447)
Hours: M-Sat. 9-5:30

A spacious, clean shop carrying nice quality secondhand men's, women's and children's clothing and accessories, as well as books and various knickknacks. Operated by the Junior League of Tacoma, all proceeds are funneled into the community. Dressing rooms. **Cash only**

SHOP 'N SAVE THRIFT STORE
Auburn: 30 W. Main (939-4245)
Seattle: 10114 15th SW (762-8099)
Renton: 936 Harrington NE (226-6352)
Kent: 425 W. Meeker (852-8349)
Hours: M-Sat. 9-9; Sun. 10-6 (all stores)

Shop 'n Save stores are outlets which sell clothing and other miscellaneous items donated to the American Diabetes Association. Merchandise arrives daily with a good variety for the entire family. Every Sun. 30% off on everything. All sales final.
Checks, M/C, VISA

SHOW AND SELL
Kent: 232 S. Railroad (854-5165)
Hours: M-F 10-4; Sat. 11-3

Sponsored by St. James Episcopal Church, the shop sells a little of everything: clothing, housewares, antiques. **Checks**

THE SOROPTIMIST CUPBOARD
Everett: 2811 Rockefeller (no phone)
Hours: Th, F, Sat. 10:30-4:30

Soroptimist Clubs are community-centered organizations. The club in Everett donates medical equipment, scholarships, educational equipment, etc. to various organizations in the city. This tiny* shop has a bit of everything at one time or another and all the items are well priced. All sales final. **Cash only**

**Shopper's Note:* In some cases, the tinier shops are lower-priced than the "big names." They can be easier to shop when they are well maintained, and the staff will often help you locate the best bargains.

THE SPARROW
Everett: 2202 Hewitt (259-3555)
Hours: M-Sat. 9-5

The Sparrow Outreach program benefits from the sale of goods donated to this all around thrift store. **Cash only**

TACOMA THRIFT CENTER
Tacoma: 1110 S. K (272-5211)
Hours: M-Sat. 10-5

Inexpensive prices on a full line of secondhand items: furniture, small and large appliances, knickknacks, clothing, paint and books. Nice house plants and new jewelry at good prices also available. Operated by the National Council of Jewish Women, all proceeds stay within the community. **Checks**

THIS 'N THAT
Seattle: 8310 Greenwood N. (789-1636)
Hours: M-Sat. 10-4:30

Donations of clothes, bric-a-brac, books, a little of everything sold here. The Seattle Children's Home receives the benefits from all sales. No exchanges or refunds. **Checks**

THISTLES 'N THINGS THRIFT SHOP
Bellevue: 4228 128th SE (641-6830)
Hours: W-F 10-2

Clothing 53

A charity organization, Women of St. Margaret's Episcopal Church, sells clothes, books, games, toys, tools, gadgets. The shop does take good used furniture on consignment. No exchanges or refunds. **Checks**

THRIFTCO
Seattle: 124 N. 85th (789-5357); 401 NE Ravenna (523-3206)
Everett: 8701 Evergreen Way (353-5997)
Mountlake Terrace: 6707 220th SW (774-2101)
Hours: M-Sat. 9-9; Sun. 11-6 (all stores)

Thriftco sells secondhand goods purchased for the Community Services for the Blind. You'll find a varied selection of miscellaneous household items, better used clothing, furniture, antiques—all at "inflation fighter" prices. **Checks, M/C, VISA**

THRIFT CENTER
Tacoma: 755 S. 38th (475-8860)
Hours: M-Sat. 10-7

This large store contains racks and racks of clothes, plenty of household items and knickknacks, books, furniture, military uniforms, etc. The proceeds benefit United Cerebral Palsy. On Sat. everything is 30% off. Daily half-off tickets are identified by color (i.e., all red tags may be half off on Mon., etc.) **Checks**

TRINITY THRIFT SHOP
Seattle: 609 8th (622-8279)
Hours: W-F 10-3; Sat. 9:30-12:30

A small thrift shop, located in Trinity Episcopal Church, filled with clothing, books, shoes, household items, etc. Proceeds benefit many organizations: i.e., Shelter for Teenage Children, Catholic Workers Kitchen, First Ave. Service Center. The shop is run by volunteers. All sales final. **Cash**

TRINKETS AND TREASURES
Seattle: 517 15th E. (325-5942)
Hours: T-F 10:45-4:45; Sat. 11-3

The Epiphany Episcopal Church Women maintain this shop, which sells nice clothing for women, antiques, gift items and furniture. Most items are donated, though some consignments are taken. Missions and people in need benefit from the proceeds. **Cash only**

UNION GOSPEL MISSION BARGAIN CENTER
Seattle: 6930 Empire Way S. (723-5700)
Hours: M-Sat. 9-5

54 Clothing

A thrift store resembling somewhat a mini-Goodwill or junk store. Do not expect anything fancy. They do carry appliances, and all are marked as to their condition. All proceeds from the store go toward the support of the mission, which has 180 beds for transients and supports 40-60 people on recovery programs. They will give in-store credit if it is absolutely necessary for you to return your purchase. **Cash only**

VOLUNTEERS OF AMERICA THRIFT STORE
Everett: 2801 Lombard (259-3191)
Hours: M-Sat. 9-5

Volunteers run this thrift store, and all items are donated. You can expect to find everything from "soup to nuts" in this nice-sized location. They do receive appliances, which are serviced and carry a 30-day guarantee. Otherwise, all sales are final, no refunds. The proceeds help support a children's camp for retarded as well as normal children. **Checks, M/C, VISA**

THE WISE PENNY
Seattle: 4744 University Way NE (524-8585)
Hours: M-Sat. 10-5:30; Th 10-9

The Wise Penny sells donations from members of the Junior League of Seattle. Men's, women's and children's clothing and accessories are top quality for used merchandise. Knickknacks are also sold. Sometimes small furniture is available. A fantastic toy sale is held early in December every year. All toys that are donated are held for this sale. If interested, you can be put on a mailing list for The Wise Penny's 2 great half-price sales: winter and summer. Just give them a call. Layaways available: 20% down and the remainder within 10 days. **Checks**

Y'S BUYS THRIFT SHOP
Seattle: 4217 Admiral Way SW (935-3983)
Hours: T-Th 10-4; F, Sat. 11-5

This thrift shop benefits the YWCA Daycare Center in West Seattle. You'll find a little of everything here including clothes, shoes, books, knickknacks; however, no furniture. All sales final. **Cash only**

CONSIGNMENT SHOPS

Used clothing that is too good to give away ends up in consignment shops. Here the shop and the original owner split the money received for a garment or other product. Style-conscious women turn over their wardrobe frequently by consigning clothes for resale. Because owners receive 15-25% of the price, clothing in consignment shops will be newer and less worn than clothing found in charity resale shops or rummage sales. Clothing in consignment shops will be varied, in broken sizes and ready to wear with minor alterations. Prices are at least half off—frequently more, particularly at seasonal sales. If you're not interested in purchasing secondhand clothing, use the consignment shops as an outlet for recycling your own used clothes.

We've deleted all consignment information for each individual shop, as to when they consign, if a fee is charged, how much the consignor makes, etc. Check the policies of each local shop owner.

ACCENT ON FASHION
Seattle: 8337 15th NW (782-8745)
Hours: M-Sat. 10:30-5

Men's and women's clothing, shoes, jewelry and purses. The 99¢ bin offers a potpourri of T-shirts, scarves and similar small bargains. There's a dressing room for trying on clothing before you purchase—a good idea since all sales are final. **Checks**

ACT II, INC.
Federal Way: 1707 341st Pl. (927-7190)
Hours: M-F 10-5:30; Sat. 10-5

Looking for a way to beat inflation? Visit Act II, a spacious consignment boutique, selling a fine variety of men's, women's and children's used garments, as well as antiques and crafts. All sales final. **Checks**

ALLEY CAT
Seattle: 1906 Post Alley (682-8886)
Hours: T-Sat. 11-5

The Alley Cat bills itself as a "classy consignment shop," and we'll definitely attest to that. The small shop is attractively and neatly filled with women's used clothing (sizes 6-16), all in excellent condition and selling for great prices. Their stock consists of skirts, blazers, dresses, blouses and pants, as well as shoes and accessories. You'll also find a few samples.

The Alley Cat does allow layaways. Dressing room. All sales final. **Checks**

APPAREL DÉJA VU
Kirkland: 12087 124th NE (821-7090)
Hours: M-Sat. 10-5:30

As the name indicates, the main intent of the owners of this shop is to stock good-quality, "gently worn" clothes. They will also carry new items when they can get them at good enough prices to offer near-wholesale savings. The store is well merchandized and comfortable. They carry women's clothing in sizes 1-18. All sales final. **Checks**

APRÈS-VOUS CONSIGNMENTS
Kent: 23639 104th SE (859-0393)
Hours: T-F 10-5; Sat. 10-4

This consignment shop resembles a "little department store." They have a bit of everything—clothing, small furniture, household items. Clothes are currently styled and in good condition. All sales final. **Checks, M/C, VISA**

B.J.'S CLOSET
Bellevue: 15015 Main (747-8085)
Hours: T-Sat. 10-6

A smaller consignment shop carrying men's and women's clothes, as well as knickknacks, housewares, accessories. Layaway with a third down. All sales final. **Checks**

BUDGET BOUTIQUE
Everett: 1917 Broadway (259-1285)
Hours: T-Sat. 10-5

Men's, women's and children's previously worn clothing is sold in this small, neat, well-priced consignment store. The garments were in good shape. **Checks**

CINDERELLA'S CLOSET
Tacoma: 3812 Steilacoom Blvd. (581-4472)
Hours: M-Sat. 11-5:30

"Gently worn" consigned women's clothing, accessories and knickknacks are found here. The owner asks that the clothes should look new! You'll also find lots of samples, selling for usually 25-33% off regular retail. All sales final. It is possible to arrange for an approval, but you must do so before you purchase. **Checks**

CLOTHES ENCOUNTER
Auburn: 906 Harvey Rd. (735-1076)
Hours: T-Sat. 10-5:30

Clothes Encounter stocks only consigned women's clothing and accessories. All sales final. **Checks**

THE CLOTHES MENAGERIE
Seattle: 22335 Marine Dr. S. (878-4510)
Hours: M-F 10-5; Sat. 10-4

"Gently" worn women's and children's clothing and accessories, as well as a nice stock of new and handcrafted items. The owner will accept nothing over 3 years old, and everything consigned must be in very good condition. There is a 2-day approval policy. **Checks**

CONSIGNMENT CLOSET
Renton: 265 Rainier S. (228-7054)
Hours: T-F 10-5:30; Sat. 10-4

Nicely used women's clothing, jewelry, bags, shoes can be found here. The shop also stocks items for infants through size 5. Items must be in mint condition if you wish to consign. **Checks**

CONSIGNMENT SHOP
Burien: 929 SW 152nd (243-5254)
Hours: T-Sat. 10-4

You'll find this small shop located on the first floor of a 2-story red house. This spot is best for its selection of blouses and shirts. Returns are allowed within 24 hours, if you talk to the owner first.
Checks

THE CRACKER BARREL
Bellevue: 2251 140th NE (Evans Plaza) (641-3855)
Hours: T-Sat. 10-5

Bellevue's original consignment shop. The Cracker Barrel sells men's and women's clothing, jewelry and accessories. Dressing room. All sales final, but you can arrange to take things out on a 24-hour approval. **Checks, M/C, VISA**

THE DARK HORSE
Bellevue: 11810 NE 8th (Midlakes Center) (454-0990)
Hours: T, W, F 10:30-5:30; Th 10:30-8; Sat. 10:30-5

Women's dresses, jackets, hats, shoes, belts, jewelry, coats, pants, blouses, and men's pants, shirts, suits and ties are sold on consignment. Good selection and variety of sizes. No children's things. Dressing rooms. Exchanges permitted only if you make arrangements to take things home on approval. Layaway plan.
Checks, M/C, VISA

ELFIE'S CONSIGNMENT BOUTIQUE
Tacoma: 6332 S. Park (423-0130)
Hours: T-Sat. 11-6

You'll find women's clothing with some infants' and children's things. All kinds of dolls, stuffed toys and floral arrangements also fill the shop. All sales final. **Checks**

Clothing

ENCORE BOUTIQUE
Tacoma: 8006-8010 27th W. (564-4515)
Hours: T-F 10-5; Sat. 10-4

A consignment store featuring women's and children's clothing, as well as antiques, knickknacks and collectibles. All sales final, though there is a layaway plan available.

Checks, M/C, VISA

ENCORE CONSIGNMENTS
Lynnwood: 17905 Hwy. 99 (no phone)
Hours: T-F 10-4:30; Sat. 12-4:30

It is amazing the amount of clothing that can be consigned in only 900 square feet! There's a large girls' rack and an equally large boys' rack. Also men's and women's sections. Consigned goods have 60 days to sell or be picked up before they appear on the $1 rack. That's a super bargain spot, as is the 25¢ reject bin. The owner strives to stock clean clothing in good condition; this applies also to the few giftware and accessory items. **Checks**

ENCORE FASHIONS
Renton: 326 Union NE (Renton Highlands) (226-2088)
Hours: T-Sat. 10-5

A small shop stocking mostly women's and children's clothing with some accessories and shoes. These are previously owned items. All sales final unless an approval is arranged ahead of time!

Checks

THE FAMILY CLOSET
Lynnwood: 19722-B Hwy. 99 (775-1116)
Hours: T-Sat. 11-5

This consignment shop allows you to take things out on approval—an especially helpful policy if you're shopping for other members of the family. The Family Closet consigns men's, women's and children's clothing and accessories as well as knickknacks. Dressing rooms. All sales final. **Checks**

FAR FETCHED
Bellevue: 112 Bellevue Way SE (451-0551)
Hours: M-F 10-6; Sat. 10-5; Sun. 12-5

A newcomer among Bellevue's consignment stores, Far Fetched carries a large, varied stock of men's, women's and teens' used clothing as well as jewelry, gift items, accessories—all in nice condition. The shop does allow a 24-hour approval (talk to the salesperson to arrange) and a 30-day layaway. All sales final.

Checks, M/C, VISA

THE FIG LEAF
Redmond: 16128 NE 87th (881-3103)
Hours: T-Sat. 10-5

The Fig Leaf, a relatively new consignment shop in Redmond, stocks previously owned women's and children's clothing as well as jewelry and some gift things. All sales final, though sometimes you can arrange for a 24-hour approval. **Checks**

THE FINDERY
Tacoma: 1205 Regents Blvd. (565-3503)
Hours: M-F 10-5:30; Sat. 10-4

A nice, spacious consignment shop selling top-quality women's clothing and a few infants' and children's items. Their back room has a couple of sales racks with things marked way down. No refunds or exchanges. **Checks**

FOXY LADY ANONYMOUS
Bellevue: 106 102nd NE (454-9377)
Hours: M-Sat. 10:30-5

Recycle your wardrobe at a fun consignment shop. You'll find top-quality, slightly used and new women's clothing and accessories here, at affordable prices. The shop has a layaway service, dressing rooms, and clothing can be taken on approval. **Checks**

GENA'S RESALE FASHIONS
Tacoma: 10227 Bridgeport Way SW (588-6848)
Hours: M-Sat. 10:30-5

A very tiny consignment shop, but don't let this deter you. Gena stocks top-quality women's clothing, shoes and accessories. Many look as though they've never been worn—which they probably haven't. Everything is very clean, neat, pressed and in top-notch condition. All sales final, but layaways may be possible. **Checks**

GENERAL STORE
Bellevue: 6401 Lake Wash. Blvd. SE (112th exit off 405) (228-7371)
Hours: T-F 10-6; Wed. 4-8; Sat. 10-5

You'll discover men's, women's and children's clothing, handcrafted items, small housewares and accessories filling this shop. The clothing and housewares are used. All sales final. **Checks**

GLORIA'S BUDGET BOUTIQUE
Puyallup: 15201 Meridian S. (848-8856)
Hours: T 12-5; W-Sat. 10-5

Find the address, then go around to the back to discover this consignment shop which stocks clothing for the entire family, as well as small housewares. All sales are final. However, the owner might allow a 24-hour approval. You can put things on layaway.

Checks

KATHY'S KLOSET
Seattle: 4540 Roosevelt Way NE (523-3019)
Hours: M-F 10:30-5:30; Sat. 10-5; Sun. 12-4

Kathy's Kloset is geared toward the young crowd. You'll find nice, used fashions, men's and women's, for students and the young professional. Dressing rooms. All sales final. **Checks**

KATHY'S OTHER PLACE
Seattle: 8410 5th NE (527-0776)
Hours: M-F 10-5:30; Sat. 10-4

Kathy's Other Place carries quite a few samples as well as "nicely used" consigned clothing for women only. You'll find home and party attire, moderately priced dresses, blouses, suits and handbags. All sales final. **Checks**

LIBERTY'S CONSIGNMENT CLOTHING AND COLLECTIBLES
Seattle: 424 1st W. (283-5537)
Hours: M-Sat. 12-5:30

A great place to look for wedding, bridesmaid and prom dresses. We discovered a long rack of new Gunne Sax dresses selling for half price. Several used wedding dresses were also in stock. The shop occupies several rooms in a house. It contains women's clothing and accessories of all sorts—casual to dressy, new and used. All sales final. Layaway available. **Checks**

MARY'S POP-INS
Seattle: 2123 Queen Anne N. (282-5151)
Hours: W-Sat. 12-5

A consignment shop selling men's and women's clothing. All sales final. **Checks**

NANDY'S BRIDAL
Edmonds: 8311 212th SW (774-2056)
Hours: T-F 3:30-5; Sat. 11-5

This is truly a unique consignment shop, selling a good selection of previously owned bridal dresses, bridesmaid dresses and bridal accessories. What a great idea and great way to cut wedding costs! You'll find mainly long dresses on hand. The store also carries maternity clothes and is desperately looking for more. Take in what you no longer need. All sales final. **Checks**

NEARLY NEW SHOP
Tacoma: 2814 6th (627-0812)
Hours: M-Sat. 10-5

A variety of men's, women's and children's apparel and accessories sold here, as well as a few books, knickknacks, and toys. This good-sized shop hums with activity, which indicates its success—for both the shopper and the consignor. Dressing rooms. **Checks**

ONE MORE TIME
Redmond: 8117 161st NE (881-5434)
Hours: M-Sat. 10-5:30

A consignment shop selling women's and children's clothing and accessories, as well as some knickknacks and gift items. You may find some antiques. All sales final. **Checks**

PANDORA'S BOX
Bellevue: 10867 NE 2nd Pl. (455-3883)
Hours: M-Sat. 10-5

Pandora's Box features "Today's Fashions at Yesterday's Prices." A consignment shop selling new and nearly new men's and women's clothing and accessories. Clothing may be taken out on approval for a 2- to 3-day period. The shop also provides a layaway service, dressing rooms, and will hold articles up to 3 days. **Checks**

PANDORA'S CASTLE
Seattle: 2026 NW Market (782-5717)
Hours: M-Sat. 11-5

Top-quality antiques and collectibles, including furniture, glassware, decorative items sold on consignment here. Quite a line of jewelry and a limited amount of clothing also available. **Checks, M/C, VISA**

PEAK EXPERIENCE—See Index

PHASE TWO
Auburn: 130 E. Main (735-3153)
Hours: M-F 10-5; Sat. 10-4

Consigned used clothing for the entire family, as well as small household goods. All sales final. **Checks**

RAGS TO RICHES
Kent: 25625 102nd Pl. SE (859-1582)
Hours: T-Sat. 10-5

Rags to Riches carries women's and children's clothing. The stock depends upon what's been brought in for consignment. You'll find some new items along with the used. **Checks**

REDRESS
Bellevue: 513 156th SE (746-7984)
Hours: M-Sat. 10:30-5:30; Th 10:30-7

The Redress advertises "gently used" clothing on consignment. The store sells women's, misses and juniors' clothing, as well as accessories—all in a nice, open atmosphere. Those of you thinking about weddings might want to scout out this shop. We saw several nice wedding gowns on our last visit. Redress has a 24-hour approval policy, which you must prearrange when making your purchase. It also has a 30-day layaway. Dressing room available. **Checks, M/C, VISA**

REWEAR APPAREL
Spanaway: 16217 Pacific Ave. (531-6031)
Hours: M-Sat. 10-6

Consigned women's clothing. Call ahead to see if someone is there. All sales final. **Checks**

SAX OFF FIFTH AVE.
Edmonds: 419 Bell (771-9515)
Hours: W-F 10:30-5:30; Sat. 11-4

Another consignment store selling only women's clothing. We found a nice selection of sweaters, pullovers and cardigans when we stopped by. All sales final. **Checks**

SECOND AVENUE
Edmonds: 925 Puget Dr. (771-5667)
Hours: T-F 10-4; Sat. 11-5

Second Avenue carries only women's clothing and only "really nice" consigned used clothes. It looks for designer-quality items suitable for the professional woman. The stock turns over rapidly. All sales final. **Checks**

SECOND EDITION
Everett: 607 SE Everett Mall Way (347-4995)
Hours: T-F 11-4

Second Edition carries used men's, women's, children's clothing and accessories. They had a few new jeans at the time we stopped by. All sales final. **Checks**

2ND TIME AROUND
Tacoma: 606 S. K (627-6201)
Hours: M-Th 10-5; F 10-6; Sat. 11-4

As the name indicates, this shop specializes in "2nd time around" merchandise. One portion of the store carries nice, used men's, women's, children's clothing and accessories, which are all consigned goods. Another part of the establishment sells furniture (everyday and antiques) and collectibles, which the owner bids on and then buys. All sales are final, unless you arrange to take something out on 24-hour approval. **Checks**

SECOND TIME AROUND SHOPPE
Federal Way: 33320 Pacific Hwy. S. (927-7777)
Hours: M, F 12-7; T-Th, 10:30-5

A consignment store selling men's, women's and children's clothing and accessories. All sales final. Layaway available. **Checks**

SKI RACK SPORTS—See Index

SUNNBONNET
Everett: 2112 Broadway (259-7092)
Hours: T-F 10-5; Sat. 11-4

Women's and men's clothing, shoes and accessories can be found here. They usually have a good selection of used clothing, though they were low on jeans when we stopped by. All sales final. **Checks**

TOP DRAWER
Seattle: 12518 Lake City Way NE (364-6217)
Hours: T-F 10:30-6; Sat. 10:30-5

Her card reads "Top Drawer, the classy consignment shop," and Charlotte intends to keep her tiny shop stocked with nice clothes at wonderful prices. We watched her price a designer blouse at $7.50—reluctantly because that is her "high." Blouses sell for $5 and $7.50, and *all* costume jewelry is $2 (needless to say, she does a brisk trade in it). As you might expect, the caliber of her standards periodically attracts nice pieces of china and bric-a-brac. If you intend to consign, clothing must be stylish, in excellent shape and seasonal. All sales final. **Checks**

A TOUCH OF CLASS
Kent: 209 W. Meeker (854-6487)
Hours: M-F 10:30-5; Sat. 10-4

This small store (700 sq. ft.) is filled with a good selection of classy secondhand women's and children's clothing. Infant furniture can also be found here, but it sells quickly. **Checks**

TURN ABOUT
Edmonds: 10024 Edmonds Way (775-7022)
Hours: T-F 12-5; Sat. 12-4

This consignment store stocks only ladies' wear—all in very good condition and up-to-date. Dressing rooms. **Checks**

TWICE AS NICE BOUTIQUE
Bothell: 19215 Bothell Way NE (483-1991)
Hours: T-Sat. 10-5

All types of ladies' apparel and accessories can be found here. These are previously owned items. All sales final. **Checks**

YESTERDAY'S
Lynnwood: 19628 76th W. (771-4225)
Hours: T-F 10:30-5; Sat. 11-4

Yesterday's bills itself as a "classic" consignment shop. They do take special pains to keep the shop stocked with nice things for women, children, infants and men in current fashion. Quality, not quantity, is the essence of this store. Wedding gowns are a house specialty. The ones we saw were lovely—and the prices were terrific. All sales are final unless otherwise arranged with the owner. **Checks**

FACTORY OUTLETS

Generally these factory stores sell irregulars and/or overruns. When clothing is cut and sewn, irregularities occur with some frequency—nobody's perfect. In factory outlets, expect to find a full range of sizes, a mixture of seasonal merchandise that changes frequently, less than plush surroundings, possibly not even a try-on booth and sales for cash with no returns or exchanges. Examine each piece for flaws unless you are assured a garment is an overrun and not an irregular. Most flaws are unnoticeable and do not affect wearability. Others may be painfully apparent in a highly visible location. Whatever the flaw, decide if you can live with it before taking it out of the shop because you can't bring it back—sales are "as is" and final. You may also find salespeople's samples among the stock.

Clothing

BOSS MANUFACTURING (GEORGE A. JOHNSON CO.)
Seattle: 433 N. 34th (634-0938)
Hours: M-F 8-12, 1-5

This factory outlet store sells seconds of waterproof clothing. You'll find foul-weather pants and jackets in men's sizes, S-XL, selling at press time for $14 each. A small men's size will usually fit a woman. Goods are yellow or green, manufactured from good, sturdy, waterproof fabric. Don't be disheartened when you walk inside the door; ask someone in the office about the seconds and irregular samples. You'll find the people accommodating. All sales final. **Cash only**

CASCADIAN SPORTSWEAR
Everett: 2701 Colby (252-0555)
Hours: M-F 8-4

Cascadian primarily sells boys' and men's jackets and vests. These are not the fancy, high-fashion styles, but simple "generic" ones which are manufactured for some local department stores. They are a good, sturdy quality. The stock depends on what's being produced in their factory at that particular time. We saw some men's heavy, winter, wool plaid jackets with fleece lining selling for $28-$30—an outstanding price. If you are in the Everett area, be sure to drop by. Dressing rooms. No refunds or returns. **Cash only**

COAT OUTLET NORTHWEST (ITEM HOUSE)
Tacoma: 2920 S. Steele
Hours: M-F 10-5; Sat. 9-5

Item House used to open its factory store only for special sales, but now you can shop anytime. It's worth the time if you want a smart suit, good-looking separates, coat or rainwear. Their summer suits at 2 for $89 ($59 for one) were less than half store retail. When they can get them, you will find designer label suits as well as their own handsome merchandise. A few men's coats were on a small rack when we visited. You may exchange merchandise or take a store credit. *Shoppers note:* This is also a factory outlet for quality work gloves from the North Star Glove Company around the corner. **Checks**

THE COMPANY STORE
Gold Bar: U.S. 2, Stevens Pass Hwy. (1-793-0221)
Hours: M-Th 10-6:30; F-Sun. 10-7:30

While not exactly next door, The Company Store does such a business we can't ignore it. Originally the factory outlet for the

66   Clothing

Gold Bar Manufacturing Company, goods were limited to backpacks and similar equipment. It is still the factory outlet, but now the store sells ski and sport jackets from a variety of manufacturers. One jacket manufacturer in Seattle told us he sends all seconds to Gold Bar. The store also sells hiking boots and cross-country skiing equipment. Jackets vary widely in styling and price and are discounted because of their ancestry. Seconds are marked and offer the best bargain.   **Checks, M/C, VISA**

THE DOWN FACTORY (DON SHINGLER, INC.)
Seattle: 500 15th E. (322-0800)
Hours: M-Sat. 9-5

This is a factory store outlet selling first-quality (not seconds) men's, women's, juniors' and children's down parkas and vests, pants, tops and warm-ups with name-brand labels. Down-insulated apparel sells for 30-50% off normal retail. The store also sells down quilts and comforters. Dressing room available. Exchanges; refunds.   **Checks, M/C, VISA**

FACTORY FALLOUTS
Seattle: 721 Virginia (622-1926)
Hours: M-Sat. 11-5

We've discovered another great place to look for children's (infants-14, boys and girls) clothing. The way things get worn out, savings on children's clothing is always a fantastic plus! Factory Fallouts stocks a good selection of pants, blouses, warm-ups, etc.—some well-known name brands. When we visited, they had a large stock of the smaller children's sizes, all at good prices. This would be a good spot to buy baby gifts.

Besides clothing, this factory outlet carries women's (sizes 5/6-14/16) pants, skirts, blouses, coats—also at good savings. Dressing rooms. Exchanges allowed on nonsale items only. No refunds.   **Checks, M/C, VISA**

FARWEST GARMENTS
Tukwila: 18375 Olympic S. (251-5010)
Hours: T-Sat. 10:30-2

If anyone has found a cheaper place to buy children's parkas, please call us. This factory outlet is well stocked with children's, men's and women's parkas. They are sturdy, basic styles and well-made—some carry "Made for Alaskan Wear" tags. Prices are incredibly low during special sales which run periodically as the seasons shift. Standard pricing is 10% below wholesale. Sales may cut another 20% off. Men's and women's sizes run S-M-L-XL, and children's sizes start at 3 and run all the way up.

Stock is mostly seconds with a few samples mixed in. Flaws or a description of the problem is written on the tag. The outlet also sells zippers, cuffs, buttons, belt buckles, fabrics and other accessory items at discount prices. Exchanges; no refunds. **Checks**

GREEN RIVER SPORTSWEAR, INC.
Tacoma: 2901 Court A (383-4925)
Hours: T, Th 12-4:30; Sat. 10-4

We love these bona fide factory outlets! Smart seamstresses will appreciate their large selection of remnants and bolt ends (stretch knits, denim, duffel, quilted goods, fiberfill) and accessories (zippers, belt buckles, elastic, buttons, etc.). If you don't want to create your own sportswear, check out the jeans, jackets, shirts, skirts, swimwear, vests, etc., most of which are manufactured across the parking lot. They do purchase overstocks from other manufacturers. There is a separate rack for "seconds." Most items run close to the wholesale price. They allow size exchanges with proof of purchase or trade for equal or more valuable items, but *not* on sale merchandise (which must be way below the wholesale price). There are stark fitting rooms. **Checks**

JANA IMPORTS
Seattle: 2126 Westlake (624-6265)
Tukwila: Pavilion, 17900 Southcenter Pkwy. (575-0211)
Hours: *Seattle* **M-F 9-4; Sat. 9-5;** *Pavilion* **M-F 10-9; Sat. 10-6; Sun. 11-5**

You'll enjoy visiting these shops with their attractively arranged and colorful merchandise. Most of the dresses, caftans, skirts, purses and quilted jackets are made from imported fabrics in batik-looking prints. Jana sells goods made of 100% cotton and some silks, for 30-40% off regular retail. Merchandise consists of discontinued styles, overstocks, last season's seconds or slight flaws. We noticed very few flaws, and if there were any, they were marked with masking tape. Everything we saw looked lovely, and the prices even lovelier. An $80 item was selling for $38, a $30 one for $18. Sizes range from juniors' to women's. Dressing room. Exchanges allowed; however, no cash refunds.

Checks, M/C, VISA

THE KATY DID
Renton: 309 2nd S. (226-1615)
Enumclaw: 422 Griffin (825-6907)
Federal Way: 1640-B S. 312th (941-6677)
Auburn: 416 & 512 E. Main (939-2775)
Kent: 218 1st S. (852-6210)
Hours: 10-6 (all stores)

68 Clothing

Another famous-maker jeans outlet! We can hardly believe how they have proliferated over the years since we began this book! You can acquire 2 name-brand jeans for the price of one. They also stock seconds for $10 and less. Parkas and vests (when they stock them) are sold at one low price. Other stock, seasonally, includes sweat outfits and windbreakers. There are no seconds except in the jeans. Children's sizes run 4-18; men's 26-60 in jeans; women's sizes are an incredible 1-18. Shirts are stocked from toddlers' size to full-growns' extra large. Dressing rooms at all locations. Returns are not given, but exchanges for size will be made gladly. The Katy Did salespeople specialize in friendly, low-pressure, knowledgeable help. **Checks, M/C, VISA**

LAWSON MANUFACTURING CO.
Everett: 2221 Everett Ave. (259-1812)
Hours: M-F 9:45-3:45; Sat. 9-1

Call before stopping by Lawson Manufacturing Co., as they may not be open between seasons and/or they may not have much in stock. This is truly an old-styled manufacturing operation—so don't be alarmed when you walk in the door! You'll discover a few racks of extremely well-made, top-quality garments; misses and juniors' coats, pant coats and pant suits (sizes 6-18, 3-13). The coats and suits are beautifully made with great care given to detailing. You'll find no flaws or irregularities. The styles tend to be simple and more tailored, made from 100% wool, wool blends and poplin. They sell for about half regular retail price, but they *are not* inexpensive even then. A few children's coats, priced $25, were available the day we visited. All sales final. **Checks, M/C, VISA**

MOUNTAIN PRODUCTS
Seattle: 306 Occidental S. (628-0728); *Pavilion,* **17900 Southcenter Pkwy. (575-3394)**
Hours: *Occidental* **T-Sat. 10-5:30;** *Pavilion* **M-F 10-9; Sat. 10-6; Sun. 11-5**

Mountain Products is an outlet for Sportscaster and carries the same merchandise. Refer to write-up on Sportscaster. Other Mountain Products outlets are located in Bellingham, Longview, Wenatchee.

PACIFIC TRAIL SPORTSWEAR
Seattle: 1310 Mercer (682-8196)
Hours: M-Sat. 9-6

Pacific Trail is an outlet for parkas, ski pants, sweaters, jackets, rugby shirts, tennis wear. In price range, Pacific Trail fits between Sportscaster and Farwest. The shop is well stocked, but goods change seasonally. All their lines are well styled, and many are carried in boutiques as well as large stores. Look for 30-50% discounts here. Watch for seconds as they are *not* marked. Men's sizes are small to a few XXL's, women's are S-M-L and children's sizes run from 2-14. Fabrics are available at very good prices. One-of-a-kind buttons, too. Most of the items are outerwear. No returns, no exchanges, no repairs—so check your selection carefully. **Checks**

POWDER RIVER, INC.
Sumner: 908 Cherry (863-2281)
Hours: M-F 9-4; Sat. 9-3

Here's an address to record for a visit when it's daffodil season or time to visit the Valley for some fresh farm products. Powder River manufactures for several labels, so their stock of overruns (and sometimes seconds) is unpredictable. Ladies' jackets, pants vests and blazers are often found, although this is a tiny outlet with a few nice styles rather than lots to choose from. Sewing items are a great bargain and include webbing, fabrics, piping, elastic and bias tape. They will accumulate a bag or more of batting scraps upon request. Powder River has opened a factory outlet in Bothell. **Checks**

RAINY DAYS
Seattle: 2013 4th (622-8404)
Hours: M-F 8-5

This quality manufacturer of women's rainwear sells some samples and discontinued styles in sizes 6-18 at discount prices. We can best describe the styling as conservative and add that the fabrics are lovely. Even at 30% off, coat prices are not inexpensive. Nothing is marked. When bolt ends are available, fabrics can be a good buy. All sales final. **Checks, M/C, VISA**

SPORTCASTER CO., INC.
Seattle: 160 S. Jackson (624-2748)
Hours: M-Sat. 9:30-5

Sportcaster has to be the fashion-conscious skier's paradise. Their basement outlet store is not a bad spot for the nonskier either. Sportcaster's good-looking, quality outerwear is sold here at factory outlet prices—about 40% off retail. Some specials cut prices even more. But Sportcaster products are not low cost. If you are in the market for a low-cost parka, go to Farwest. Sportcaster's outlet stock is tremendous and varied. Goods are mostly surplus, but seconds are supposed to be marked. Check the "reject box" for seconds also. This company manufactures warm-ups, men's raincoats, ladies' leather-look jackets, down

70   Clothing

hoods, backpacks, cross-country equipment and parkas for everyone in the family. Men's and women's sizes are S-M-L-XL, and children's start at size 6. Sweaters, zippers and fabrics are also available at good prices. A small dressing room is available. All sales final. **Checks, M/C, VISA**

WALIA'S OF INDIA
Tacoma: 4413 6th Ave. (759-6893)
Hours: M-F 8:30-5:30

This is the warehouse, office, factory outlet and retail shop for a big importer of East Indian clothing. You will find samples and overstocks and clearance items "out front" in the shop. There are also some seconds. Prices run from 20-50% off retail depending on the garment and the reason it is on the sales floor. You can order from their regular line (in back), but you pay full retail. We were intrigued with the variety of colors and styles. There's a lot more here than the usual unpressed cotton goods we are used to seeing in import shops. No returns on anything priced less than full retail. Women's clothing runs sizes S-M-L. Dressing room.
Checks, VISA

FULL-LINE THRIFT STORES

DESERET INDUSTRIES THRIFT STORE
Lynnwood: 17935 Aurora N. (542-9447)
Hours: M-Sat. 10-6

The Church of the Latter Day Saints operates this spacious, well-merchandised thrift store which is also a sheltered workshop for the handicapped. They claim there are over 20,000 clothing items with an average price tag of $1.75 on their racks. Besides the copious racks of clothes, you will find the usual bric-a-brac and housewares, toys, etc. plus new mattresses and some new furniture made in their Salt Lake factory and shipped to Seattle. Twin mattresses were $61 to $101, depending on the grade. A *sturdy* bunk bed was $225. The store is very well groomed. The TV's are on, just like in an appliance shop. This is a good spot for used appliances because of the "in-house" workshop where they are checked over and repaired. They will accept some returns with receipt. **Checks**

GOODWILL INDUSTRIES
Federal Way: 31319 Pacific Hwy. S. (941-0386)
Tacoma: 714 S. 27th (272-7030)
Hours: *Pacific Hwy. S.* **M-F 9:30-8; Sat. 10-7; Sun. 12-5;** *S. 27th*
  M-F 9:30-8:30; Sat. 9:30-7; Sun. 11-6

Clothing

These two retail stores are not a branch of the Seattle Goodwill, but they are very similar as far as merchandise and operation. You'll find less furniture, but plenty of clothing, shoes, knick-knacks, small appliances, books and other small ware. **Checks**

GOODWILL SHOPPING CENTER
Seattle: Rainier S. & S. Dearborn (main store) (329-1000)
Lynnwood: 5421 196th SW (774-6157)
Burien: 455 SW 152nd (246-0835)
Everett: 2726 Lombard (252-6163)
Hours: *Rainier & Dearborn* **M-F 10-8; Sat. 10-6; Sun. 12-6;** *196th SW & SW 152nd* **M-Sat. 10-6;** *Lombard* **M-Sat. 9-5**

Plan to spend the day in the enormous main store. It's been billed as the largest store of its kind in the world. Guinness might take issue, but that's no deterrent in finding some incredible buys, both new and old. Many items are restored to good condition by Goodwill trainees, and it's not uncommon for local merchants to donate new items. There's no way to predict what you will find exciting: a bicycle, new styrofoam centerpiece form, clothes for all ages, yard tools, toys, dishes and glasswear, furniture, jewelry, paintings, shoes, skis, and so on *ad infinitum*. Check the blackboard as you enter for specials; these are usually "10¢ for all boys' T-shirts" kinds of bargains. During holiday periods special seasonal items are in abundance, usually on 1 or 2 tables. tables.

Thirty thousand copies of books (new, used and rare) are stocked here with about 15,000 changes monthly. Plan on spending time browsing because the books are not catalogued.

Checks, M/C, VISA

ST. VINCENT DE PAUL
Seattle: 1001 Fairview N. (623-1492); 17712 15th NE (364-1492)
White Center: 9835 16th SW (763-2130)
Auburn: 926 Auburn Way N. (833-0400)
Everett: 6430 S. Broadway (355-3504)
Federal Way: 14424 Ambaum Blvd. SW (243-6370); 35002
  Pacific Hwy. S. (838-7476)
Tacoma: 4009 S. 56th (474-0519)
Hours: Call stores for hours

St. Vincent de Paul stores carry a wide and ever-changing assortment of secondhand merchandise—books, furniture, clothing, bedding, dishes, etc. Appliances are guaranteed and in working order. All sales final. **Checks, M/C, VISA**

SALVATION ARMY THRIFT STORES
Seattle: 1010 4th S. (Main Store, As Is, & Antique) (624-0200 & 622-9117); 8404 Greenwood N. (784-8586); 520 2nd (622-2650)
Lake City: 12526 33rd NE (363-1606)
Lynnwood: 16530 Hwy. 99 (745-5725)
Everett: 2817 Rockefeller (252-8143)
Bremerton: 606 Park Ave. (373-1881)
Renton: 422 S. 3rd St. (255-0171)
Tacoma: 309 Puyallup Ave. (627-8118); 2805 6th (272-5427)
Mt. Vernon: 1101 E. College Way (424-6441)
Hours: Call store for hours

The Goodwill may have it all under one roof, but the Salvation Army has it all over the place. We shopped the Main and First Avenue stores; they vary greatly in size. First Avenue is very small, so it stocks clothes and small items. The Main store is mid-sized and well ordered. The As Is Store in the basement of this store is hereinafter referred to as "The Pit." We're not sure any unusual project around our house could be completed without a visit to The Pit, from putting together a child's kitchen to enlarging a round table by 12 in. We've never come out empty handed, but there's such a wild assortment of items down there that it's hard to describe accurately. Presumably this is the dead end for overly damaged donations, thus the name, "As Is." No Returns.

From The Pit to Paradise is a short leap upstairs where the Antiques 'n' Things shop is located. The trains and dolls are worth the visit if you are an antique buff in either class or if you want to show your youngsters some classy classics. **Checks**

VALUE VILLAGE THRIFT STORES
Seattle: 2929 27th S. (723-5000); 12548 Lake City Way NE (365-8232)
Burien: 131 SW 157th (246-6237)
Renton: 1222 Bronson Way N. (255-5637)
Lynnwood: 5912 196th SW (775-1944)
Tacoma: 5424 S. Tacoma Way (475-4150)
Hours: M-W 9-7; Th, F 9-9; Sat., Sun. 10-6

Value Village sells some new, but mostly secondhand goods donated to the Northwest Center for the Mentally Retarded. Furniture, clothing and other items are similar in all stores. No refunds. **Checks, M/C, VISA**

Clothing 73

LOW-OVERHEAD OUTLETS

ANDERS CLOTHING CLEARANCE CENTER
Bellevue: 3640 128th SE (Loehmann's Plaza) (641-8090)
Seattle: 2007 4th (223-0271)
Lynnwood: 19800 44th W. (771-3232)
Hours: *Loehmann's Plaza* **M-F 10-9; Sat. 10-6; Sun. 12-5;** *4th Ave.* **M-Sat. 9-9; Sun. 11-5;** *44th Ave. W.* **M-Sat. 10-9; Sun. 11-5**

The area's only pipe-rack operation offers men a chance to save at least 40-60% off on nationally advertised and designer apparel. This is a *good* place, guys, but you'll have to overlook the atmosphere. On looks, the downtown store rates about a one; Lynnwood and Bellevue are "comfortable," due to the effect of carpeting. But your comparisons with prices you've paid elsewhere should convince you that you save money at this no-frills outlet. You'll quickly spot the best buys in suits, shirts, ties, slacks, sportcoats, outerwear, sweaters, etc. Pure silk ties are $8, with an everyday 3/$20 special. Or you can get 3 poly-dacron ties for $10. Suits run from $69.90 to $199.90, and we've seen $100 suits that were ticketed double-plus in nicer surroundings. Sizes run from 36 short to 56 extra long (plus portly sizes).

All merchandise is first quality. There are no seconds or irregulars. Alterations are *very* reasonable, and there are fitting rooms. The "Anders Promise" states that you may return any unaltered purchase (with receipt) within 7 days. No questions asked.

Checks, M/C, VISA

FELL & COMPANY
Tukwila: 4100 West Valley Hwy. (575-8383)
Hours: M-Sat. 9-5:30; Sun. 12-5

If you are among the millions of Levi fans, it's worth your while to find your way to this warehouse outlet. The problem is in locating it—tucked in an industrial area about a mile south of Southcenter. Fell & Co. concentrates on offering bargains, not atmosphere. The store's philosophy is to offer basic clothing at reduced prices. They have the largest stock of Levi's in the northwest AND they guarantee to be below everyone else by at least 25%. Some items run to the 50% savings, especially if they are irregulars or seconds (all of which are marked). If you have qualms about selecting an irregular or a second, check with the owner, Anthony Fell. There's lots to choose from among the shirts, jackets, slacks sweaters, blouses—and, of course, the ubiquitous jeans. Top sellers are the "Bend Over" pants and Levi's Men's Action slacks. Oskhosh, Lee and Kennington garments also hang on racks. Clothing shipments arrive from El Paso every Thursday.

74   Clothing

Special features are the Queen and Petite sections. About a fourth of the store is devoted to children's clothing, although this quantity varies. One of the nicest things about the store is their friendly return policy and their guarantee on everything they sell. **Checks, M/C, VISA**

JEANS 'N STUFF
Lynnwood: 188th & Hwy. 99 (775-5848)
Hours: M, T, Th 10-6; W, F 10-8; Sat. 10-6

Yes, you *will* find some hot prices on fashion jeans and shirts here. This is a small shop full of current-fashion men's and women's casual wear (some children's also), and we highly advise that you comparison shop them when you need to add to your jeans and tops wardrobe. Seconds, which are not indicated but are priced very low, are the best buys of all, and usually these are on hand in both Brittania and James Jean lines. You will note that some items are stock fill-ins or high-demand items ordered for customer convenience and not nearly as discounted. When they run a sale, the savings get even better. **Checks, M/C, VISA**

JEANS TO GO
Bellevue: 11822 NE 8th (453-9517)
Hours: M-F 10-9; Sat. 10-6; Sun. 12-5

You can find something here for the entire family if you are looking for jeans. The savings vary on the store's inventory. Some things are discounted only slightly (less than 10%), while others may be more. Be sure to compare brands and prices to other retail outlets. Dressing rooms. No cash refunds. You can exchange or take an in-store credit if the jeans haven't been worn, shrunk or abused. **Checks, M/C, VISA**

LEATHER PALACE
Bellevue: 300 120th NE (Benaroya Bus. Park) (455-3430)
Hours: M-F 11:30-7; Sat. 11-5:30

If we had discovered this spot before purchasing a suede coat, we could have saved 30-40%. Leather Palace is a warehouse, and low overhead means savings. The Leather Palace sells first-quality, imported leather and suede coats and jackets—both men's and women's. All the merchandise is new and current—no flaws. An excellent selection of styles, sizes and colors available. All sales final. **Checks, M/C, VISA**

FURS

We found it! Fabulous fur discount sales held by national fur liquidators. These "scavenger" fur companies gather new and

Clothing 75

used fur coats, capes, stoles, ponchos, scarves, collars, etc. from sources all over the USA. Among their suppliers are department stores and furriers disposing of returns and unclaimed layaways and insurance companies with a recovered heist on their hands. The sales are held at various locations and are truly classics in bargain shopping. Be there at opening. Prices can range from $5-$10 for small items to $6,500 (original value, $17,000). Expect to save from 25-85%. All furs are labeled according to federal regulations, and the FTC inspects the parent company. Watch for the ads entitled "Unclaimed Furs" or "Preowned & New Furs" in both Seattle papers.

TUXEDOS

If you are contemplating a tuxedo, check into a recycled one. Used tuxedos are available at most rental shops at low prices. One-of-a-kind tuxes may also be available at a bargain price (these tend to be "way-out" in styling). Some large stores hold clearance days for used goods and include shirts, ties and vests in their sale.

OUTLET STORES

BI-LO CLOTHING
Tacoma: 6400 S. Yakima (473-6457)
Hours: M-Th, Sat. 10-6; F 10-9; Sun. 12-4

We are intrigued with these small, out-of-the-way shops where exsalesmen settle down to market national brands at low, low prices. This is the case at Bi-Lo and a growing number of other outlets in the area. The owner takes his markdown at the point of purchase: he buys in assorted lots from his friends in the business at about 30-50% below the normal wholesale, so he can then offer the goods to the public at the same discount. Women's, men's and children's large-sized clothing plus costume jewelry are the specialties at Bi-Lo. The overall stock is gradually expanding. Many of the labels are familiar, some aren't. Refunds and exchanges are welcome—*except* on special sale items. The latter are so far below wholesale that that seems a reasonable policy!
Checks, M/C, VISA

THE CLOTHES CLUB
Burien: 121 SW 152nd (244-0201)
Hours: M-F 10:30-6; Sat. 10:30-5

Membership is $5/year and opens the door to better-quality and designer fashions at cost plus 10%. This is a great place for those who like the feel of well-made, good-looking clothes or like to dress in the latest fashion looks (not the trendy looks—the designers behind these labels have been around for a long time.) The clothes are nicely merchandised and displayed. And there's plenty of free parking. It would be easy to rave on and on about the stock: separates and coordinates, resort and evening wear, etc. Amazingly, sizes run from petites through queens. The wholesale tickets are left on the garments to verify that the savings are authentic.

There's more to come! Bargain hunters can pay well below wholesale prices in the "retail" side of the store. It's confusing, but "retail" only means that you don't have to be a member to shop on this side. The stock is the clearance items from the Club side. Past-season merchandise is reduced to low levels. Since the Club's fashion lines appear preseason, often before the stores themselves have them, the outlet's fashions are often just right for wearing the day you buy them. Retail side or wholesale side, we don't see how you could miss by shopping here.

Checks, M/C, VISA

COATS GALORE, INC.
Puyallup: 106 S. Meridian (845-7131)
Renton: 441 Renton Way (Renton Mall) (226-7800)
Hours: *Puyallup* **M-F 9:30-7; Sat. 9:30-5:30; Sun. 11-5;** *Renton* **M-F 10-9; Sat. 10-6; Sun. 12-5**

We happened upon this outlet one day and consider it to be a stroke of good fortune. We exited with a purse and a fabric wallet for less than half of retail and have been back for raincoats and scarves. That by no means exhausts the inventory: there are coats for every occasion, all priced 30-50% below retail. In fact, if you can't find a coat here, you probably aren't in the mood for one. The stock is fresh with new looks and fabrics as well as the good old standbys. They buy from many coat manufacturers; labels are intact. Costume jewelry is also nice quality and a great buy. The stock is so diverse, and the size range so great (6 petite to 24½) that this is a good place to take a young teen as well as a grandmother. The Renton store is much more spacious, but both locations are well stocked. Returns are accepted with your receipt and within 5 days. **Checks, M/C, VISA**

FASHION CLUB
Lynnwood: 19700 37th Ave. W. (771-2582)
Hours: M-F 10-6; Sat. 10-5

This entry has more unique side-lines than any other discount clothier in the *Shopper*. It will have immense appeal to some of you, and be of little interest to others, so we suggest you stop by to decide for yourself whether the Fashion Club's merchandising approach is for you. The $10 annual membership fee is more than your ticket to 25-50% savings on clothing. It includes complimentary fashion coordination, phone-ahead shopping, informational mailings, 2 open houses/year for members to preview new lines and "men's shopping nights" during the holiday season. There's also free gift wrapping, a 3-day hold policy, $5 off on your next purchase if you bring in a new member, gift certificates, special orders and layaways. You want more? How about complimentary beverages for you (and your children) while you shop? The owner's philosophy is to pamper people on a budget while offering them quality clothing (labels you'll know at once) at a savings. The merchandise arrives before the season, just like "up-town." Career clothes, resort wear, evening wear, separates, dresses—even jeans—are sold in this small outlet. For busy women, this may be just the ticket for dressing better and paying less. There's a large communal dressing room and a small private one. Returns are accepted. Nonmembers are welcome, but must pay full price for selections. **Checks, M/C, VISA**

FRUGALMAN'S
Seattle: 3rd & Marion (Seattle Trust Ct.) (622-9499)
Hours: M-Th 9:30-5:30; F 9:30-7:00; Sat. 10-5

The Trust Court's boutique atmosphere goes well with the quality menswear at Frugalman's. This is definitely a place where the well-dressed man can save money if he is a sage shopper. Suits and sportscoats are consistently priced at least 25% below suggested retail, but keep an eye out for specials and sales. Ties are nearly half off or better; silk ties sell for $7.90 (comparable $20). All garments are first quality, labels intact, and Frugalman's stands behind everything they sell. Exchanges or in-store credit accepted, but no cash refunds. **Checks, M/C, VISA, Amer. Exp.**

GLAD RAGS AND GREAT THINGS
Bellevue: 102-A Bellevue Way NE (451-0770)
Hours: T-Sat. 10-6

Opening with the motto "quality is a style not a price tag," Glad Rags and Great Things stocks a unique selection of women's (size 4-14) fashions: designer and quality fashions from New York and Paris. The clothes look and feel elegant in a simple, understated way. They were of natural fibers: cottons, silks, linens. The shop is not large, but it is attractively arranged to show off the clothes. You'll find separates, pants, skirts, blouses as well as jewelry and accessories, which sell anywhere from 20-50% off normal retail. Even with the discount, things are fairly expensive so don't go in expecting to find $10 blouses or $15 skirts. However, do go take a look. You'll find the owners extremely friendly and helpful—and you may just want to splurge. All sales final. **Checks, M/C, VISA**

GREAT CLOTHES
Kirkland: 401 Parkplace, Suite 325 (827-5444)
Tukwila: Pavilion, 17900 Southcenter Pkwy. (575-8515)
Hours: M-F 10-9; Sat. 10-6; Sun. 12-5

There is no disputing the quality of the clothing in these 2 stores. The labels from the big names are intact and the looks are classy, classic and chic. Prices are in the 20% off range, unless you find something on the sale rack or take advantage of one of their many coupon offerings. (Put your name on the mailing list). We found some items that were not discounted, so read the tickets carefully and ask if you are uncertain. The Kirkland store is large, spacious and well lit. The salespeople at both locations are pleasant and helpful. Our opinion is that if you are into nice clothes, you'll enjoy your visit, appreciate the caliber of the merchandise and get a little discount on the side. They accept returns courteously. Women's sizes run 1-20 and men's S-XL. Juniors and petites are available. **Checks, M/C, VISA**

JAY JACOBS WAREHOUSE
Seattle: 5th & Pine (Basement of Jay Jacobs) (625-5400)
Hours: M, F 10-7; T-Th, Sat. 10-6:30; Sun. 12-5

Wow, has this spot expanded since we first discovered it! It's almost quadrupled in size, space and inventory. A sign in the Warehouse says it all: "Jay Jacobs guarantees everything at least 50% off the original price—some lower; first quality and 99% free of flaws and imperfections; guarantees that the original price on each item was the regular retail price." Since the basement has expanded, men's clothing has been added: shirts, T-shirts, jeans, slacks. You'll also find an increased inventory of women's and girls' shirts, pants, sweaters, blouses, skirts, coats, jewelry and accessories. Sizes range from 3-13. At the end of the summer season, we found skirts selling for 80% off their regular price. Dressing rooms. All sales final. **Checks, M/C, VISA**

KUPPENHEIMER FACTORY STORE
Bellevue: 14405 NE 20th (746-8177)
Seattle: 831 NE Northgate Way (365-4350)
Tacoma: 2520 S. 38th (473-6555)
Hours: M-F 10-9; Sat. 9-6; Sun. 11-5 (both stores)

To adequately assess the bargains inside these new "factory stores" requires that you know a lot about fabrics and garment manufacture. Yes, there are suits from $89-$110 (worsted wool blends $120-$150 and all wool $149-$159), and they sell a popular worsted wool flannel or gabardine slack at less than $40. Since Kuppenheimer stores are the only outlets for the Kuppenheimer Company, the only way to assess their claim to being half the price of equivalent garments elsewhere is to compare their stock with what you already own—or would like to own. Our advice is to wear in your favorite outfit and compare it with the fabric, fit and construction of the Kuppenheimer item. They also allow "try-on" returns (ask first) and exchanges. To round out the stock, they offer Van Heusen shirts at 25% off and ties at roughly 40% off retail. There is a tailor on the premises; charges are nominal. Shirts are sized 14-17; suits 36 S to 50 XL and slacks 28-44 waists.

Checks, M/C, VISA

MATERNITY FACTORY
Seattle: 17145 Southcenter Pkwy. (575-3255)
Hours: M-F 10-9; Sat. 12-5; Sun. 12-5

What a find! Wish we'd had this one around when we were pregnant. What better way to budget? The Maternity Factory sells top-quality, name-brand maternity fashions. You'll be pleased to know there's an excellent selection of pants, tops, dresses, lingerie—all selling 25-50% off suggested retail. You'll also find a large selection of sizes (ranging from 4-24). If you're pregnant, be sure to check out this place. **Checks, M/C, VISA**

NORDSTROM'S CLOTHES RACK
Seattle: 1501 5th (628-2111)
Bellevue: Bellevue Square (455-5800)
Hours: M, F 9:30-9; T-Th, Sat. 9:30-6; Sun. 11-5; *Bellevue* **M-F 9:30-9; Sat. 9:30-6; Sun. 11-6**

The Clothes Rack in both places offers a continually changing broken stock of bargains in sizes 5-18, ladies, juniors, misses. These are not factory seconds but items sold regularly through Nordstrom stores. Men's and children's clothing is not usually stocked except during the twice-yearly sales (Jan. and July). Returns are permitted but only to the Clothes Rack. You cannot return items to any of the other Nordstrom stores.

Checks, Nordstrom's Credit Card, Amer. Ex., M/C

TRUDI'S BACK ROOM
Bellevue: 2102 140th NE (747-8881)
Hours: M-Sat. 10-6; Sun. 12-5

People are always asking us, "Where can we find large-size clothing for a savings?" Well, we've found just the place: Trudi's Back Room, located inside the Queen Size Boutique. For those of you needing large, queen-size fashions, you can't miss here. You'll find a nice, varied selection of separates, coordinates, dresses, and even coats—all selling 30-50% off normal retail. All are attractive styles and well-known brands. Make your selection carefully, as all sales are final. **Checks, M/C, VISA**

SAMPLE SHOPS

Clothing in sample shops, contrary to most goods in outlets, is top quality because salespeople sell from the samples. When a trip is over or a new season begins, the samples are sold—either by a salesperson or manufacturer's rep or to a sample shop. Samples will be widely varied in color and style, but narrowly varied in size. Most women's fashion samples will be in small sizes. Men's samples tend to be in the medium range with suits and sport jackets in regular sizes. Since many of the samples are often cut without patterns, sizes will be less uniform than production goods. Try on any sample before buying. Usually samples can be exchanged, but few shops offer cash refunds. If you are concerned, ask before buying.

The following shops sell primarily samples, but you will find some shops that sell discounted retail garments as well.

CLOTHES OUT
Seattle: 2600 Elliott (622-4342)
Federal Way: 3131 S. 320th (839-3550)
Tukwila: Pavilion, 17900 Southcenter Pkwy. (575-9440)
Hours: *Seattle & Federal Way:* **M-F 10-6; Sat. 10-5;** *Tukwila:* **M-F 10-9; Sat. 10-6; Sun. 11-5**

A dynamic spot, selling quality name-brand samples—names you'll recognize. It is a good-sized establishment stocking a large, varied selection of juniors' and women's wear. These are not irregulars or seconds. Sizes available are determined by the manufacturer's sample size, but there is a range depending on the company. New samples arrive daily. You pay 10% over the wholesale ticket price. All sales are final. Sign up for their mailing list to be kept informed of hour changes, special sales, etc.

Checks, M/C, VISA

DEEDEE'S KLOSET
Redmond: 16940 NE 79th (881-6113)
Hours: M-Sat. 10-6

Located slightly off the main drag in Redmond, this small shop, located in a house, sells some very nice samples—mainly size 9-10's, though she does get some smaller and some larger things. Call to see what sizes are on hand. You'll find name-brand women's dresses, pants, blouses, scarfs, etc. selling for approximately 30% off normal retail. We were impressed with the large variety of infant clothing which the shop also carries. Dressing rooms. Exchanges are allowed on non-sale items. No cash refunds.

Checks, M/C, VISA

FIRST STOP
Seattle: 514 15th E. (322-1414)
Hours: M-Sat. 10:30-6

What a curious name for a men's sample shop! Presumably they mean you should make this your first stop and you won't want to go elsewhere...They carry quality men's sweaters, jeans, shirts, shorts, suits, blazers, slacks and accessories—primarily in sample sizes (mediums), although the suits and jackets come in a full range and there are smalls and larges available in some lines. The store atmosphere is "up-beat," and the merchandise is sharp-looking. Dressing rooms. Exchanges are welcome or you can get a credit voucher, but no refunds. **Checks, M/C, VISA**

C. B. FINNEGAN AND CO.
Seattle: 1st & Virginia (Terminal Sales Bldg.) (622-7970)
Hours: M-F 7-11:45, 1-4

C. B. Finnegan and Co. sells a wide variety of samples at 40-50% off retail. These are name-brand samples, not seconds or irregulars, of men's, women's, children's and infants' clothing. You'll also find towels, underwear, mittens, caps and football blankets—plus many other items. **Checks, M/C, VISA**

GLAVIN'S SAMPLE SHOP
Seattle: 116 15th (325-6975)
Hours: M-Sat. 10-5

Glavin's carries women's pants, skirts, blouses, sweaters, lingerie and dresses, sizes 5-16 at savings of 30-50% off retail. These are samples and broken stock. Some things appear "dated," but the stock is worth looking at. Dressing rooms. Exchanges, but no refunds. Layaway. **Checks**

K. C. AND FRIENDS CO.
Kirkland: 220 Kirkland Ave. (822-3243)
Hours: M-Sat. 10-5:30; Th 10-8 (10-9 in summer)

Eastsiders who haven't yet discovered K. C. & Friends Co. are in for a treat. This is a super sample boutique. The racks are filled with quality clothing in current styles and classic good looks. Prices are just above wholesale. The one drawback is that the stock consists primarily of sample sizes, which means the very small and large sizes are few and far between. They do manage to obtain some styles in a full-size range, however, so if you are outside the "average" sizes, call first to see what they have on hand in your size. They carry about an equal amount of men's and women's clothing with a smaller proportion of children's things. No refunds, exchanges only. **Checks, M/C, VISA**

KAY'S SAMPLE SHOPPE
Seattle: 2nd & Virginia (Terminal Sales Bldg.) (682-0298)
Hours: M-F 10-4:30; Sat. 10-4

Kay's sells ladies' samples at wholesale prices. There's a good variety and selection of blouses, jackets, pants, long and short dresses and skirts. This well-stocked shop can save a working woman a lot of money. For that matter, any woman will find good prices on quality clothing here. You can walk a few blocks uptown to compare Kay's prices and quality to regular retail outlets. Ladies' samples are sold at wholesale prices. There's a good variety and selection of blouses, jackets, pants, long and short dresses and skirts, primarily, but not exclusively, in sample sizes. These are name-brand items—nice quality. All sales final.

Checks, M/C, VISA

LOEHMANN'S
Bellevue: Loehmann's Plaza, I-90 at I-405 (641-7596)
Hours: M, T, Th-Sat. 10-5:30; W 10-9; Sun. 12-5

Loehmann's offers the discriminating woman top designer fashions for low prices. We've seen clothing on Loehmann's racks priced 25-50% higher at other retail shops. You need to be a comparative shopper so you can spot the values. The main room carries quality name-brand (though labels have been cut out, you may recognize them) dresses, coats, blouses, skirts, sweaters, sportswear and accessories. The racks in the back room contain top designer merchandise. Merchandise changes constantly. If you don't find something the first time, try again later.

Loehmann's communal dressing room is spacious, mirrored and well lit. Don't let this throw you! We've found it to be an asset. Ask the person next to you what she thinks of the garments you're trying on. It's nice to have another opinion, especially if you can't make up your mind about which outfit looks better. And you do need to make up your mind, as Loehmann's does not allow exchanges or refunds. No alterations, no charges. **Checks**

MOSS BAY MERCANTILE
Kirkland: 7 Lake Shore Plaza (827-1116)
Hours: M-Sat. 10-6; Eves. by appointment

We were delighted to find this excellent sample boutique in our own backyard. Classic, famous-brand-name men's clothing (and some women's) sells for 30% off. Sale tables offer even greater reductions. Men's sizes generally run 15-16½ in shirts, M and L in knits, 40-42 in suits, although they do get greater size ranges in some items. Shorts, for example, come in a full size range for men and women. If you aren't a sample size, you may still find a handsome tie. They also carry boys' prep lines (sizes 16, 28 waist).

Good-looking pajamas, robes, sweaters, jackets are artfully displayed in this tasteful shop. Except for the price tags, you would never expect to save money in this type of environment. The service is outstanding. Full returns are accepted.

Checks, M/C, VISA

PIC-A-DILLY
Seattle: 1108 Aurora Plaza N. (542-4466); 10005 Holman Rd. at 6th NW (783-6343)
Bellevue: 117 106th (455-4052)
Bremerton: 3320 Wheaton at Sylvan (377-7706)
Burien: 205 SW 152nd (243-6716)
Everett: 7213 S. Evergreen Way (353-9925); 1512 S. Broadway (353-7009)
Federal Way: 31503-B Pacific Hwy. S. (839-4414)
Lynnwood: 185 3rd W. (771-1764)
Redmond: 14930 NE 24th (881-9753)
Renton: 36 S. Grady Way (228-1465)
Tacoma: 2941 S. 38th (474-5849); 10111-H Gravelly Lake Dr. SW (582-8131)
Tukwila: Pavilion, 17900 Southcenter Pkwy. (573-3460)
Hours: Generally M-F 10-9; Sat. 10-6; Sun 12-5

Pic-A-Dilly sells young women's current, name-brand-quality fashion apparel at 30-60% off regular prices. New merchandise is received every week, providing a wide, changing selection for the fashion-conscious customer. Layaways are 25% down, for 30 days.

Checks, M/C, VISA

PLAZA DEL SOL JEANS WAREHOUSE
Seattle: 3157 Elliott (282-5050)
Bellevue: 229 Bellevue Way NE (455-5575)
Hours: M-F 10-8; Sat. 10-6; Sun. 11-5

In your search for jeans, don't bypass this spot. Some of the good, name-brand jeans we saw were selling for reduced prices (25-50% off retail). However, others were not. Gauze peasant blouses were going for about half their usual retail. Dressing rooms. No cash refunds.

Checks, M/C, VISA, Amer. Exp.

THE SAMPLE SHOP
Lake Stevens: 1804 124th NE (334-8970)
Hours: M-Sat. 10-6

Size 10 and under will find a variety of women's samples selling for 40-60% less than in the department stores. The styles range from youthful and trendy to the more conservative. Exchanges are okay.

Checks, M/C, VISA

SAMPLE SHOP
Seattle: 613 Queen Anne N. (282-8780)
Hours: M-F 10-5:30; Sat. 10-5

Women's name-brand (labels intact) clothing samples at 40-50% savings. Sample Shop carries shirts, blouses, pants, sweaters, long and short dresses, some coats and jackets, robes and gowns in sizes 6-16. Dressing rooms. No cash refunds. No exchanges after 6 days. No refunds on layaways left over 30 days.

Checks, M/C, VISA

SAMPLE SHOPPE ETC.
Mercer Island: 7836 SE 28th (232-6080)
Hours: M-Sat. 10-6

The owner of this shop uses his connections with high-end clothing manufacturers and reps to obtain classically styled garments at excellent prices. He then passes on the savings to his customers. We found top-quality, well-known, name-brand clothing for men and women. There is a fair range of sizes, not just sample sizes, selling for 25-50% off regular retail. There are no seconds or irregulars and no "dated" items. Except for the price tags, you would never suspect this shop was a discount operation. Dressing rooms.

Checks, M/C, VISA

TERMINAL SALES BUILDING
Seattle: 1st & Virginia

Some manufacturers' reps rent display space in the Terminal Sales Building for showing samples to prospective buyers. They sell samples from time to time as seasons change. Look for sample sales posted on a bulletin board inside the foyer of the First Avenue entrance. However, since there is a charge for advertising on this board, not all reps use it. They may post "Samples for Sale" signs upstairs in their showroom windows. It pays off to shop this building frequently enough to know where and when the best buys can be found. Be sure to ask if you are buying seconds so you can check for flaws. No returns. Never interrupt a conversation between a salesperson and buyer, even when sample signs are posted.

It is not unusual to find salespeople's sample sales advertised under the "Garage Sale" heading of the classified section of newspapers. If you once find a rep selling what you like to buy who holds these events regularly, you can enjoy a direct pipeline to a great way of saving money.

Three sample shop in the Terminal Sales Building remain open year-round and welcome retail trade:

C. B. Finnegan and Co.   Kay's Sample Shoppe

Prasad's—See Giftware

VALERIE'S
Seattle: 5621 University Way NE (524-0073)
Hours: M-F 11-6; Sat. 10-6

Valerie's is a very chic little shop. It features a sophisticated collection of women's clothing at savings of 35-50% or better. Everything is first quality, and new stock arrives weekly. Sizes are 3-13, mostly, with some misses sizes also. Most of the labels are intact, although even without them these clothes are distinctly boutique. Some accessories such as belts and lingerie are sold at the same discount prices. Layaways and dressing rooms. Credits are given if you make an error in judgment, but generally there are no refunds. **Checks, M/C, VISA**

SHOES

THE BON SHOE RACK
Seattle: 4th & Pike (344-2121)
Hours: M-Sat. 10-6; Sun. 12-5

We're pleased to announce the Bon now has a farily good-sized shoe rack in its basement. You'll find shoes for the entire family, all marked down about 50%. These are name-brand, top-quality shoes which have previously sold upstairs for regular prices. You can return things, which is a nice advantage. The Shoe Rack works like the one at Nordstrom's—serve yourself. If you need help, ask for it. **Checks, Bon Credit, Amer. Exp.**

GORDON'S SHOELAND
Tacoma: 5914 6th (564-7261); 3121 S. 38th (473-0252)
Spanaway: 161st & Pacific (537-0552)
Lakewood: 9630 Gravelly Lake Dr. SW (582-0580)
Auburn: 402 Auburn Way S. (924-0277)
Hours: M-F 10-9; Sat. 10-6; Sun 11-6

Shoeland sells shoes for the entire family at savings of 30-50% off. Well-known brands and imported knock-offs, but overall the quality is good. This is not a no-name discounter. Buyers for these stores go direct to famous manufacturers and buy assorted lots, taking advantage of off-season production and surplus stock. We recommend that you check for defects, although seconds are supposed to be marked at the factory. With large volume buying they can slip by. Shoeland will take exchanges on defective merchandise, but there are no refunds. You will find many, many styles to choose from here. New shoes arrive weekly. Everything is arranged on self-serve racks for easy browsing and trying on. There are also socks, nylons and slippers. Mom's Note: This is one of the few places we've found children's brand-name shoes discounted and in quantity. **Checks, M/C, VISA**

86   Clothing

NORDSTROM'S SHOE RACK
Seattle: 1501 5th (628-2111)
Bellevue: Bellevue Square (455-5800)
Hours: *Seattle* **M, F 9:30-9; T-Sat. 9:30-6; Sun. 11-5;** *Bellevue* **M-F 9:30-9; Sat. 9:30-6; Sun. 11-6**

A changing broken stock of men's and women's shoes sells at sharply cut prices at the Shoe Rack in the basement of this downtown Seattle store. These shoes are sold regularly through Nordstrom stores—no factory seconds, nothing brought in. Salespersons are not available to help with fitting—one of the reasons for the low prices. Exchanges allowed but only at the Shoe Rack. You cannot return or exchange your purchase at any other Nordstrom store. No layaways.
Checks, Nordstrom's Credit Card, Amer. Exp., M/C

THE SHOE FACTORY
Seattle: 5th & Northgate Way (365-4670)
Bellevue: 3630 128th SE (Loehmann's Plaza) (746-1524)
Hours: M-F 10-9; Sat. 10-6; Sun. 12-5 (both stores)

A fantastic addition to the greater Seattle area, which has needed more shoe outlets. You'll discover an excellent and large selection of men's and women's well-known, name-brand shoes—casual and dressy styles, leather boots, moon boots, after-ski boots, jogging and tennis shoes. Prices range 30-50% off. The shoe factory also stocks some accessories: purses, socks, shoelaces.

The store allows refunds if you have your sales receipt. No returns allowed on sale merchandise. No layaway plan.
Checks, M/C, VISA

N.W. SHOE OUTLET
Seattle: 1514 6th (621-7633)
Hours: M-F 9-5; Sat. 10-4:30

Check out this shop. Well-known name brands stock the shelves, selling for 25-50% off. Savings depend on the shop's purchase price. When they get a good discount, they'll pass it on to you. Men's (6½-13) and women's (5-11) styles are available—casual, sporty, dressy and even cowboy boots. We've seen some beautiful shoes here, which sell for more money just a few blocks away. The store permits exchanges if the shoes have not been worn and if you have your sales receipt.   **Checks, M/C, VISA**

RAFF'S SHOES
Seattle: 401 E. Pine (323-6008)
Hours: M-F 9-7; Sat. 9-6; Sun. 12-5

Raff's Warehouse Retail Store sells a mixed bag of shoes at regular Raff prices, which tend to be less than other shoe retailers. It has racks of $4, $5, $9, $12 women's shoes—broken stock of sizes and styles. These are not nationally advertised shoes. All sales final. **Checks, M/C, VISA**

UNIFORMS

RE & P, INC.
Everett: 2931 Norton (259-4101)
Hours: M-F 10-6; Sat. 9-3

There are 2 very different bargains in this industrial workwear shop: (1) used work coveralls (pants, shirts, jackets and shop coats) ranging from $2-$15, in varying condition, and (2) new Wrangler western shirts in assorted sizes and colors priced at a bargain $12.95. Returns are allowed on new goods.

Checks, M/C, VISA

SUPERIOR LINEN SERVICE
Tacoma: 1012 Center (383-2636)
Hours: M-F 8-4:30

Superior is the only outlet we've found in the Tacoma area which has a thrift store for used items. When we visited, smocks were $2.95, coveralls $6, work shirts $1.89 and pants $2.98. PEERLESS LAUNDRY AND DRY CLEANERS (627-1177) sells coveralls only from their office. WASHINGTON UNIFORM SERVICES (272-4116) does the same thing. **Checks**

CHILDREN & INFANTS

BELLA'S BABY WORLD
Bellevue: 123 116th NE (453-8083)
Hours: M, W-Sat. 10-5:30; T 10-7; Sun. 11-4

This diminutive consignment shop, located on the edge of Bellevue's auto row, carries an excellent selection of nearly new and new baby clothes (infants-toddler 5), accessories, furniture. The used things had excellent prices and were in excellent condition. Some new brand names were also priced below normal retail. We also found a nice rack of used maternity clothes. What better way to save money? The shop owners also rent baby furniture. All sales final. **Checks**

BUTTONS AND BOWS
Bothell: 3808 Bothell Way SE (481-3690)
Hours: M-Sat. 10-5

Buttons and Bows, an inflation-fighting store, carries new and almost-new children's clothing and other children's items. The owners consign children's used clothing and furniture that is in top-notch condition. New items, name brand, are offered at reduced prices. All sales final on consigned things. Exchanges allowed on new things, which are samples. **Checks**

CAROUSEL CHILDREN'S CONSIGNMENT SHOP
Issaquah: 147 Front N. (392-0109)
Hours: M-Sat. 10-5

This shop has moved and grown since they were first in our book. The inventory has also grown. They've added some women's clothing, maternity, some samples and homemade fashions to their stock of children's items. They offer a 24-hour approval if agreed upon at time of purchase. **Checks**

Children & Infants

CARTER'S FACTORY OUTLET
Tacoma: 1415 E. 72nd (472-9340)
Hours: M-Sat. 10-5; Sun. 1-5

How fortunate Tacoma is to have one of the regional outlets for Carter-brand children's clothing! Irregulars and closeouts are sent here, and you stand to save at least 20-30% (off suggested retail) on everything in the store. Closeouts are first quality. The outlet also carries first-quality items from vendors of the same caliber at the same discount prices. There are definite fall, winter, summer and spring stock changes. Keep your eyes open for clearance bins and racks where savings run in the 50% range.

The store is large and comfortable. There are dressing rooms. Best of all, there's a playroom for young children so you can shop peacefully. Sizes run from full layette and toddler range to girls' 4-6X and 7-14 and boys' 4-7 and 8-14. Exchanges and refunds with your sales slip. **Checks**

CHICKABIDDY TRADING CO.
Seattle: 1720 N. 45th (633-5437)
Hours: T-Sat. 10-5

Chickabiddy sells new and used clothes, toys and baby equipment (80% is used, 20% is new). They carry maternity, infant and children's clothing through size 14. They will trade your used items for immediate credit on new or used merchandise. They also consign some handcrafted items.

The Trading Co.'s philosophy is to offer quality and practical things at a reasonable price. Your little ones are welcome to play while you barter or buy. Exchanges can be made on new items, but there are no cash refunds. **Checks**

A DOLLAR'S WORTH
Lynnwood: 19410 35th W. (774-9186)
Hours: M 11-3; T-F 10-5; Sat. 11-4

A good selection and large stock of recycled children's clothing and accessories. If you're expecting your first, drop by, as they carry consigned maternity clothes as well. **Checks, M/C, VISA**

GOLDEN GIRAFFE
Edmonds: 917 Puget Dr. (776-6262)
Hours: M-F 10-6; Sat. 10-4

If you're near Edmonds and need children's clothes (sizes 0-14, boys and girls), take a peek at the Golden Giraffe. You'll also discover toys, furniture and some maternity things. These are all consigned goods, nearly new, along with some new handcrafted items. Be sure to take your children with you, as all sales are final. **Checks**

Children & Infants

GRANDMOTHER'S HOUSE
Lynnwood: 7331 196th SW (771-4640)
Hours: M-Sat. 9:30-5:30; Sun. 12-5

What a find! And as far as we know, it's one of a kind in the Seattle-Tacoma area. Grandma buys only quality used baby and children's furniture, toys and dolls, baby accessories and mint-condition infant clothing to size 3. She will make an appointment to come see your furniture if you have some left-behinds in good condition. Upon entering the shop, we were immediately struck by the high standards and warm atmosphere. You couldn't ask for a cleaner, more inviting place to save lots of money on lovable, but often expensive, things for little ones. **Checks, M/C, VISA**

JUST FOR YOU
Seattle: 19828 Aurora N. (542-3993)
Hours: M-F 9:30-5; Sat. 10-2

A nice children's consignment shop featuring "used but not abused" children's articles (infantwear through size 14), accessories and maternity clothes as well as some new handmade gift items. All sales final, though you can arrange for a 24-hour exchange. **Checks**

THE KIDS CLOSET
Seattle: 5032 Wilson S. (723-1979)
Hours: M-Sat. 10-6

The bright and spacious atmosphere of this "new and nearly new" shop is enhanced by the warm attitude of its 4 owners. Quality items are stocked to fill the gaps in their consignment areas. You'll find Gerber baby pants, sox and bibs, the Spencer underwear line, also tights, p.j.'s and so forth (sizes 0-14). These items are marked at standard discount house prices. The Oshkosh line is well represented. Handcrafted items (including ethnic dolls and a character called Lucy Longlegs) are sold on consignment. Consignments are taken any time the store is open, and they will take anything related to children and maternity clothes. Refunds are accepted if the item is new, has the tag on and you have your receipt. There is no refund or exchange on consignment goods. **Checks**

KID'S EXCHANGE
Tacoma: 2726 N. Proctor (752-6434)
Hours: M-F 10-5; Sat. 11-4

Just what Tacoma has needed—a consignment shop totally catering to children's items. Those of you who have children and those of you expecting should definitely stop by this location. The store stocks not only clothing (sizes 0-14/16 boys and girls), but baby furniture, toys, shoes and maternity clothes. Most of these are nice-quality, used things, but they also carry some new handmade merchandise. They keep a good inventory, but things come and go quickly. **Checks**

KIDS KLOSET
Burien: 2034 SW 152nd (243-1795)
Hours: T-F 9:30-4:30; Sat. 10-4; (summers) T-Sat. 10-4

The two owners of the Kids Kloset merchandise their consigned children's (sizes 0-14) and maternity items to advantage in this remodeled and well-kept shop. They will consign anything relating to children or expecting Moms, including small toys and furniture. As a special service to customers, they display a bulletin board which may be used free of charge to advertise anything that has to do with children, i.e., day care, furniture, etc. New craft items are also sold at the Kids Kloset, such as sweaters, booties, stick horses and decorative hair ribbons. Dressing room available. Returns are not accepted. **Checks**

KID'S KORNER
Edmonds: 8311 212th SW (775-5152)
Hours: T-Sat. 11-5

Another good spot for children's consigned clothing and shoes. A nice selection (newborn-size 14) is on hand. All sales final, so be sure you have your little ones along for fitting. **Checks**

KID'S KORRAL
Kent: 216 E. Gowe (854-8807)
Hours: T-Sat. 10-4

In this spot you'll discover recycled clothing for infants through juniors. It has a variety of boys' and girls' clothes as well as shoes, toys, accessories. Exchanges are allowed—discuss at the time of purchase. **Checks**

KID'S STUFF
Renton: 10 B NE (833-7188)
Hours: M-Sat. 10-5

Another good place to check for children's clothing (infants-size 14), as well as dolls, stuffed animals, accessories. You'll find both new and used goods. All sales are final on consigned items.

ME 'N MOMS
Seattle: 8414 5th NE (524-9344)
Hours: M-F 9:30-5; Sat. 11-4

Expectant Moms and little "me's" (sized 0-14) have a choice of purchasing consigned clothing, toys, baby accessories and equipment or brand-new, discounted items. Since the store stocks slightly more used than new items, it's possible to recycle your children's wardrobes throughout the growth-spurt years. The Oshkosh line is available, including denim jumpers for Moms in sizes 0-16. Several major maternity lines of new clothing are offered at a discount. Snugli carriers are also on hand. Me 'n Moms is a bright and friendly place to start fighting the high costs of outfitting your children—right from the very beginning! Dressing rooms. Two-day return policy. **Checks**

MOUSE CLOSET
Bellevue: 521 156th SE (641-0531)
Hours: M-Sat. 10-5

This store carries a large selection of new, well-known, name-brand, sample clothes up to size 8 for boys, size 12 for girls. These clothes sell for 30-50% off regular retail. The shop also sells secondhand children's clothes (infant up to size 12) and maternity clothes on consignment, as well as handmade items. The merchandise is top quality and sells at less than half price. Handcrafts include stuffed animals, toys, quilts and knickknacks, all beautifully finished and unique. Refunds and exchanges permitted on cash sales. Dressing room. **Checks, M/C, VISA**

PUNCH AND JUDY
Seattle: 413 15th E. (324-4409)
Hours: M-Sat. 10:30-4:30

Punch and Judy carries top-quality, name-brand children's clothing at prices slightly above wholesale. The shop is bright and well stocked with a beautiful and large variety of coats, dresses, jackets, pants and shirts. Boys' sizes range from infant to size 18; girls' sizes from infant through size 12. Exchanges with receipt or tag, but no refunds. Layaway plan. **Checks, M/C, VISA**

RAINBOW'S END, FASHION OUTLET FOR CHILDREN
Bellevue: 3710 128th SE (Loehmann's Plaza) (624-6000)
Hours: M-F 10-8; Sat. 10-6; Sun. 12-5

Looking for high-fashion, top-quality children's wear? Rainbow's End sells regular name-brand merchandise at good, reasonable prices. You'll find savings from 10-30% on dresses, skirts, shirts, pants, infant items and underwear. There is a large clearance rack. These are not samples or irregulars, but complete lines so that all sizes are available: boys' 7-14, girls' 7-14, infants', toddlers'. Dressing rooms. **Checks, M/C, VISA**

RASCAL'S GLAD RAGS
Seattle: 3243 California SW (935-3127)
Hours: T-F 10-5; Sat. 12-5

There are two requirements for consigning items at Rascal's: (1) the item must have something to do with children and (2) it must be in good condition so that it will fit the description of "nearly new." Shoppers will discover that this policy has filled the small store with good-quality clothing for children (sizes 0-12) and also for mothers-to-be. Baby furniture and toys are also consigned. Handcrafted new items such as quilts, sweaters and T-shirts are also available. Dressing room. All sales are final.
Checks

ROSEBUD SHOP
Seattle: 18518 Ballinger Way NE (363-7790)
Hours: T-Sat. 11-5:30

We generally do not include stores which don't consign or buy, but at press time this newly owned shop was stocked to the brim with small children and infants clothing (sizes 0-6) at prices generally under $5 and averaging $2. Keeping children clothed is tough enough on family budgets to warrant pointing out this good spot. The owner might trade if you have nice things to offer. Equipment is also sold. Exchanges, but no refunds. **Checks**

THE SECRET GARDEN CHILDREN'S BOOKSHOP
Seattle: 7900 E. Greenlake Dr. N. (524-4556)
Hours: M-Sat. 10-6

This is a children's bookstore, probably the only one of its kind in Seattle. The shop is small, cozy and homey—the perfect place for small children and adults to browse through a wide variety of children's literature. Most of the inventory is new, but there are some shelves of used paperbacks and hardbacks selling at good prices. All proceeds from the shop benefit children's projects.
Checks

TOYS R US
Tukwila: 16700 Southcenter Pkwy. (575-0780)
Lynnwood: 18601 Alderwood Mall Blvd. (771-4748)
Hours: M-Sat. 9:30-9:30; Sun. 11-5 (both stores);
  M-Sat. 9:30-midnight; Sun. 9:30-10
  (holiday shopping season at both stores)

If you haven't visited Toys R Us yet, you are in for a treat. Each store contains 43,000 sq. ft. of inventory which ranges from infant formula, disposable diapers, toys and clothing to video games and science kits. Just about everything you can imagine in the way of bikes, games, crafts, records, model trains and gym sets, not to mention the vast selection of toys. And if you're giving a party, they carry favors and giftwrap, plus seasonal items for Halloween, etc. The price is right, too. They do not run sales, but we have yet to be disappointed by their price structure. Bicycle assembly is reasonable and fast (2 days maximum). We would like to thank whoever thought to put in the nice, clean, large restrooms. It was probably the same thoughtful person who came up with a midnight closing time for holiday shoppers and the "no questions asked" return policy (your money back, provided you bring along the sales slip). Leave the item in its box and have all the component parts. **Checks, M/C, VISA**

THE TREE HOUSE
Redmond: 15742 Redmond Way (885-1145)
Hours: M-Sat. 10-5; Sun. 12-5

An impressive consignment shop for children's clothing (sizes 0-10) and children's furniture. The day we visited, they had a large, excellent selection, and all in topnotch condition—at good prices! There is a yearly $1 consignment registration fee. **Checks**

THE UNICORN
Kirkland: 12700 NE 124th (823-4868)
Hours: M-Sat. 10-5; Sun. 11-4

It's easy to miss this location, but well worth the finding. The racks are full with consigned children's clothing. There is a lesser quantity of "in" items for juniors, maternity and ladies wear plus baby furniture and toys. The owner runs a regular children's clothing shop elsewhere, so she is able to stock this shop with new items at reduced prices. When we stopped in, there were 2 large racks of new young children's clothes at half off. Dressing rooms. New clothes are returnable (with your receipt), and used clothing will be taken back *only* if returned by 10 the next morning. **Checks**

THE VILLAGE CRAFTSMAN
Seattle: 5208 Ballard NW (783-5575)
Hours: T-F 10-5; Sat. 10-2 (usually)

Here's a factory outlet on behalf of your children! Clever little wooden toys are made here and distributed to gift and tourist shops. Seconds of paddle boats, ferries, cars, trucks and other handcrafted wooden toys can be purchased at a third off or better at prices ranging from 25¢ to $5. **Checks**

HOME FURNISHINGS

APPLIANCES

AJAX ELECTRIC, INC.
Seattle: 2911 1st S. (622-9945)
Tacoma: 747 S. Fawcett (383-3446)
Hours: M-F 8-5; Sat. 8-4

Ajax is the factory-authorized parts and service shop for Mirro, Farberware, Hamilton Beach, Mr. Coffee, Water Pik, Moulinex, West Bend and other well-known manufacturers. They sell an array of small appliances which have been factory serviced. All carry a guarantee, some are 90 days, some for a full year. Factory-serviced items are not returnable unless they are defective. We suggest using the Jafco catalog for price comparisons.
Checks, M/C, VISA

BAYSIDE SUPPLY COMPANY
Everett: Call first 259-4994
Hours: Call after 4 or all day Sat.

First, shop around for the new appliance you want. Then call to make an appointment to check Bayside's catalog prices. They sell all the major brands by order only—there's no showroom— and no overhead! **Checks**

BOTHELL APPLIANCE AND TV
Bothell: 10042 Main (485-0551)
Hours: M-Sat. 9-5:30 (both stores)

Once a year you can save at least 25% on slightly used ranges, washers, dryers, refrigerators and freezers. These appliances have been loaned to local school districts for instructional purposes. They are on loan for a 9-month period. When the school year is over, they're sold at a good savings. They look and operate like new. All factory warranties are included. This program is sponsored by the manufacturer, so it is of no cost to the taxpayer. If you're in the market for a large appliance, check this store at the end of the school year. **Checks, M/C, VISA**

REMCO
Tacoma: 6824 W 19th St. (565-7373)
Hours: M, F 10-8; T, W, Th 10-7; Sat. 9-6

Remco sells rental returns (appliances, TV's, stereos, microwaves) the same way the rental furniture stores do. The difference is that there is a 90-day limited warranty on parts and labor plus whatever remains on the original appliance warranty from the factory. The sale price is determined by the number of months the equipment has been rented, so you can reap the benefit of someone else's rental dollars. Most returned items are put up for sale after they are 6 months old, so these are generally much newer pieces of equipment than you find in the used appliance shops. *Note:* Merchandise is not on the floor, and at times there may not be much available. **Checks, M/C, VISA**

REMINGTON SHAVER FACTORY SERVICE
Seattle: 1909 4th (682-1522)
Hours: M-F 9-5: Sat. 9-3

If you are in need of an electric shaver, be sure to check this out. You can bring in a used, broken shaver (even a 20¢ BIC will do) and trade it in for a new one at about a 20% discount. Price examples are: a $35.99 shaver sells for $29.99; a $54.99 shaver went for $44.99 **Checks, M/C, VISA**

SARCO
Seattle: 2420 2nd (682-5977)
Hours: M-F 8:30-5:30; Sat. 9-1

SARCO, Seattle Appliance Repair Center, has a few rebuilt small appliances which they sell with a 90-day guarantee. You may find a razor, toaster or blender, but call first to check what's on hand before going in. You may also special order almost any electrical hard-to-find item. **Checks, M/C, VISA**

THE SHAVER CENTER
Everett: 5108 Evergreen Way (252-9735)
Hours: M-F 9-5:30; Sat. 9-3

This shop repairs personal-care appliance products and sells accessories and new appliances. When they take trade-ins on shavers, they repair them and resell them at great prices ($12.95-$25). Tell them which shaver brand and model you want; they'll put your name on their want list, and when they get one, they'll repair it and call you. Rebuilts are guaranteed for 6 months. You may have to wait *several* months for a call, so don't put your name down unless you can wait. A small stand in the front of the shop holds clearance miscellany and a few repaired appliances, such as dryers. **Checks, M/C, VISA**

SUNBEAM OSTER APPLIANCE SERVICE COMPANY
Seattle: 333 Westlake N. (624-7855)
Hours: M-F 8:30-5

This store sells reconditioned Sunbeam appliances with a one-year guarantee. These excellent buys are slightly used demonstrators, display models, carton-damaged items and factory closeouts. Only lawnmowers are rebuilt from trade-ins. Expect to save 10-25% off discount store prices. Watch for extra-special bargains, which can run in the 40% or better range. **Checks**

WAREHOUSE KITCHEN SALES
Auburn: 233 D NW (833-6340)
Hours: M-F 9-5; Sat. 10-4

This wholesale/retail distributor for a cabinet manufacturer stocks over 40 styles and colors of wood cabinets. The only nonwood styles are the European laminates. It's worth the phone call or visit to check their prices on quality bath and kitchen cabinets and equipment. **Checks, M/C, VISA**

CARPETING & FLOOR COVERINGS

One of the best ways to save money on this important purchase is to use these sources as a starting point for gathering price comparisons. Word-of-mouth advertising from your friends and a thorough knowledge of carpet quality are your best allies in this important purchase. Almost every carpet store also sells remnants. Some of the best bargains are in the remnant corners of the large department stores.

We strongly advise carpet buyers to shop around before making a final selection. The savings more than make up for the extra time expended. The shops we've listed consistently offer low prices, and their stocks frequently change. Typically they will carry both high and low grades of carpet—often side-by-side and unlabeled as to quality.

ARDIES CARPETS
Everett 3516 Paine (258-9241)
Hours: T-Sat. 10-6

The employees at Ardies now own this mill-direct carpet store. Their goal is to get the customer the best value for the money. They accomplish this by selling directly from huge rolls as well as from selected samples which are carefully picked to meet their criteria of good price and good value. We like the philosophy and some of the buys were outstanding. We do feel obliged to remind you that you should always compare price and quality in at least 3 places when purchasing big ticket items. Ardies will cut according to your measurements for free, or you can have them install for $2/yd. Installation is guaranteed for one year. **Checks**

BENOY'S CARPET
Tacoma: 54th & S. Washington (475-3434)
Hours: M-Sat. 10-6

A good-sized carpet store which houses a large assortment of roll ends and remnants. Lots of the roll ends contained many yards of carpet, so you're not restricted to just doing a small room. These are nationally known brands and attractive pieces. Check their prices. We feel they're well worth looking at. Installation is available. **Checks, M/C, VISA**

CAL-GA-CRETE NORTHWEST, INC. (THE TILE FACTORY)
Woodinville: 12400 Bothell-Woodinville Rd. (488-1288)

This is a manufacturing plant outlet for a new type of high-density concrete tile paver (for exterior or interior installation). The tiles come in 40-50 colors and 25 different shapes and cost about $1/sq. ft. less than comparable products in stores. The Tile Factory also brokers ceramic tile which can save you 20-30% compared to retail elsewhere. When they decide to clear out stock, they usually run an ad, and tile pavers can run as low as 50¢/foot. **Checks**

THE CARPET EXCHANGE
Seattle: 1251 1st S. (624-7800)
Federal Way: 30820 Pacific Hwy. S. (952-6768)
Lynnwood: 19902 40th W. (771-1477)
Bellevue: 12802 Bel-Red Rd. (455-8332)
Hours: M-Sat. 9-6; Sun. 12-5 (all stores)

These stores carry the largest carpet inventory in the state. They are also the largest volume retailer and stocking dealer in Washington. They must be doing something right. They advertise that they will save you at least 40% on your carpet purchase, and suggest that you shop elsewhere first so that they can prove it. Besides the regular inventory, there are discontinued styles and colors and literally thousands of roll ends. **Checks, M/C, VISA**

CARPET WAREHOUSE
Tacoma: 2620 Bay E. (572-2050)
Hours: M-Sat. 9-5:30

In the market for floor covering? Check here! A large warehouse-type location, filled with rolls of carpeting and some vinyl flooring. A good, varied selection was on hand when we visited. Prices appeared to be 20-30% off regular retail. They will also install if you need it done. **Checks, M/C, VISA**

CONSOLIDATED CARPET WAREHOUSE
Seattle: 5935 4th S. (762-6270)
Hours: M-F 9-6; Sat. 10-5; Sun. 11-5

Authentic carpet bargains are available as remnants here. Remember, a good remnant buy is only a bargain if it's also a good grade remnant. You'll find a large collection to choose from. The store carries a good selection of 12 × 18' and 12 × 20' sizes but fewer 12 × 28's. Ask about discontinued rolls if you need a large size, as prices may be nearly as good for them as remnants. Few tags exceed $150 ($200 was tops in grade and size); most 12 × 10's were priced under $100. Returns are always made in case of flaws, but not usually for other reasons. **Checks, M/C, VISA**

CONTRACT FLOORS, INC.
Kent: 7847 S. 180th (251-8250)
Hours: M-F 8-5 (or by appointment)

The term "contract" has traditionally meant wholesale to contractors and builders. Contract Floors, Inc. has decided to open up its wholesale carpet, vinyls, hardwood and ceramic business to the general public at wholesale prices. We highly recommend that you include them in your comparison shopping when you are in the market for flooring (and window treatments). They carry well-known brands, and they will estimate your needs from blueprints or floor plans. **Checks**

DALTON CARPETS
Seattle: 1515 12th (329-0767)
Hours: By appointment only

Home Furnishings

Dalton's used to be in Redmond and used to own the Final Yard (roll ends). Now they do primarily large-yardage installations, but you can make an appointment to discuss carpet, vinyl, tile and hardwood products for single-home projects. With their wholesale margin and factory-direct buying, you can expect *very* competitive prices. Roll ends from big jobs are sometimes available.
Checks

DICK WYNNE FLOOR COVERING
Seattle: 200 N. 85th (784-2822)
Hours: M-F 9:30-5:30; some Sat. mornings

Dick doesn't advertise and "Dick sets the prices." It may be worth your while to discuss your carpet and vinyl needs with him. You can order from samples or select from carpet on the floor. The latter consists of large roll ends left over from large installation jobs (like condos and apartments)—priced accordingly.
Checks, M/C, VISA

DIRECT CARPET SALES
Bellevue: 13000 Bellevue-Redmond Rd. (453-2050)
Seattle: 12048 Lake City Way NE (364-9601)
Hours: M-F 10-7; Sat. 10-6; Sun. 12-5 (both stores)

Direct Carpet buys from large mills and as a result gets good discounts which they can pass on to customers. They sell some "generic" carpeting from some of these mills. There's no identification as to manufacturers, but it's good quality. Large roll ends run up to 25% off regular retail; remnant roll ends up to 40% off. Their other carpeting, which you can order, also sells for less here. They had a tremendous selection in Bellevue when we stopped by, and the prices were excellent, even including installation and pad.
Checks, M/C, VISA

DON'S TACOMA CARPET SALES & CLEANING
Tacoma: 3902 S. 56th (474-0509)
Hours: M-F 8-5; Sat. 9-1

You will find a few roll ends and used carpeting at Don's at excellent prices. They also offer a "cash & carry" discount on carpet and floorcoverings from major brands. As a sideline to their carpet cleaning business, they sell carpet care products in bulk and concentrated form. This does not explain the presence of the concentrated laundry and dishwashing compounds. Don's buys from S.V. Chemicals (see Index) and repackages the products in quantities smaller than those sold at the plant.
Checks, M/C, VISA

THE FLOOR SHOPPE
Kirkland: 503 6th St. S. (827-0665)
Hours: M-F 8-5; Sat. 10-4

Ask to see their roll ends in the warehouse. We found a weird cut for $10 which was the best buy we've ever made on a piece of carpet. Out front they sell enough carpet to keep the roll-end stock ever changing. **Checks, M/C, VISA**

FRAN'S CARPETS & INTERIORS
Lynnwood: 5716 Evergreen Way (353-2122)
Hours: M-Sat. 9-5:30

Fran's stock area contains a good selection of quality roll ends at some of the best prices in the north end. There are no seconds. Remnants are also available at even better discounts. They will cut and piece carpeting for a nominal fee. Some vinyl flooring roll ends are also available. **Checks, M/C, VISA**

FRANK'S RED CARPET STORES
Seattle: 12325 Lake City Way NE (362-2732)
Hours: M-F 10-6; Sat. 10-5

Frank discounts all the brands he carries 20-30%. There are no remnants or roll ends. He's been in the carpet and vinyl flooring business for 14 years, so he is well qualified to point out the differences in carpet grades, durability, etc. We saw good-quality samples in his small, no-frills showroom. **Checks**

FUZZY WUZZY RUG CO.
Seattle: 815 Eastlake E. (623-2957)
Hours: M-F 8-5; Sat. 9-12

Fuzzy Wuzzy sells rugs that were not picked up (after 90 days and repeated reminders) for the cleaning cost plus overhead. They also sell "border" rugs which they make up from the remnants of other projects. Savings on these can be as great as 65% below the comparable retail price, but the selection and colors are limited to stock on hand. **Checks**

MILLER'S INTERIORS
Lynnwood: 15615 Hwy. 99 (743-3213)
Hours: M-F 9-5; Sat. 10:30-4

This popular north-end carpet store prices their merchandise to save you 18-20% off department store prices and 3-5% off other carpet outlet stores. Next door is their large carpet warehouse where roll ends are available at 50% savings. **Checks**

102   Home Furnishings

THE RUG BARN
Spanaway: 14803 Pacific (537-1473)
Hours: M-F 10-5

Quality and selection vary, but you will find used carpeting, "pull-ups" (carpets which were installed and pulled up again in a relatively short time), remnants and roll ends.

Checks, M/C, VISA

DRAPERIES, FABRICS & BEDDING

AMERICAN DRAPERY FACTORY
Renton: 700 S. 3rd (226-5920)
Hours: M-F 9-6; Sat. 10-5

This is the retail outlet for the workroom of a major supplier of apartment houses and condos. In addition to excellent drapery prices on their own output of closeouts, selected seconds, display and sample draperies, they also buy stock at auctions. Accessory items are discounted. Drapery yardage is plentiful and remnants are always available.   **Checks, M/C, VISA**

ANDY'S DRAPERY CO.
Seattle: 11413 Des Moines Way S. (246-2922)
Hours: M-F 8-5:30; some Sat. mornings

If you are ordering mini-blinds, call this manufacturer for a price quote. If you like the price, and we believe you will, go in to discuss the advantages of his blinds over the "name brand." (Note for frustrated mini-blind owners: he will soon stock a new brush designed to work on those impossible-to-clean nooks and crannies.)   **Checks**

B & B UPHOLSTERY
Redmond: 2653 151st Pl. NE (881-7773)
Hours: M-F 9-5:30; Sat. 10-2

B & B Upholstery offers good bargains in top-quality fabrics. You'll find 30-40 roll ends of velvets, brocades, herculons, nylons, etc. displayed in the front office. Most contain enough yardage to cover a large sofa. Most of the roll ends sell for $10/yd.; 3/yds. and under rolls are $5/yd. They would cost 2-4 times that amount elsewhere.   **Checks**

BEDSPREAD WAREHOUSE
Seattle: 10744 5th NE (365-9920)
Bellevue: 3640B 128th SE (Loehmann's Plaza) (747-1115)

Home Furnishings 103

Hours: *Seattle* **M-F 10-8; Sat. 10-6; Sun. 12-5;** *Bellevue* **M-F 10-9; Sat. 10-6; Sun. 12-5**

Take a look here and compare prices for bedspreads, comforters, pillows and draperies. Expect to be pleasantly surprised. They stock some top-quality, attractive merchandise. However, make certain your purchase is what you really want. No refunds are accepted. You can exchange or take a store credit—but it must be done within 7 days of purchase and with sales receipt.

Checks, M/C, VISA

BRANAM
Kent: 19036 72nd S. (251-9059)
Hours: M-F 8-4:30

When Branam runs their $199 drapery special, you can get up to three 5-ft. windows custom draped for the price of the fabric alone. And they run the special whenever they have an excess in selected fabrics. They also have a rack of assorted drapes that were ordered but never picked up. These sell for at least half of what it would cost to order the custom equivalent. If you are considering new carpeting, ask whether they are running a carpet special or have one coming up: they sell selected carpets at $1/yd. over cost during these specials. Branam is not easy to find, tucked back in an industrial park, but their specials are worth hunting for.

Checks, M/C, VISA

BUR-BANK DOMESTICS, INC.
Seattle: 2213 15th W. (282-1551)
Hours: M-F 8:30-5

A sandwich board announces "Warehouse Sample Sales" outside the retail outlet for this linens wholesaler. Irregulars and samples of towels, quilts, sheets and other domestics are sold individually. If you need a large stock of linens, visit the office and inquire about buying in package lots. They have $100 minimum but will sell to smaller accounts who are willing to pay the 10% service charge on anything under the minimum. You also need to buy according to specified quantities which vary with the item. You have a choice of assorted colors and grades. **Checks**

CALICO CORNERS
Bellevue: 210 105th NE (455-2510)
Hours: M-Sat. 9:30-5:30

A super fabric store, Calico Corners sells beautiful decorative fabric seconds. These seconds have slight imperfections of color or design. You can save from 30-50% on fine drapery, slipcover and upholstery fabrics. Stock is extensive, and new shipments arrive often. Trained salespeople provide information about fabrics and help you figure yardage needed for a project. A bolt of fabric may be borrowed for a 24-hour color test in your home (full deposit required). Always buy enough fabric because the pattern or color may not be available later. If you do not intend to sew your own, ask the salesperson to recommend a reliable custom workroom. Friends have found these workrooms to have good craftspeople who work at reasonable rates. No refunds or exchanges. **Checks, M/C, VISA**

CASCADE CO.
Bellevue: 13300 SE 30th (746-4949)
Hours: M-F 8-5

Cascade supplies motels, hotels, etc. with linens. They sell *white* sheets (as well as towels, pillowcases, and some bedspreads) by the dozen at wholesale prices. They will break allotments and sell 6. They're well worth looking into. **Checks**

CRAM'S INTERIORS, INC.
Tacoma: 2621 70th Ave. W. (565-3980)
Hours: M-F 10-6; Sat. 10-5

This shop produces custom-order draperies and shades. When orders do not get picked up, the items are sold at a good cost savings so that the shop does not have to keep them in stock. Call to see what might be around. **Checks, M/C, VISA**

DRAPERIES, INC.
Edmonds: 8402 Bowdoin Way (776-9875)
Hours: M-F 10-5:30; Sat. 10-4

We found a few bolt ends of fabric and some "customer-didn't-want" draperies the day we shopped. In this category, you are either lucky enough to find what you want or must be flexible enough to make do with what you find. **Checks**

EIDEM'S CUSTOM UPHOLSTERY
Seattle: 5420 Ballard NW (783-1519)
Hours: M-F 8-6; Sat. 10-4:30

Have a small do-it-yourself upholstery project? Eidem's carries a limited quantity of fabric remnants which are left from upholstery jobs. Most pieces are small (a few yards), but sell for approximately 50% off regular retail. **Checks**

EVERETT TENT & AWNING CO
Everett: 2916 Hewitt Ave. (252-8213)
Hours: M-F 8-4:30

Canvas bolt ends are available, but it just depends on what they have been working on. A big box of scraps sits in the front window if you can use little pieces of canvas. **Checks**

FACTORY DIRECT DRAPERIES BUDGET SHOP
Seattle: 8300 Aurora N. (525-7932)
Bellevue: 141 106th NE (454-7909)
Hours: M-Sat. 9:30-5:30; W 9:30-9 (both stores)

These outlets for the Factory Direct Draperies stores sell good-quality drapery and upholstery fabric at a fraction of regular retail prices. You'll find an excellent and large selection of sheers, velvets, brocades, cottons and other fabrics at values up to 50% off Factory Direct's regular prices. Beautiful custom-made draperies, which were not picked up or were fabricated to the wrong size, sell at 50% savings. You can sometimes find top-quality woven blinds at a 50% savings. And fabric, regularly $7.99-$14.99/yd., selling for $1.99/yd. No returns or refunds.
Checks, M/C, VISA

HANCOCK FABRICS
Seattle: 6034 Empire Way S. (723-6859); 3922 SW Alaska (932-1110); 15th NW & Holman Rd. NW (783-2434); Lake Forest Park Center (363-7767)
Burien: 148th & 1st S. (242-5095)
Bellevue: 15625 NE 8th (641-2970)
Tacoma: Villa Plaza Shopping Center (585-1232); 3121 S. 38th (474-8681)
Hours: M-F 10-9; Sat. 10-6 (all stores) (Lake Forest Park open Sun.)

This nationally successful company offers first-quality goods at the lowest prices possible. Seconds are priced very low (and not always marked). Remnants purchased from mills throughout the country end up on Hancock special price tables. Dozens of fabric bargains are usually available in these stores. You'll see top-quality names as well as unknowns. The stores all carry accessory items, a full line of patterns and rows and rows of fabrics. They have a very reasonable return policy, but you must have your sales slip. Unopened patterns and accessories may be returned.
Checks, M/C, VISA

HUBBARD'S BARGAIN BASEMENT
Bellevue: 10429 NE 2nd (454-9500)
Hours: M-Sat. 9:30-5:30

Hubbard's has been a fixture in Bellevue for years, but not so their bargain basement. For those of you unaware of its existence,

106   Home Furnishings

you'd better take a look, especially if shopping for drapery or upholstery fabrics, rods, trims. We even saw some Levolor blinds and woven wooden blinds priced 65% off. Rods were also selling for 65% off regular price. Though the basement is small, it was packed with bargains the day we stopped by. Make your selection carefully, as all sales are final. **Checks, M/C, VISA**

JACK MURRAY CO., INC. (VOLUME INTERIORS)
Woodinville: 14221 NE 190th (624-5740, 1-800-562-6924)
Hours: M-F 9-5:30; Sat. 11-2

Jack Murray Co., Inc. specializes in draperies for condominiums, apartments and businesses. At times, they have unclaimed orders on hand; therefore, you'll not find a large selection as to colors, etc. Remember, draperies can be altered if you're handy as a seamstress.

Volume Interiors is a service operating out of Jack Murray and offers very low competitive prices on made-to-order window covering. **Checks, M/C, VISA**

JEN-CEL-LITE CORP.
Seattle: 954 E. Union (322-3030)
Hours: M-F 8:30-3:30

This factory supplies quilted fabrics and battings to outerwear garment makers and sleeping bag manufacturers. Quilt scraps (outer fabric plus batting) are sold in large bags when available. 30-yd. rolls of batting may be purchased; prices range from under 50¢ to nearly $3/yd. Call before you visit to place an order for the type you need and to assure it will be ready. Calling ahead saves time for everyone. **Checks**

JENSEN DRAPERIES
Everett: 2814 Rockefeller (252-6116)
Hours: M-F 9:30-5:30; Sat. 9:30-1

Check out the bin of bolt ends ($1.50/yard), pillow-size fabrics and occasional leftover window coverings. The selection is limited, but the quality is good and the prices are low. **Checks**

PACIFIC LINEN OUTLET
Lynnwood: 44th W. & 200th St. SW (774-7700)
Tukwila: Pavilion, 17900 Southcenter Pkwy. (575-9440)
Bellevue: 152nd NE & NE 24th (454-9911)
Tacoma: 3815 S. Steele (475-2880)
Hours: *Tukwila* **(see PAVILION);** *Tacoma* **M-F 10-9; Sat. 10-6; Sun. 11-5;** *Bellevue* **M-F 9-6; Sat. 10-5; Sun. 11-5;** *Lynnwood* **M-F 10-9; Sat. 10-6; Sun. 11-5**

"Pacific Linen Outlet announces the 365-day white sale." That's truly what you'll find here. The large inventory features name-brand bedspreads, towels, sheets, napkins, tablecloths, curtains, bed pillows, quilts, shower curtains, bath rugs, etc. Everything is priced at factory outlet prices or "white sale" prices. Some examples of cost savings: $45 items selling for $35, $50 for $30, $10 for $6.95. You can return things if you have your receipt. For returned items valued over $50, they process your return and have cash waiting for you within 10 days. Since Pacific Linen has expanded from one store to 4 in less than 2 years, somebody besides us thinks they are great! **Checks, M/C, VISA**

PERFECT FIT/McDONALD CO.
Seattle: 414 Boren N. (682-7161)
Hours: M-F 8-4:30

McDonald's sells foam and batting—just to eliminate any confusion over names. Shredded foam sells in 20-lb. minimum quantities. They cut sheet foam to order. Call ahead to place an order. They sell synthetic batting in rolls 30 in. wide × 30 yds. long at around $1/yd.—but you must buy the full roll. Scraps of foam are sometimes available in 50- to 100-lb. bales at around 45¢/lb. Unless your order is a huge one, be prepared to defer to regular commercial customers. Try to complete your purchase as quickly as possible. Calling ahead is really a must, as their stock and supply vary. **Checks**

PLENTY OF TEXTILES
Seattle: 2909 NE Blakely (524-4383)
Hours: M-Sat. 10-6; Sun. 12-5

This small but money-saving fabric outlet features mill ends, remnants and sample cuts. Originals sent to designers for selection or rejection are called sample cuts. You could end up with a one-of-a-kind purchase. Plenty of Textiles formerly sold by the pound, but now almost everything is sold by the yard. You'll find a wide variety of fabrics, and prices are good. They have quite an extensive wool selection at substantial savings. Month-old pattern books may be purchased for $2.75, except Vogue which is $5.50.
Checks, M/C, VISA

SHAMEK'S BUTTON SHOP
Seattle: 709 Pine (622-5350)
Hours: M-F 10-5:30; Sat. 11-4

If for some reason you need scores of buttons, here is a place to visit. They have surplus buttons that they will sell for as little as a "penny apiece." **Checks**

Home Furnishings

SPRING CREST DRAPERY CENTER
Lynnwood: 6820 196th SW (775-0090)
Hours: M-F 9:30-5:30

Fabric bolt ends are always on hand. The supply of mismeasured draperies is less predictable. **Checks, M/C, VISA**

TACOMA TENT & AWNING
Tacoma: 121 N. G (627-4128)
Hours: M-F 8-5

This multi-purpose company does canvas construction for residential, commercial and marine jobs. Because of the variety of their production, they have a large inventory of bolt ends which start at $2.50/yd. and go up to over $15/yd. for the kind of stuff that can withstand Alaskan waters in the winter. It's a good idea to call first to let them know you'd like to browse for some canvas, tent or tarp fabrics. Roll ends are merely a by-product of their production and not considered a part of their primary sales. **Checks**

WELLWORTH'S
Everett: 2631 Colby (252-4303)
Hours: M-Sat. 9:30-5:30

Wellworth's sells custom draperies and bedspreads. They also stock one of the best buys in the Puget Sound area: ends of quilted bedspread fabrics. These 2-3 yd. ends can usually be matched up to make your own bedspread at about one-sixth the cost. The ends are also popular for comforters and for patchwork items. Smaller, quilted pillow squares run under $1. We found their prices on small, made-up pillows to be reasonable ($9-$15). There are usually outstanding fabric buys on drapery and upholstery fabric roll ends. Mismeasured drapes and overstocks of bedspreads, when available, offer super savings. Check the store policy on refunds and exchanges—it will vary depending on the item purchased. **Checks, M/C, VISA**

WESSCO
Seattle: 3208 15th W. (285-5455)
Hours: M-F 9-6; Sat. 10-5

Wessco offers outstanding prices on window coverings: Levolor and Verosol blinds. They sell Levolor Riviera—Type 1, the original type which costs a little more than Type 2, but is higher quality with better construction and more design options. They sell these for about 55% off the list price. When comparing prices, be sure you check Type 1 against Type 1 not Type 2. Prices on Verosols are also approximately 50% off suggested retail and carry a 3-year warranty. When we ordered ours over a year ago, we thought we'd hit upon a special sale, but these are their everyday prices. **Checks, M/C, VISA**

WIGWAM TENT & AWNING
Everett: 2933 Broadway (259-1260)
Hours: M-F 8-5

Wigwam almost always has a window full of canvas shopping bags ($2.75) and wood totes ($6). Poly tarps are also available at fair prices. They generally have a limited selection of canvas bolt ends (3 ft. wide). **Checks**

THE WORK SHOP
Tacoma: 5046 S. M (472-4373)
Hours: T-F 8-4:30 (call first)

Call ahead if you want to shop their bolt ends. There are many lovely drapery and bedspread fabrics tucked away in a back room, and the prices are right. But this *is* a workshop, not a retail outlet, so we suggest only serious shoppers (as opposed to browsers) call to say they'd like to stop by. **Checks**

FURNITURE

Furniture discount stores are not included here because of the difficulty of establishing consistent bargains. We did find stores offering used, sample and/or damaged furniture. Some furniture stores have in-store clearing places for flawed, damaged or other furniture, i.e., Scan/Design, Budget Floor (Bellevue), 2nd Scan Import, Levitz (Tukwila). These items sell for less, usually all sales final.

AFCO FURNITURE RENTALS, INC.
Bellevue: 12002 NE 8th (455-4280)
Kent: 6822 S. 190th (251-5730)
Tacoma: 5412 S. Tacoma Way (475-4300)
Hours: M-F 9-6; Sat. 10-5 (generally)

Used furniture stock is returned rental furniture at this sales outlet. Great price savings, as they do not ordinarily refinish items before selling. Sometimes minor repairs are made, and upholstery is sanitized, but the best bargains on the floor will require some labor. **Checks, M/C, VISA**

BOB STAFFORD (BURIEN BUDGET FURNITURE)
(854-7300)

While he looks for a new site for his retail business, Bob is brokering furniture. Call him for price quotes. His shop may be

gone, but his pleasant help and savings-oriented service are still available to customers. The savings in paying cash and doing your own delivery (and Bob's low, low overhead) can be great.
Checks

BUDGET FURNITURE RENTALS
Everett: 9730 Evergreen Way (355-4879)
Hours: M-Sat. 10-6

In need of some furniture and don't want to pay an arm and a leg for it? Try here! They sell rental returns, which are different types of home furnishings: tables, chairs, couches, etc. What's available depends upon what's been returned. Remember, these have been used, so look them over carefully. **Checks, M/C, VISA**

CONTINENTAL FURNITURE
Seattle: 2200 Western (625-9848)
Hours: M-Sat. 9-5; Sun. 12-4

When furniture rented out by Continental Furniture Rental is returned, the pieces (after sanitizing) show up here. Most items offer good savings, but look over selections carefully: some are damaged. Many pieces show relatively little wear. All sales final.
Checks, M/C, VISA

GRANTREE FURNITURE RENTAL
Seattle: 13400 Interurban S. (246-6882)
Lynnwood: 4027 198th SW (774-3512)
Tacoma: 3802 S. Cedar (474-0571)
Hours: M-F 10-9; Sat. 10-6; Sun. 11-6 (generally all stores)

Grantree's returned rental furniture is sold at these stores. Damaged returns are usually repaired before being sold, though "as is" items are sometimes found. No returns on sales. The Interurban S. location gets rental *office* furniture returns. The inventory is fairly good and you can ask if other items are available in the warehouse. **Checks, M/C, VISA**

KEN'S SUBURBAN FURNITURE CLEARANCE CENTER
Bellevue: 905 Bellevue Way NE (next to Albertson's)
  (454-2474)
Hours: W 12-6; Th, Sat. 10-6; F 12-8; Sun. 12-5

The Clearance Center is just what it sounds like—a clearing house for Ken's Suburban Furniture. You'll find the same top-quality goods here and a nice selection of dining, bedroom, living room furniture and accessories—all at considerable savings. These are pieces that have been misordered or overstocked at Ken's regular store. We bought some top-line outdoor webbed

Home Furnishings 111

chairs for $79 each, elsewhere usually priced at $120. The manager is extremely accommodating! All sales final.

Checks, M/C, VISA

NATIONAL FURNITURE RENTALS AND SALES, INC.
Seattle: 2440 1st S. (682-8680)
Tacoma: 5617 S. Tacoma Way (475-6217, 838-1750)
Hours: *1st S.* **M-F 9-8; Sat. 9-5;** *S. Tacoma Way* **M-F 9-6; Sat. 9-5**

National Furniture Rentals sells "as is" rental returns, discounted 30-40%. No returns, so ask if you want a trial period.

Checks, M/C, VISA

OFF CENTER FURNITURE WAREHOUSE
Tacoma: 2926 S. Steele (627-2862)
Hours: M-Sat. 10-6; Sun. 10-5

The garish "sale" signs posted outside are in direct contrast to the merchandise inside. There are many high-quality pieces of furniture in this bona fide warehouse setting. We talked with several customers who had saved over 50% on earlier purchases and were happily returning. This family-owned and operated business relies on large volume and low overhead to keep their prices at an average of 50% below retail. Items are strictly cash and carry, although the warehousemen will deliver in the evenings on their own time. We've been in a lot of "discount" furniture stores, but few can compete with the quality and prices we found here—*and* you can compare prices elsewhere because this is not off-brand or overstock merchandise. There are *no* seconds, and the stock is current. **Checks, M/C, VISA**

SAMPLE MART, INC.
Seattle: 85th & Greenwood (782-8945)
Tukwila: 17686 Southcenter Pkwy. (575-0775)
Hours: M-F 10-9; Sat. 10-6; Sun. 12-5 (both stores)

The Sample Mart carries factory showroom samples, warehouse surplus stock and factory overruns *only*. Convertible couches, sofas, dining sets, bedroom groups, lamps and tables are all new and first quality. Furniture sales/showrooms turn over their samples twice a year to display new lines seasonally. Other pieces of furniture show up in the Sample Mart, between the January and May markets, when a store elects not to take delivery for some reason or other. Prices range from 35-60% off retail. Financing and delivery can be arranged. **Checks, M/C, VISA**

SCAN IMPORT FURNITURE
Bellevue: 12130 Bellevue-Redmond Rd. (454-4220)
Hours: M-Th, Sat. 10-6; F 10-9; Sun. 12-5

Scan Import sells Scandinavian furnishings made from top-quality hardwoods: cabinets, dressers, beds, sofas, chairs, accessories. All exhibit fine workmanship! So how do you save on such quality furniture? By taking home the furniture in its box and assembling it yourself. You can save up to 35% by doing this. Walk through their gorgeous display room and choose what you want. Most pieces have 2 price tags, so you can see the price difference between assembled and unassembled pieces. Warehousing is right there, so there is no delay or waiting for your furniture. You can also talk to the salespeople about taking something out on a trial basis. **Checks, M/C, VISA**

SCHOENFELD'S
Tacoma: 1423 Pacific (272-4171)
Hours: M, F 9:30-9; T-Th, Sat. 9:30-6; Sun. 12-5

The 7th floor of this Tacoma establishment houses 2 different types of furniture bargains. The first you'll see when you step off the elevator. This is the F.O.D. department—"Factory Outlet Division." All the furniture located here is new but being closed out by *leading* manufacturers. You'll find some complete sets, some odds and ends, some one-of-a-kind—all at a guaranteed 40% minimum savings, most ranging 50-80% off regular retail. The other bargain on the 7th floor is Schoenfeld's "Economy Store." Here you'll discover low-priced new, unfinished and used furniture—many prices as much as 50% off.
Checks, M/C, VISA

SEATTLE FURNITURE FACTORY
Kent: 20834 84th S. (872-8989)
Hours: M-F 9-6; Sun. 10-4 (no Sat.)

This factory has an interesting way of keeping furniture costs down. They show you 11 different styles of sofas, and you select the one you want, plus the fabric you like, and they "custom" build it for you at a savings of 30-50% off comparable merchandise. Any sofa can become a queen-size sleeper for an additional $69. All sofas carry a 5-year warranty on craftsmanship. Loveseats, chairs, ottomans and kiddie chairs are also available.
Checks, M/C, VISA, Amer. Exp.

MATTRESSES

Many local manufacturers sell from their own retail stores—factory outlets in one sense. Due to the nature of the business, you will find very cheap and very expensive mattresses. Here price more or less reflects quality. A mismatched set (different fabrics on the mattress and box spring) can be an excellent buy. Most of the factors that distinguish quality in a mattress are hidden beneath the cover, but you can tell a lot by testing them out in the store. The real test for a mattress is to sleep on one for a while—a long while. With these disclaimers the following sell locally made mattresses. You will save considerably by shopping carefully for the price and quality to meet your needs.

Note: Warranties on mattresses are prorated like tire warranties. They are not a guarantee that a product will last 10, 15 or 20 years. Guarantees may be limited or unconditional—read the fine print!

ARTY'S CUSTOM-BUILT
Tacoma: 5415 S. Puget Sound (474-4800)
Hours: M-F 8-5

Arty's rebuilds your mattress for less than a third the cost of a new mattress—which he also manufactures at this location. A new queen mattress runs $150 (one price for all firmnesses) while a comparable rebuilt runs less than $90   **Checks, M/C, VISA**

EVERREST MATTRESS
Seattle: 1907 15th W.
Hours: M-F 7:30-5; Sat. 9-4

Everrest is a small, independent manufacturer of mattresses. When you go in, you'll see a factory, not a showroom. The company has been run by the same family for 43 years. They stand behind their product and sell top-quality mattresses for less than what you find in regular retail stores. Check them out if you need to purchase a new mattress. They will quote prices on the phone and offer free, prompt delivery. We found them extremely helpful.   **Checks, M/C, VISA**

GRAND MATTRESS CO.
Seattle: 3206 S. Hudson (722-1202)
Hours: T-F 10-5; Sat. 10-3

Mr. Lacker, who owns and operates this factory, says he will produce any grade mattress you want. He also rebuilds, renovates and does custom work. He contracts for large orders, for institutions, apartments, etc., and sometimes closes his shop until finished. Call first.   **Checks, M/C, VISA**

IMPERIAL MATTRESS CO.
Seattle: 462 N. 34th (632-2240)
Hours: M-F 9-5; Sat. 9-1

Imperial wholesales rebuilt and renovated mattresses by the truckload. You can save money here because the owner buys mattresses that have been fumigated (by law) from charity organizations and rebuilds them—an intelligent form of recycling. Many of the old, reusable materials may be better than new products. Or if you prefer, have your own sagging sleepset renovated here. You'll pay far less than buying a new one. Check prices elsewhere and compare. Stop in and see for yourself; call first to be sure the owner will be there. **Checks, M/C, VISA**

MATTRESS AND MAPLE SHOP
Tacoma: 9606 40th SW (582-3483)
Hours: M-Sat. 9-5

The Mattress and Maple Shop sells mattresses and maple furniture (primarily bedroom) for good prices. The mattresses come from well-known manufacturers. They've been display models, pattern changes or damaged in shipping, and therefore are marked well below regular retail. We saw a twin, extra-firm set selling for $129. All are in mint condition. If damaged, they've been repaired. The maple furniture also sells for less than suggested retail. All prices are cash and carry. All sales final.
Checks, M/C, VISA

RESTMORE MATTRESS & FURNITURE CO.
Tacoma: 1541 Market (272-2429)
Hours: M-F 8-6; Sat. 9-1

Take advantage of factory-direct savings from Restmore and save at least 25% over nationally touted names. Their mattresses are comparable to the moderate and top-line brands and come with a full 10-year unconditional guarantee. They will replace or repair your purchase if there's any defect or problem during this time. **Checks, M/C, VISA**

SLUMBER EASE MATTRESS CO., INC.
Marysville: 1327 8th (659-8458)
Hours: M-F 8-5:30; Sat. 10-4

Here's the old cliche at work again: if you (a) eliminate the middle person and (b) avoid products with expensive national advertising costs, you stand to save money. How much depends on the mattress you choose, but one top-line comparison at Slumber Ease for a king size was $569 vs. a $1,000 ticket on a big name brand. This factory builds their own mattresses and will also rebuild your mattress. They do commercial work as well as retail work. Their mattresses carry a 10-year unconditional guarantee. **Checks, M/C, VISA**

The following stores are direct outlets for locally manufactured mattresses, and they can often save you money over nationally advertised brands:

EASTSIDE MATTRESS CO.
Redmond: 7858 Leary Way (885-2156)

SEATTLE BETTER BEDDING CO.
Seattle: 714 Taylor N. (282-1433)

SLEEP-AIR MATTRESS CO.
Seattle: 19022 Aurora N. (523-6744); 6110 Roosevelt Way NE (523-3702); 2444 1st S. (682-4063)
Bellevue: 13120 Bellevue-Redmond Rd. (454-0310)
Bremerton: 1550 NE Riddle Rd. (479-2663)
Midway: 25447 Pacific Hwy. S. (839-6003)

PICTURE FRAMES

BOND'S PICTURE FRAMES
Tacoma: 6400 S. Yakima (474-5542)
Hours: M-F 9-9; Sat. 9-5

For years Bond's used to sell only to licensed artists. They have relocated and are now open to the general public, although they still cater to the professional. Because they either buy direct or manufacture their own, they offer good prices on stock frames, both with and without linen, gold and sienna liners. There is no minimum purchase; licensed artists receive 10% off. They will construct odd sizes. They also stock a full line of artists' supplies including bulk thinner, stretched or rolled canvas and stretcher bars, but your best savings (30% off retail) are on the rows and rows of premade frames. Returns may be made on cash purchases.   **Checks**

L.A. FRAMES
Renton: 309 S. 3rd (228-1693)
Hours: M-F 9:30-6; Sat. 10-5

If a new piece of art needs framing and it's variety you're after, L.A. Frames has the largest selection of ready-made frames in the Northwest. Because there is no middle person, you can expect substantial savings here. If you are currently enrolled in an art class, they will offer you a 25% discount on frames and 15% on art supplies. They do custom framing, but the best buy is to select your frame from the huge inventory, have them cut your mats and glass, take it all home and assemble it yourself. For us, it's worked out to be cheaper than the do-it-yourself shops, and far, far easier. Returns on ready-made frames are accepted within 30 days and with receipt.   **Checks, M/C, VISA**

116 Home Furnishings

LAKE CITY FOREST PRODUCTS
Seattle: 14028 Lake City Way NE (363-2100)
Hours: T-F 9-6; Sat. 9-3

We'd like to hear about it if this isn't the cheapest place in the Seattle area for picture framing. With some distress, we discovered we could have saved nearly 50% on several of our own framing projects—even over the do-it-yourself shop prices. This shop relies on volume buying and minimum labor charges to cut costs. That means you will have to take the materials home and mount your own picture, clean the glass, seal the framed piece and put on the wire (they do the mat and glass cutting and make the frames). With a few instructions, your part is a cinch. There are many mouldings to choose from and also racks of completed frames which are about the same price. A few rejects in this category are cheaper. Orders placed on Tuesdays will be ready at noon on Friday. If you only need the glass, it can be cut while you wait. **Cash**

TRU ART PICTURE FRAME CO.
Tacoma: 2609 6th (572-7972)
Hours: M-F 10-6; Sat. 10-4

Their own line (mostly solid oak) of standard sizes costs about 60% less than custom frames. There are 13 different profiles. Artists receive a special discount plus a quantity discount. **Checks**

SEATTLE DESIGN STORES
Seattle: 406 Broadway E. (324-9700); 1621 Westlake (625-0500); 2943 NE Blakeley (523-7500)
Bellevue: Bellevue Square (455-4300)
Hours: *Broadway* **M-F 10-9:30; Sat. 9:30-9:30; Sun. 11-6;** *Westlake* **M-F 9:30-7; Th, Sat. 9:30-6; Sun. 12-5;** *Blakeley* **M-Sat. 10-6; Sun. 12-5;** *Bellevue* **M-F 9:30-9; Sat. 9:30-6; Sun. 11-6**

Seattle Design buys in quantity and sells contemporary plastic box frames at 40% off regular retail, and metal frames at 25% off. The matboard is not included. Watch for ads announcing special sales events when the prices on these frames go even lower. **Checks, M/C, VISA**

STORE OUTLETS

FURNITURE WAREHOUSE SALES CENTER (THE BON)
Tukwila: 17000 Southcenter Pkwy. (575-2164)
Hours: M-F 10-9; Sat. 10-6; Sun. 12-5

Bon's outlet for home furnishings and appliances carries clearance, overstocked, damaged ("as is") and just plain "on sale" items. Prices are always below the regular Bon sales floor except in the case of some sales for which all stores have floor stock. Look for rug remnants, TV's and outdoor furniture. You have probably noticed their well-advertised clearance sales. It's the same Bon quality, and the same return policies apply.

Checks, The Bon Card, Amer. Exp.

JAFCO'S ROUND THE CORNER STORE
Tukwila: 17500 Southcenter Pkwy. (575-2540)
Hours: M-F 10-9; Sat. 10-6; Sun. 12-5

Slightly marred, overstocked and clearance items find their way to this warehouse. The stock changes considerably and quantity of merchandise available varies from season to season. Bargains range from excellent to so-so, but Jafco's regular prices are easy to check next door at their Southcenter showroom. Many items carry original tickets. We make a practice of popping in and out to check the bargains if we're in the area. Returns if accompanied by the receipt. **Checks, M/C, VISA**

MONTGOMERY WARD AND CO.
Tacoma: 9530 Bridgeport Way SW (582-9000)
Hours: M-Th, Sat. 9:30-5:30; F 9:30-6; Sun. 11-4

Some of the merchandise is overstock of catalog items and sells for approximately 25-33% off. They had quite a bit of surplus clothing the day we went by, but this is not always true. Many other things were regular price, so look carefully. Exchanges allowed. **Checks, M/C, VISA**

SEARS BARGAIN BASEMENT STORE
Seattle: 1st S. & S. Lander (344-3389)
Hours: M-Sat. 9:30-6
SEARS BURIEN SURPLUS STORE
Burien: 500 SW 150th (344-3140)
Hours: M-W, Sat. 9-6; Th, F 9-9; Sun. 12-5
SEARS SURPLUS STORE
Tacoma: 8720 S. Tacoma Way (584-8160)
Hours: M-Th, Sat. 9:30-6; F 9:30-9; Sun. 12-5

If you can imagine the Sears catalog come to life, you'll get an idea of what can be found at these 3 stores. Surplus and discontinued items arrive at the basement store daily. Clearance items and some seconds also find their way here. Count on finding clothes for everyone in the family plus decorator items, such as bedspreads, drapes, pillows, shower curtains, etc. Irregulars are labeled, though the flaws may not be readily apparent.

The Burien store is spacious and very well organized. We found many more items available in all categories at this store—especially in children's clothing.

Tacoma also has a Sears catalog come to life. It's very similar to the Seattle locations, stocking surplus and discontinued items, some clearances, and some irregulars or seconds. The store is good sized and filled with clothes, housewares, bedding, shoes, window coverings. A large selection of family clothing was on hand when we visited. Many were 50% off, some down to a quarter of their original price.

Items are exchangeable or returnable between the 3 locations, as long as you have a receipt. Toys are not returnable.

Checks, Sears credit card (all stores)

SEARS RETAIL OUTLET
Seattle: 4786 1st S. (767-8361)
Hours: M-Sat. 9-5

Sears' own brand furniture and appliances which are surplus, returns, "as is," or freight-damaged end up here. All items carry a regular Sears NEW guarantee. The tags showing Sears' regular price and the marked-down price generally indicate 20-25% savings on appliances and nearly 50% savings on furniture. Maintenance agreements are available, and delivery can be made for a nominal charge. The salespeople are very knowledgeable. If you are shopping for a Sears product, especially an appliance, start at the Surplus Store, as their floor stock in appliances is quite large. Mattresses are also in abundance. Other furniture varies from week to week, as do TV's and nonfurniture items. Sears stands behind all its products no matter whether you purchase them here or "uptown." The return policy is the same here as at all Sears stores.   **Checks, Sears card, credit terms**

HOME ACCESSORIES

WALLPAPER AND PAINT

Wallpaper and paint stores included here offer a large selection of papers generally warehoused in Seattle and available in a day or less. Many papers are closeouts or discontinued patterns. Best price bargains are on fairly old patterns of cheaper papers, but occasionally you'll find an excellent buy on new stock. Discontinued stocks are best buys too; buy plenty because it may never be available again. Watch for the wallpaper sales in fall and spring with savings up to 50%. Call your favorite dealer to see when he or she plans his or her next sale. *Note:* Ask about obtaining old sample books after closeouts. Children can spend hours creatively with the old samples.

MAJOR BRANDS
Seattle: 2424 1st S. (623-3550)
Hours: M, F 9-9; T, Th, Sat. 9-6

This is a one-store version of a bigger chain with a similar name. They carry paint, tile, wallpaper, floor coverings, laminates plus an assortment of general hardware items. The big savings are in closeouts, dropped patterns or colors, and damaged merchandise. Specials are tagged around the sales floor, and some are super bargains. You're on your own as far as price and quality comparisons are concerned. **Checks, M/C, VISA**

McLENDON's—See Index

120   Home Accessories

POST WALL COVERING DISTRIBUTORS
1-800-521-0650
Hours: M-F 9-5

The more expensive the paper, the more you save by using this toll-free number. They can get any wallpaper, including designer lines. You need only the name of the book, the pattern number, the number of rolls and the manufacturer's suggested retail price per single roll. *Every* roll is discounted 27%. Add a 50¢ charge per roll under 24 rolls of one pattern. There are no deposits, no COD fees, no freight fee or sales tax. Your order will arrive COD, and you can pay the driver cash, check or money order. Post also discounts all lines of Levolor blinds and woven woods a full 27% of the suggested retail price.

STANDARD BRANDS
Seattle: 1702 4th S. (682-7887); 9701 Aurora N. (522-6666)
Burien: 636 SW 152nd (246-8804)
Bellevue: 14625 NE 24th (747-5555)
Edmonds: 21558 Hwy. 99 (774-8711)
Tacoma: 4820 S. Tacoma Way (475-8444)
Hours: M-F 9-9; Sat. 9-6; Sun. 9-5:30 (all stores)

These stores stock quantities of wallpapers, paints, resilient flooring, carpet remnants and every imaginable accessory necessary to complete a home do-it-yourself decorating project. Prices are definitely discounted, and specials are advertised frequently. Price is not necessarily an indication of grade due to their large-volume buying. Standard Brands now sells their own paint almost exclusively. They offer a 100% money-back guarantee on their product. You can save 30% or more over nationally advertised brands. All stores will refill your own gallon metal can with paint thinner for 89¢. You'll also find newsprint pads and artist supplies at very good prices. Remnants and other floor coverings are priced low, but quality varies. Floor coverings range from well-known to unknown brands. Selections vary in the six stores; all carry remnants. Their return policy is outstanding.

Checks, M/C, VISA

WALLPAPERS TO GO
Bellevue: 2245 148th NE (747-0150)
Tukwila: 17456 Southcenter Pkwy. (575-4035)
Tacoma: 2901 S. 38th (472-9679)
Lynnwood: 19417 36th W., Suite J (774-9646)
Hours: M-F 10-9; Sat. 9-6; Sun. 12-5 (all stores)

The perfect spot for a "do-it-yourselfer." Wallpapers To Go carries around 1,200 different patterns with an inventory of about 30,000 rolls: vinyls, prepasted, textured, corks, foils, flocks. The merchandise, all first quality, comes straight from factory sources, so the savings are passed on to the customer. Rolls are guaranteed refundable or exchangeable. Odds and ends sell for a quarter the original cost. Some of the regular stock was priced 25-50% off normal retail. Be sure to comparison shop if you have a large room to paper. The store offers free paper-hanging demonstrations and has a trained staff to answer questions and assist the customer. It also offers custom mini-blinds, wood blinds and fabric blinds at good prices. **Checks, M/C, VISA**

LOCAL PAINT COMPANIES

Many companies manufacture paint locally. Prices vary. Quality probably varies too, but we are not qualified to judge between brands. A contractor might help if he or she buys from different suppliers. We've listed the companies contacted and indicated whether they are local manufacturers or distributors for a national product. Usually, you'll save by buying local paint at company stores rather than through a dealer. Bargain hunters should look for "boneyards." They all have them. Boneyard is the term for paint that is discounted around 50% because it's the wrong shade (called a "mismatch"). If you're out to tackle a small job or just want to sample a product, it's the cheapest way to go. If mismatches aren't stacked in an obvious place, ask. Almost any store that mixes paint will have at least a few around.

COWMAN-CAMPBELL PAINT CO. (C AND C PAINTS) (MFR.)
Seattle: 5221 Ballard NW (783-8835) (call for other locations nearest you)

DANIEL BOONE PAINTS, INC. (MFR.)
Tukwila: 103 Nelson Pl. (228-7767)

DUTCH BOY, INC. (DISTR.)
Seattle: 3414 4th S. (622-1950)

FARWEST-MATSON PAINT MFG. CO. (MFG.)
Seattle: 4522 S. 133rd (244-8844)

JARVIE PAINT MFG. CO. (MFR.)
Seattle: 760 Aloha (284-1040)

KELLY-MOORE PAINT CO. (MFR.)
Seattle: 6101 Airport Way S. (767-3140); 20230 Ballinger Rd. NE (364-5920)
Kirkland: 11200 Kirkland Way (822-6092)
Kent: 10460 SE 256th (852-6250)

MILLER PAINT CO. (DISTR.)
Seattle: 1500 NW Leary Way (784-7878)

PITTSBURG PAINTS CENTER (DISTR.)
Seattle: 234 Dexter N. (624-0305)

RUDD PAINT CO. (MFR.)
Seattle: 1630 15th W (284-5403)

CLEANING SUPPLIES

ALL CITY VACUUM & JANITORIAL
Everett: 9023 Evergreen Way (355-9194)
Hours: M-F 9-7:30; Sat. 10-5:30

This is the Kleenco (see their entry) distributor for the north.
Checks

CHRIS LOKEN & CO.
Everett: 2807 Rockefeller (259-6137)
Hours: M-Sat. 9-5:30

Loken's carries (or can get) all Northcoast Chemical products (see their entry). They also carry mops, brooms, etc. You must factor in durability when you check prices on this type of equipment.
Checks

COAST BRUSH COMPANY
Seattle: 400 N. 35th (633-5475)
Hours: M-Sat. 10:30-5:30

Professional-quality brushes and brooms of all sorts, for windows, floors, etc. These are top grade and sell at prices equal to brushes of inferior quality. Coast Brush sells to professional window washers and janitorial services where brushes need to last and not wear out after a few weeks' use.
Checks

GAGNON SUPPLY CO.
Everett: 3614 Smith (259-2124)
Hours: M-F 8-5 (out for lunch from 12-1)

Gagnon can supply anything you need to clean and maintain your house. Some items (like bowl cleaner) come in quart sizes, most in gallons which are highly concentrated and should last you the better part of a year. For your first visit, pick a Friday (or call first) when the salesmen are usually on the floor. They can give you a complete rundown on their products.
Checks

KLEENCO, INC.
Bellevue: 1415 134th NE (641-8888; 1-800-562-3291)
Hours: M-F 8-5; Sat. call first

This manufacturer of industrial cleaners sells quality products for home use as well. You won't get these prices off a supermarket shelf, either! Buying in quarts, gallons, tubs and large cartons at Kleenco can cut your cleaning costs drastically. Their products include: window cleaner, laundry and dishwasher detergent, degreaser, oven cleaner, bowl cleaner, dish detergent, shampoo, liquid handsoap and their own exclusive shower cleaner for fiberglass which has gotten rave reviews. They also sell a line of *professional*, heavy-duty tools (mops, brooms, squeegies and brushes) that are priced about the same as in a hardware store. It's not necessary to call ahead (except Sat.) and there's no minimum order. If you want them to ship to you, you'll pay the UPS charges. **Checks, M/C, VISA**

MURTOUGH SUPPLY CO., INC.
Tacoma: 702 Pacific Ave. (627-1171)
Hours: M-F 8-5; Sat. 8:30-12:30

COAST WIDE SUPPLY
Tacoma: 6701 S. Adams (475-8940)
Hours: M-F 8-5

WESTSIDE SUPPLY
Tacoma: 2809 Rochester W. (564-3215)
Hours: M-F 8:30-4:30 (closed for lunch 12-1)

These three janitorial supply businesses will sell you commercial-grade cleaning equipment and chemicals, generally in bulk concentrate form. Their product lists are lengthy and include waxes, soaps, paper products, dispensers, cleaners, deodorants, etc. You can save by buying nonadvertised products alongside the professionals and be assured of products that work. They may also be able to help you find a specialized product for a difficult cleaning or maintenance task. **Checks**

NORTH COAST CHEMICAL CO., INC.
Seattle: 6300 17th S. (763-1340; Tacoma 272-3505)
Hours: M-F 8-4:30

Northco produces household chemicals, such as dishwasher detergent, shampoo concentrate and cleaning solutions, and sells in bulk sizes, generally 1- to 5-gal. containers. All their products are biodegradable and formulated specifically for Northwest water and weather conditions. Savings can be extraordinary, since you are buying bulk supplies in concentrated form. Orders have to be made in advance, and there is a $25 minimum. When possible pick up 2 or 3 orders at a time.

Directions: Exit 161 on I-5. Located between the railroad tracks and the freeway.
Checks

S V CHEMICALS
Tacoma: 1918 Milwaukee Way (383-3692)
Hours: M-F 8-5

S V sells industrial, automotive and residential cleaning products. Their smallest sizes are gallons in liquids and 50 lbs. "dry" (i.e., laundry soaps). Most are highly concentrated and represent tremendous savings over retail-size containers of nationally advertised brands. *Note:* If you don't want to buy in this size until you've tried a product, you can get many of the same chemical compounds at Don's Carpet (see Index) in smaller sizes.
Checks

VERAX CHEMICAL COMPANY
Maltby: 20102 91st SE (481-5353, 668-5186)
Hours: M-F 10-5

Verax has a complete line of cleaning supplies and equipment. They manufacture some of the cleaning chemicals they sell. Their product list contains items to clean or care for everything from swimming pools to septic tanks, from yachts to Volkswagon bugs. They also stock aerosol products. *And* they import coco mats directly from India: you can purchase different grades and sizes. There is no "showroom," but you can pick up a product list and discuss your cleaning needs at the office before you place an order.
Checks

WESTERN SOAP AND SANITARY SUPPLY
Seattle: 1314 E. Union (322-2721)
Hours: M-F 8-5

Good prices on all types of cleaning agents: liquid soaps, washing detergent, dishwasher detergent, all-purpose cleaners, etc. These are concentrated and sold in large quantities only—sizes used by janitorial and restaurant people. Laundry soap sells in a 50-lb. tub at 70¢/lb. You only need to use about $1/8$th of a cup, so good savings are definitely there. We were pleased with the dishwashing compound we tried (50-lb. container at 85¢/lb.). Don't go in unless you're willing to purchase large quantities.
Checks

RESTAURANT EQUIPMENT & SUPPLIES

AAA NEW & USED RESTAURANT EQUIPMENT
Kent: 7835 S. 212th (872-7474; 622-2525)
Hours: M-F 8-5; Sat. by appointment

AAA is unique among our entries of this type because they specialize in such a variety of *used* restaurant equipment (from silverware to walk-in freezers) and because they have a showroom where you can view the used items without an appointment. Savings on used equipment can range from a low of 25% to a high of 95%. **Checks**

ALLIED RESTAURANT AND GOURMET SHOP
Seattle: 1242 6th S. (447-9113)
Hours: M-F 8-6

Allied Restaurant sells both wholesale and retail at lower prices. You'll find commercial-grade kitchenware: mixing bowls, electrical appliances, saucepans, baking pans, glassware, casseroles, etc. Prices appeared good, but more important, you'll not find many of these items in a regular kitchen store. For example, we saw a 24-cupcake baking pan, an 8-qt. colander, a 10-qt. saucepan, 60- and 80-qt. kettles—and being of commercial grade, they'll last a lifetime. **Checks, M/C, VISA**

BARGREEN-ELLISON, INC.
Tacoma: 6626 S. Sprague (474-9201)
Hours: M-F 8-5; Sat. 9-12

This is the gourmet cook's heaven! When you've outgrown the frilly (and expensive) varieties in the specialty shops and want to get serious, plan to spend plenty of time browsing. Check prices and you will find that durable items, which are built to last and last, are far better investments over time and use than those designed for the consumer market. Not that you won't find some very eye-appealing glassware, flatware, china and furniture here. Ever since the restaurant decorators decided to make them look like the living room we'd like to own, the selection at restaurant supply houses has gotten classier and classier. It would take pages to describe the contents of this showroom, from cocktail napkins (with or without jokes) to cleaning supplies to specialty drink mixes—everything a restaurant or bar owner needs to run his or her business. We have found that name brands sold elsewhere will be very close to regular retail (i.e., Wilton), but that restaurant specialty items not sold in other shops represent good buys. It's a mixed bag. A giant potato masher ($7.64), a set of Goliath-sized tongs ($2.40) and a huge Whisk ($11.15) make kitchen art for the wall at about 30% less than retail. **Checks**

126   Home Accessories

KALBERER RESTAURANT EQUIPMENT
Seattle: 914 Virginia (623-6976)
Hours: M-F 8-5; Sat. 9-11:30

Kalberer sells a large assortment of new and used restaurant supplies: flatwear, cutlery, china, glasses, chairs, tables, etc. You don't need to be in the restaurant business to shop here. We found many items that could outfit a mountain or beach cabin or one's own home. It never hurts to take a look. All sales final.
Checks

MOUNTAIN STATES RESTAURANT AND BAR
Bellevue: 2021 130th NE (1-800-562-5923)
Hours: M-F 8:30-5

Looking for the unusual to equip your remodeled kitchen? This business sells new and used restaurant and bar appliances and equipment, from large walk-ins to small, heavy-duty mixers. They also sell dishes and glassware by the case. If you need a quantity, you can buy them here at wholesale prices.   **Checks**

RESTAURANT EQUIPMENT BROKERS
Lynnwood: P.O. Box 5111 (774-4303)
Hours: Call for appointment

Along with the new wave of interest in gourmet foods and equipment, there has been a move towards restaurant-quality kitchens. Restaurant Equipment Brokers sells used (as well as new) equipment and furnishings.   **Checks**

RESTAURANT MART
Seattle: 2851 Eastlake E. (322-4900)
Hours: M-F 8:30-5; Sat. 10:30-3

A wholesale and retail restaurant supply store that sells to the public—everything from glasses to pizza ovens to bar taps. They have commercial-grade electrical appliances. Items like glassware, silverware, dishes must be bought in bulk (one dozen at a time). We found the prices to be good (a little above wholesale), and ended up purchasing a 15″ pizza pan for $2.96.
Checks, M/C, VISA

PATRICK-HART, INC.
Tacoma: 1002 S. 30th (272-0321)
Hours: M-F 8:30-5:30; Sat. 8:30-noon

This is a smaller version of the Bargreen-Ellis restaurant supply store. They sell cookware, utensils, dishware, flatware, furniture, gadgets, etc. Their closeouts and specials are dynamite. Other items are good buys if you want restaurant-quality goods.

We find the glassware to be more resistant to child and dishwasher damage, and the pizza cutter ($2.41) cuts even our wildest creations with ease. We suggest you check all boxed items.

Checks

ODDS 'N ENDS

A & R CUTLERY SERVICE
Seattle: 5633 Airport Way S. (762-1231)
Hours: Variable, call first

A & R is a cutlery rental service for meatcutters. Used knives run about half original retail, and you may find used cook's knives and French knives among the butcher knives. **Checks**

CACALLORI MARBLE CO.
Seattle: 1535 S. Albro Place (767-6300)
Hours: M-F 7:30-5; Sat. 9-12

Making a marble paperweight? Planning an elegant marble entry or bathroom fixture? Call to see when you can drop by the Cacallori Co. to price this natural stone that artistic people have prized for centuries. We're serious about the paperweights— make your own with an inexpensive marble chip and compare your savings against the ones sold in specialty gift stores. Marble pastry "boards" make wonderful gifts. **Checks**

GRAND CENTRAL MERCANTILE
Seattle: 222 1st S. (no phone)
Hours: M-F 12-3; Sat. 12-5

Grand Central has an outlet for their closeouts, overstocks, sales items, etc. It is located in the basement, so ask for directions. You'll discover top-quality kitchen items, pottery goods and baskets. The inventory varies constantly. We found some lovely placemats and napkins, top-notch salad spinners, some handcrafted tiles and Arabia stoneware. It's an excellent place to look for shower gifts, wedding gifts or just something special for yourself. All sales are final, so make certain of your purchase.

Checks, M/C, VISA

KEEG'S DISCOVERY ROOM
Seattle: 310 Broadway E. (325-1771)
Hours: M 9:30-9; T-Sat. 9:30-6

Located in the basement of Keeg's Interiors, the Discovery Room contains odds and ends of merchandise. We found some glassware, a few linens, lamps, gift knicknacks and a couple of chairs on our sojourn. Savings vary depending on the item—

33-50% off. Terms available on furniture. All sales final; no returns. If in doubt, the store is happy to hold furniture items for 24 hours. **Checks, M/C, VISA, Amer. Exp.**

THE NICEST THINGS
Seattle: 4855 Rainier S. (725-8446)
Hours: M-Sat. 10-6

This small shop carries a truly diversified variety of gift items and collectibles. Merchandise sells from 20-50% off regular retail. The day we dropped by, we found stationery to toys and much more. New items arrive weekly. **Checks**

PLANTS

BAKER & CHANTRY ORCHIDS
Woodinville: 18611 132nd NE (483-0345)
Hours: M-Sun. 10-5

Orchids are the only product at this specialty growers' greenhouses. At least twice a year they hold open houses with special sales, drawings, give-aways and refreshments—the works! During these times they clear out their excess inventory. You'll find orchid plants priced at $1-$3. If you are interested in—or already have—the orchid habit, call and ask to be put on their mailing list. Even if you don't buy, the open houses offer a free education in orchids. You may need directions on locating Baker & Chantry, so call first. **Checks**

BOTANIC DESIGNS
Tacoma: 625 Commerce (627-6132)
Hours: Call first

Three times a year Botanic Designs holds plant clearout sales. Call to be put on their mailing list. If you can't wait, you may buy "office trained" plants, bug-free and Florida raised if you are willing to make a $25 minimum purchase. That's easy, because these plants are specially bred and raised to thrive indoors and are priced accordingly. **Checks**

CHERYL'S INTERIORS IN GREEN
Seattle: 1130 NW 85th (784-4312)
Hours: M-F 9-5:30; Sat. 10-4

Here's a "seconds" outlet for indoor plants! Cheryl's sells "used" plants from their interior plant maintenance business for 50% less than normal retail—or less. The plants need some TLC and some good light, but they are all bug free.
Checks, M/C, VISA

GROWING GREEN GARDENS
Seattle: 711 N. Northlake Way (632-2022)
Hours: M-F 8-5

Growing Green Gardens periodically holds a distressed plant sale. These plants are rentals returned from offices, banks, etc. When we visited, a 5-ft. ficus sold for $5, and 2 5-ft. scheffleras sold for $10. We were told that this sale may be held every 3 months or so, but it is not advertised. Call if you have healing powers where plants are concerned. **Checks**

INTERIOR PLANT DESIGN
Redmond: 3860 Bellevue-Redmond Rd. (883-4455)
Hours: Call first

Put your name on their mailing list for "distressed" and overstock interior plant sales that are held at least every 6 months. If you drop by (usually after 3:30) and someone is there, they will also sell whatever they have on hand at the time. **Checks**

K & J DISTRIBUTORS
Woodinville: 18808 142nd NE (483-9292)
Hours: M-F 8-4

Clay flower pot seconds are available, but you need to call first to be sure someone is there and to check the stock on hand. Decorator pieces (i.e., clay animals that serve as planters) and saucers are also accumulated in the seconds pile. Once a year K & J holds a warehouse sale to clean out their seconds, but you are welcome to shop in between sales. Sizes run from very small to very large pots. **Checks**

LARRY'S NURSERY, INC.
Renton: Renton Shopping Center (271-8311)
Hours: M-Sat. 9-6

This must be a one-of-a-kind consignment shop. Larry will take plants on consignment *only* if he feels they are in good condition and will sell. He also consigns chain saws.
Checks, M/C, VISA

NORTHWEST GROUND COVERS & NURSERY
Woodinville: 17420 Woodinville-Duvall Rd. (483-0123)
Hours: M-F 8-4:30

This grower specializes in native plants and general ornamentals. Although they do have different prices for wholesale and retail customers, the retail scale is graduated so that large purchases will net you close to the wholesale price (and far below retail elsewhere). Paying in cash will also help your bargaining position, especially on large orders. This is a good find for those who plan extensive landscaping. **Checks, cash preferred**

PLANTS & PLANTING GREENHOUSES
Puyallup: 7722 48th St. E. (922-6994; 838-0254)
Hours: M-Sun. 8-4:30

If you love indoor plants, this will be a trip worth taking whether or not you want to fill a solarium or find the perfect single specimen to add a decorator's touch. In fact, if you get a hankering to return to the jungle, it's a lot cheaper to come here to satisfy the urge. In 9 greenhouses in total profusion, you will find plants in 6-in. pots, 2-story trees and everything in between. The best buys are on overruns—literally. These varieties threaten to take over and are cleared out. We selected a 6-in. pot of a big, spreading variety which we've never seen in the multipurpose stores for $3.98. Trees, while dramatic, aren't cheap. It's a good idea to research prices in advance so you'll know which ones represent the best buys. Quantity buyers ($200 plus) may be able to arrange a discount, but only licensed florists and interior landscapers get wholesale. The greenhouses are on the Levee Road side of the Puyallup River; turn left off 70th and right onto 48th E. It's a jungle out there! **Checks**

Shopper's Note: While romaine was pushing 90¢/head, we found beautiful, freshly picked ones for 59¢ at GARDENS WEST on the other side of the river (5430 66th E.—848-7345).

SQUAK MOUNTAIN GREENHOUSE
Issaquah: 7600 Renton-Issaquah Rd. SE (392-1025)
Hours: M-Sat. 9-6

This greenhouse operation sells wholesale as well as retail. Last spring, we bought top-quality bedding plants (flowers and vegetables) for good prices. They stocked an excellent selection of geraniums, petunias, fushias, begonias, impatiens, tomatoes, to mention a few. We feel you should check them out, and make some comparisons. They also sell their own grafted rhododendrons. **Checks**

POTTERY & CERAMICS

CLAY ART CENTER
Tacoma: 4320 Pacific Hwy. E. (922-5342)
Hours: M-F 10-5:30; Sat. 10-4 (except during July & Aug.)

If pottery is your bag, visit this pottery supply and workshop. We stopped in to check out their stock of seconds on the Red Tag Shelf and discovered a large, pleasant gallery full of quality clay

Home Accessories

pieces. The seconds were in good condition and very well priced, albeit there's not usually more than a shelf-full (that's probably a testimony to the skill of the potters). The Clay Art Center is a year-round shop outlet for the hand spun merchandise you find in mall shows and art fairs. If you've been to the Bellevue or Tri-Cities art fairs, you'll recognize the styles. Since this is the "factory," some prices may be lower. **Checks, M/C, VISA**

FABRIK
Seattle: 321 Broadway E. (329-2110)
Hours: M-F 10-6; Sat. 10-5:30

Fabrik offers attractive seconds, 40-50% off retail—all beautifully displayed in very attractive surroundings. The stock includes cups, plates, saucers, bowls, serving bowls, serving platters, salt and pepper shakers, and sugar bowls. You do not have to buy a complete setting; any piece can be bought individually. However, there are added savings if you buy 4 or more place settings. Fabrik stoneware is microwave- and dishwasher-safe. Each piece is hand finished and hand glazed, leading to a nice variation in glaze tones and a truly handcrafted look. All pieces stack solidly. The store also carries seconds in Alleniana hand silk-screened fabrics from Port Townsend. Depending on what they've discovered at the time you visit, you may find placemats, napkins, wooden toys from Oregon, ironworks by Enclume, stocking stuffers for the holidays, etc. Some exceptional bargains show up. Keep your eye on this spot. **Checks, M/C, VISA**

OLD TOWN POTTERS
Tacoma: 2202 N. 30th (572-9570)
Hours: M, W, F 10-5; T, Th 10:30-5; Sat. 10-4

Old Town Potters has the largest selection of pottery markdowns we've ever seen. The 5 shelves in the back of the gallery contain yellow and red tag specials. The yellow tag indicates a true second (poor glaze, crack, etc.); the red indicates pieces that have been in the shop long enough to become clearance items. Returns are not taken on yellow or red tag items, but if you purchase one of the many tempting items in the front, you may exchange it (keep the receipt). Old Town Potters sells the wares of many local potters. You'll find variety in both style and price. **Checks**

WASHINGTON POTTERY CO.
Seattle: 13001 48th S. (243-1191)
Hours: M-F 7-3:30

Seconds in clay flower pots are available here in 7-12 in. sizes. Prices are excellent on the seconds, and we found them to be in good condition. If not available, check the price on their first-quality pots before shopping elsewhere. These pots range from 1-12 in., and saucers from 3-12 in. Broken clay pots are sold by the cubic yard (for walks or roadbeds). No returns. Call first to check hours and availability of pots.

Directions: Take the Tukwila/Interurban exit off I-5 south; turn right at the stop sign, and right again onto 48th Ave. South.

Checks

CRYSTAL, GOLD & SILVER

CARROLL AND ASSOCIATES
Seattle: 316 Securities Bldg. (621-1148)
Hours: M-F 9-3; 9-4 (winter)

Words cannot and will not describe adequately what you'll discover here. We were truly overwhelmed with the beauty plus the cost savings. Carroll's merchandise is not inexpensive—it may be the most expensive in this book. However, the values are phenomenal as far as percentage in savings.

Mr. Carroll is the third generation of his family to be involved in the silver, gemstone and gold business. He buys sterling, gems and gold from estates, trust departments and some smelters—*before* the silver is melted down. He dislikes seeing things melted down. Items are then polished, buffed, etc. Scratches are removed from the sterling. In the end, what you see looks brand new. Silver here sells for approximately half of the best store sale price. Half of the stock consists of sterling silver candlesticks, tea services, etc. He has a few silver-plated pieces, but only if they're unique and have some value. There is an open stock on 200-250 sterling patterns. The other half of the business deals with gems and gold. As stated before, this is not an inexpensive place, but the savings are there.

Checks

GOLD, SILVER & GEM EXCHANGE
Seattle: 17524 Aurora N. (542-5568)
Hours: M-F 9-6; Sat. 9-1

We must advise that you are on your own when it comes to buying jewelry, but we can point you to some places that sell gold and silver by the weight, and whose prices therefore fluctuate daily. Since a high markup is not the main factor (and the markup on jewelry is very high), you can often get excellent buys in low-overhead shops like this one, but you had best shop around first so you can compare quality and prices. They will take returns with receipt within a reasonable amount of time.

Checks, M/C, VISA (on jewelry)

MARCI JEWELRY
Bellevue: 925 116th NE #207 (455-4561)
Hours: Wed. only 10-6; 3 weeks prior to Christmas open M-Sat.

We thank Buffy for letting us know about this one. She's been taking her bus tours there for the past several months. Marci's is a wholesale jewelry company and this is the showroom. The manufacturing of their jewelry is done on the premises. You'll find an excellent large selection of 14 K gold chains, sterling silver chains, diamonds and colored gemstones—all selling for significant savings (wholesale prices)—about 50% off the price you'd expect to pay for comparable jewelry elsewhere. All chains are sold on a weight basis. We saw one gold chain priced at $28. It would be suggested retail at $96 somewhere else. Their diamonds are certified stones. The diamonds and gems exhibit themselves beautifully in their settings. Marci's does do custom design work for people, as well as sell what they have already made-up.
Checks, M/C, VISA

C. RHYNE & ASSOCIATES
Seattle: 110 Cherry (623-6900)
Hours: M-F 10-5:30

C. Rhyne & Associates is not for everyone. They carry 14 K and 18 K gold chains, gold coin jewelry, pendants, custom-designed investment gemstones, certified diamonds, rubies, emeralds, sapphires. They mainly deal with people who want to invest in precious metals. They sell Krugerrands, gold sovereigns, gold coins. Their gold chains are worth a price comparison. **Checks**

WEST COAST GOLD & SILVER EXCHANGE
Seattle: 539-A NE Northgate Way (367-0313)
Hours: M-F 10-5

This company buys and sells sterling silver, silverware, gold jewelry and coins. We crosschecked prices on a set of sterling flatwear and found them to be just about 50% less than the current sale prices downtown. Fourteen carat and pure gold jewelry prices were also very good. Their stock comes from individuals and estate sales, so it's a good idea to call first to see what they have on hand. Silver-plated flatwear is sometimes in stock, as are odds and ends, such as silver candlesticks and serving pieces. We believe the buys we noted at West Coast to be very, very good. We also believe that anyone dealing in precious commodities should know prices and merchandise before investing.
Checks

134 Home Accessories

KOKESH CUT GLASS CO.
Seattle: 301 NE 65th (527-4848)
Hours: T, Th, F 11-5; W 6:30-8; Sat. 10-1

We recommend Kokesh Crystal as a place to shop for wedding and anniversary gifts. They offer a wide selection in the $7.50-$25 range, and the stock is very attractive. Kokesh may hold a yearly sale of accumulated seconds and closeouts. The date of the sale will vary from year to year, so watch for their ad. **Checks**

KUSAK CUT GLASS WORKS
Seattle: 1303 Rainier S. (324-2931)
Hours: M-F 9-4:30

Once a year Kusak sells their year-long collection of blems and seconds (no chips or cracks) at a fairyland sale of lovely cut crystal. Pieces are 30-50% off retail. The sale begins around Halloween and lasts for 10 days. When you attend a sale, fill out a card to be notified in advance of the following year's sale. Pieces are all imported crystal, and prices range from a $5 item to more than $100. You may shop at Kusak any time, but prices are not lower there than at their retail outlets except at sale time. Returns are accepted during the sale if you discover a chip or crack. Twice a year they will refinish chipped and scratched crystal (first week in April and mid-October). Kusak glass can be brought in for repair year-round. **Checks**

MISCELLANEOUS

BALTAM TRADING, INC.
Seattle: 1419-C Elliott W. (282-3060)
Hours: M-F 9-5

Go to the second floor where you'll find shelves of seconds in imported giftware. The stock on hand could be crystal, wood or copper items. Actually, it could be just about anything you would find in a giftware department. There wasn't much available the afternoon we visited, but the quality was nice. In this category it is always a question of happening upon what appeals to you.

Checks

IRWIN BRENNER PAPER CO.—See Index

K AND K COMPANY
Seattle: 4442 27th W. (284-0827)
Hours: Two yearly sales; call for an appointment at other times

K and K manufactures scarves, napkins, 49-in.-square tablecloths. Twice yearly they open their doors for a special sale of discontinued styles and patterns, factory seconds, overruns and

Home Accessories 135

overprints. The sales include scarves, napkins, cloths, fabric gift bags, place mats, some fabrics and baskets. The sale is not advertised—a mailing list is sent out. Give them a call to make sure you get on the mailing list. You can leave information on their answering machine. The fall sale is a great place to purchase holiday gifts. All sales final.
Checks

LUND'S LITES
Auburn: 131 30th NE (939-5385)
Hours: M-F 9-5 CLOSED IN SUMMER

This is the outlet for Lund's Candle Factory. Lund's normal retail is strictly via home candle parties, but seconds, damaged candles and overstocks are cleared out here at savings up to 50%. Besides the unique candles, you will find candle holders and nifty gift items like their sawdust "muffins" for lighting fires without kindling.
Checks, M/C, VISA

PHILCO IMPORTS
Seattle: 12010 Des Moines Way S. (242-1108)
Hours: M-F 9-5

Philco is the moniker for a Philippine import company which produces, wholesales and retails buri-rattan furniture, baskets, wall decorations, jewelry, oriental vases, sea chimes, etc. The shop specialty is baskets, and they are plentiful and inexpensive. Returns are taken within 3 days of purchase only.
Checks, M/C, VISA

PRASAD'S
Seattle: 1932 1st (624-4809)
Hours: M-F 10:30-4:30 (closed 1-2)

This tiny shop is packed to the brim with outstanding giftware buys. Prasad's is the outlet for an importer specializing in brassware, soapstone with inlay work and rosewood, sheesham wood and brass boxes. You'll also find silk scarves in all sizes, Indian garments and men's ties. Items come from India, Pakistan, Hong Kong, Taiwan and Germany. Some items are samples, some overstocks and some are only sold here. If you are looking for something you don't see, ask if it's in the warehouse, on its way or can be ordered. Exchanges are welcome, refunds only if the item is defective.
Checks

RINDLER DISPLAY
Seattle: 2601 Elliott, Suite 1306 (Seattle Trade Center)
   (623-3145)
Hours: M-F 8:30-5

Have fun exploring here! Rindler's has a vast assortment of ribbons, giftwrap, silk, and preserved flowers and seasonal display items for Christmas, Easter, back-to-school and just about any other decorable event, such as a wedding. They are wholesalers in the store fixture and display business, but they have opened their spacious 2 floors of merchandise to the general public for browsing and buying at wholesale prices. In fact, they graciously welcome shoppers. Exchanges are given gladly, but no refunds. **Checks, M/C, VISA**

RITZ EMPORIUM
Lynnwood: 4520 200th SW (774-8800)
Hours: M-F 10-9; Sat. 10-6; Sun. 12-5

Gift items, jewelry (coral, jade, cloisonné), dinnerware, home accessories, glassware, furniture—search no further! The Ritz has lovely, top-quality merchandise. Items sell for a few dollars to a few hundred. However, no matter what the price, you're going to save compared to normal retail. The owner tells us he keeps costs down by buying directly, therefore cutting out the middle person. You'll find a changing inventory. When the owner can get hold of a good buy, he does it and passes the savings on to you. Returns are allowed, if in perfect condition and within 30 days. *If you take this book with you to the Ritz and show the clerks this page, you'll receive an additional 20% off on your purchases.* **Checks, M/C, VISA**

SEATTLE CARD MART, INC.
Mountlake Terrace: 5503 232nd SW (778-3951)
Hours: M-F 8:30-4:30 (Labor Day through Christmas)

The Card Mart lists themselves as "the fund raisers' center," but individuals also find savings on boxed greeting cards, napkins, novelties, wrapping paper, imprinted Christmas cards and other items. The boxed greeting cards are among the best buys, although you will find their overall retail prices to be quite low. Group buyers pay wholesale prices. There's a $10 minimum on all orders, as they are primarily geared to large purchasers. You'll find the proprietors to be pleasant and helpful. There's almost always a shelf or two of super clearance bargains marked 50% and 75% off. All sales are final (except samples, which are guaranteed). **Checks**

TRADEWINDS
Bellevue: 3640-A 128th SE (Loehmann's Plaza) (746-2226)
Hours: M-F 10-9; Sat. 10-6; Sun 12-5

Shopping for wedding presents, birthdays, Christmas gifts? Be sure to take a look at Tradewinds. You'll be sure to find something for someone among the excellent stock of brass items, crystal, pottery, straw baskets. You'll be pleased also to find a wide assortment of prices, so you can pick up a $3 gift or a $75 gift, depending upon what you need. The discounts are good. We found a china doll marked down 50% of retail. Exchanges are accepted. **Checks, M/C, VISA**

TRULAND GREETING CARD CO.
Seattle: 12055 5th NE (365-5534)
Hours: M-Th 8-12

Truland has a $50 minimum, and you must purchase cards in packs of 6 of the same design and message. These limitations generally rule out the individual shopper. Their stock is the type that charity groups often purchase for fund raising. Businesses might keep a supply on hand for appropriate occasions. Gift wrap, ribbons and stationery packs are 33% off retail, cards are 50% off. Gift items are sometimes available. **Checks**

WINDFALL
Seattle: 4712 University Way NE (522-1220)
Hours: M-F 10-6; Th 10-9; Sat. 10-5; Sun 12-5

We almost missed this one, and we're certainly glad we didn't. Windfall specializes in factory overruns and closeouts. The shop has a large selection of quality gift items at reasonable prices. Not everything inside the store is discounted, but you'll find at least half of the stock priced 20-50% below suggested retail. We discovered good buys on napkins, dinnerware, picture frames, shorts and tops, glassware, top-quality rubber boots—just to name a few. We were also pleased to come across a former favorite (Enclume pot racks, fireplace tools, etc.) now sold here. Stock changes frequently, as good buys don't last long. You must go see for yourself. **Checks, M/C, VISA**

OFF-PRICE MALL

THE PAVILION OUTLET CENTER
Tukwila: S. 180th & Southcenter Pkwy. (575-8090)
Hours: M-F 10-9; Sat. 10-6; Sun. 11-5 (some holidays 11-5; late opening during the holiday shopping season)

If you haven't heard about The PAVILION, or if you've heard but are skeptical, we advise you to visit the Northwest's first enclosed off-price mall as soon as possible. This recommendation is not based on our always finding spectacularly low prices that make a bargain shopper weak-kneed. Rather, we believe that this is the most comfortable way to shop and save on the greatest variety of goods in the Puget Sound area. The mall is pretty, the restaurant is very pleasant, the shops are well appointed, you only have to park once and the odds of your paying full price for anything are very slim. Naturally, the clever will ferret out the big buys as well as the disappointments, but even the novice is going to do pretty well just by virtue of the mall's determination to exist as an off-price center and attract off-price and factory-direct merchants. Some of the shops are discount outlets for regular retail stores "uptown," including the beauty shop, which is Gary Bocz' contribution to looking better for less.

All of the stores, by virtue of being in The PAVILION, have made a commitment to be at least 20% below retail on every item. They actually range from 20-50% below retail, and sometimes even more. However, the mall management can't enforce this on every price tag. PAVILION management encourages shoppers to advise both the individual store and the mall information desk or management office of any specific complaints. These malls are big business back East, and you can expect to see some big names in the off-price world coming to The PAVILION in the future.

Returns and refund policies are up to the individual stores, as are check and credit card acceptance. All stores must remain open during mall hours, however.

Off-Price Mall

A nice feature for out-of-town visitors: The PAVILION operates a free shuttle from the major airport and Southcenter hotels. Call the information number for details. They will also arrange special shopping tours and free merchandise-related programs for clubs and groups. And being a mall, they offer their share of fun events and entertainments for shoppers throughout the year.

We could easily devote the better part of this book to describing the variety of bargains under one roof at The PAVILION, but unfortunately, space does not allow us to describe each location in detail. We have settled for a brief listing and the phone number of each outlet. Allow plenty of time to explore for yourself, and ask lots of questions. The employees are very helpful and are oriented towards pointing out the best bargains they have to offer.

ANDERS CLOTHING CLEARANCE CENTER (575-3630)*

BARONE BROTHERS (575-0999)

Fine hand-cut crystal and engraving, plus porcelain, china and giftware.

BERGMAN LUGGAGE COMPANY (575-4090)*

BIG CITY GIRL (575-8496)

Fashion concepts in large and half sizes. Quality and value in pants, tops, coordinates, separates. Everything in your "special size"—36-52 and 14½ to 26½.

THE BIG DEAL (575-1606)

Men's apparel, jeans and sportswear. Arrow, Levi Strauss, Calvin Klein, James Jean, Haggar, Sassoon, Jordache, Brittania, Generra and Union Bay. Sizes S, M, L, XL.

BONAFIDE SHOE FACTORY OUTLET (575-4021)

Thousands of pairs of quality ladies' and men's shoes. A large selection of current styles and colors.

CARACO'S GENERAL STORE (575-8880)

An outlet for manufacturers and wholesalers featuring only top-quality merchandise—much of it famous name brands you'll find at retailers for 25-75% more. They turn over their merchandise rapidly with new merchandise every week.

CHAMPION PARTY AND COSTUME SHOP (575-1925)

One-stop party and costume shop featuring decorations, balloons and helium, plastic and paper party supplies at quantity discounts, plus costume rental and accessories. Also a complete line of theatrical makeup.

CHIPPER'S (575-4653)

Black Hills gold, largest collection in U.S. Also 14-karat gold, diamonds, pearls, opals and turquoise.

THE CLOTHES OUT (575-9440)*

COATS, ETC. (575-8484)

Vast selection of first-quality suits and coats, including rainwear, furs, wools, quilts, from well-known junior and misses manufacturers.

CUT-THE-CORNER FRAME SHOPS (575-8272)

Custom picture framing at you-frame-it prices, plus a large selection of framed and unframed original works, limited editions, prints, posters and graphics, all at substantially discounted prices.

ENCORE BY GARY BOCZ (575-9134)

Full-service hair salon, offering professional beauty supplies, cosmetics, sun beds.

FIRENZE LEATHER GOODS (575-9320)

Representing Italian manufacturers; 20-50% off fine-fashion men's and women's shoes, belts, wallets, women's purses and attaché cases for men and women.

GREAT CLOTHES, INC. (575-8515)*

IMPORTS EAST (575-0244)

Importers and wholesalers of quality gifts and home decor, Oriental art goods, brass, porcelain, stoneware, wood, toys, housewares, cloisonné and other popular-priced jewelry.

JACQUELINE JEWELRY (575-4367)

Direct importer of diamonds, gems and cultured pearls. Manufacturer of fine jewelry at affordable prices.

JANA IMPORTS—FACTORY OUTLET (624-6265)*

JEANS ENCOUNTER (575-8070)

Men's, women's and children's name-brand jeans and tops.

JEHLOR FANTASY FABRICS (575-8250)

Over 1,000 specialty fabrics, sequined and metallic sheers, lamés, georgettes, silks and 80 colors of chiffons, plus over 600 trims. Metallics, sequins, beads, jewels and maribou for costumes, evening and bridal fashions, and special everyday wear.

KATIE'S DANCE BOUTIQUE (575-3086)

Featuring a complete line of dancewear—leotards, tights, ballet slippers, legwarmers—plus swimwear, skating skirts and exercise clothes.

KID'S MART (575-8585)

Name-brand children's and infants' clothes at greatly reduced prices; sizes infants through 14.

LABELS FOR LESS (575-8555)

A designer and better brand-name discount boutique, specializing in quality clothing for the fashion-minded, cost-conscious woman.

LEATHERMAN FASHIONS (575-9353)

Men's and ladies' leather coats and jackets at direct-import savings.

LITTLE FOXES (575-3797)

Beautiful bottoms and tops for pre-teens and juniors. Fashion names like Normandee Rose, Calvin Klein, Pulse, Esprit, Lawman, James Jean, Brittania, Sara Jean, Levi Strauss, etc. Big names. Big choice. Little prices.

ME AND MY BABY (575-8557)

Brand-name apparel and lingerie for pregnant women; clothing and accessories for newborns and infants to 24 months.

MIMI'S PETITE CORNER (575-8525)

Today's fashions for the woman 5' 4" and under at prices she can afford. Coordinates, separates, blouses, jeans, dresses; sizes 0-14. Discount alterations available.

THE MIRROR IMAGE (575-9310)

Custom-designed mirrors, mirror clocks, selected framed pictures and a large variety of unique gift items—all at savings direct from the designer.

MOUNTAIN PRODUCTS (575-3394)*

NATIONAL SAVINGS COMPANY (575-3612)

National-brand men's sportswear, suits, sport coats and accessories from such famous manufacturers as Haggar, Levi Strauss, Arrow, Van Heusen and others. All current styles.

OVER AND UNDER (575-3838)

Thousands of leisure tops for adults and kids; transfers and lettering done while you wait. Underwear and sweatsuits too.

PACIFIC LINEN OUTLET COMPANY (575-3999)*

PAVILION BOOKS (575-1939)

Full range of hardbacks, paperbacks and children's books. Current New York Times best sellers. Publishers' overstock and sale books.

PIC-A-DILLY (575-3460)*

PLANTS II

Common to exotic trees, houseplants and cut flowers. Knowledgeable personnel to assist you 7 days a week. Main floor Atrium.

QUEST FOR THE HOME (575-0250)

Casual wicker furniture, baskets, silk flowers and arrangements, decorative accessories, brass and copper designer accents, year-round Christmas decorations and supplies. Designer decor at outlet prices.

REGINE FINE CHOCOLATES (575-0801)

Fine-quality chocolates and nuts made locally in Seattle to ensure freshness. Featuring Ducklings, Aplets and Cotlets, Almond Roca, Jelly Bellies and imported fine candies.

ROCKBOTTOM BOOT RANCH (575-4011)

Factory discount western wear store featuring Tony Lama, Justin and Double H workboots. Plus name-brand western shirts, fur felt and straw hats, belts, buckles and western accessories.

SAM HELLER MEN'S CLOTHING (575-0368)

Suits, sportcoats, slacks, many designer labels found in other fine men's stores, meticulously tailored, so you can trust the quality and fit. Plus dress shirts, ties and rainwear. Alterations available on premises.

SCHEHERAZADE (575-8393)

Elegant, distinctive clothes and unique fashion accessories for today's well-dressed woman. Specializing in natural fibers, Indian cotton, voile and silk.

SEATTLE DIAMOND & GOLD CENTER (575-8510)

Gold, bullion, finest Italian chains, loose and mounted diamonds, colored gemstones. Diamond and gold brokers.

THE SHOE PAVILION (575-0196)

All famous brand-name women's shoes. High-fashion dress, casual and sports styles.

THE SPORTS DIRECTOR (575-8536)

Featuring a full line of name-brand sporting equipment, athletic footwear, clothing and accessories.

THE STRAPPED JOCK (575-4400)*

SWANS & DAUGHTER (575-3751)

Top-quality costume jewelry, fashion accessories and cosmetics at prices below prevailing retail.

TRADER JOHN'S (575-8887)

Personalized gifts, home accessories and the unusual.

TUKWILA SOCK EXCHANGE (575-8484)

Socks for the entire family; legwarmers, knee-highs, tights, pantyhose, novelty shoe laces plus seasonal gift items.

VALU-TRONICS (575-8885)

Sight and sound savings on the latest consumer electronics—TV, video recorders, projection TV, home audio, portable cassette recorders and car stereo, plus the latest releases on album and cassette.

VISION LAND (575-9307)

Huge savings on complete glasses packages (lenses *and* frames) with designer and popular brand frames and sunglasses.

*See Index for write-up with more information and other locations.

PERSONAL CARE

A-1 BEAUTY SUPPLY
Bellevue: 133 106th NE (454-2852)
Hours: M-F 10-6; Sat. 10-4:30

A-1 is 95% retail and carries mostly professional merchandise sold in professional quantities. These larger sizes make for savings. A-1 also sells some products that are impossible to buy at drug stores or cosmetic counters; lash and brow tint is one example. You'll also find hair ornaments, acrylic nails, hair rollers, purses, hats, combs, brushes, blow-dryers, perms, shampoos, conditioners, rinses, etc. There's everything and anything. We're convinced that you can't lose and you'll certainly save—at least 30% on most merchandise. If you purchase in large quantities (half-dozen allotments for example), you can save an additional 10%. There are a few products, but not many, which the store has to sell at the suggested retail price, and they will be honest with you as to which these are. Be willing to try some new products. The owner is extremely helpful and knowledgeable.
Checks, M/C, VISA

EVERETT CASH AND SAVE BEAUTY SUPPLY
Everett: 7207 Evergreen Way (347-5866)
Hours: M-W, F 9-5; Th 9-9; Sat. 10-5

Beauticians with a license may shop behind the counter, non-beauticians may not, but they may purchase everything except chemical products (such as permanents and hair coloring).
Checks, M/C, VISA

GENERIC MAKEUP
Bellevue: 3720 128th SE (Loehmann's Plaza) (643-6880)
Seattle: 1525 4th (223-1353)
Tacoma: 925 Tacoma Mall (473-6544)
Hours: *Bellevue, Seattle* **M-F 9:30-6; Sat. 9:30-5;** *Tacoma* **M-F 9:30-9; Sat. 9:30-6; Sun. 11-5**

Generic Makeup offers "designer quality" discount makeup and free makeup lessons. Generic cosmetics are purchased from the same labs that produce many name-brand lines, but Generic eliminates the fancy packaging and charges less—25-50% off what you'd pay for a top-line department store cosmetic. You can call and make an appointment for a free half-hour makeup lesson. Be honest with the trained salespeople as to what you want—a natural look or a more professional make-up look.

Personal Care

They'll create something for your individual lifestyle and personality. We think you'll be pleased with your consultation as well as their cosmetic prices. **Checks, M/C, VISA**

KARIN'S BEAUTY SUPPLIES, INC.
Seattle: 10017 Holman Rd. NW (782-0577)
Lynnwood: 4001 198th SW (775-3212)
Renton: Renton Shopping Center (271-7145)
Tacoma: Tacoma Mall (472-1288)
Hours: *Holman Rd. NW & 198th SW* **M-F 10-6; Sat. 9-5;** *Renton Shopping Center* **M-F 10-9; Sat. 10-6; Sun. 12-5;** *Tacoma* **M-F 10-9; Sat. 10-6; Sun. 12-5**

You'll find Karin's competitive, as far as prices, with other beauty supply outfits around town. A large selection of products, covering most brands, is available: perms, rinses, shampoos, dryers, irons, capes, artificial nails. Newly developed products appear at Karin's as soon as they're on the market. If you're wondering about some of these, ask the salespeople—all are licensed hairdressers. You'll also want to check into Karin's monthly sales. **Checks, M/C, VISA**

K'S BEAUTY SUPPLY
Everett: 1001 Hwy. 99 N., Suite A-8 (258-2866)
Hours: M-F 10-6; Sat. 10-4

This small shop carries beauticians' lines only, and among these brands you'll find some outstanding bargains. We recommend that you tell them what you are currently using in a retail product and ask them to show you the beauticians' version of that product. One of the best buys in the shop is the generic knockoffs of the famous-name brands. The generics and the brand names are chemically labeled so you can compare ingredients. **Checks**

MARQUIS BEAUTY PRODUCTS
Federal Way: 1706 S. 320th (839-5881; 927-6153)
Hours: M-F 10-6; Sat. 10-5

The shopping is pleasant in this nicely appointed beauty supply outlet. We discovered new items we hadn't encountered elsewhere and found information we were given to be especially helpful. Marquis carries products for men and women. If you haven't yet tried saving money by buying professional beauty products, this would be a pleasant spot in which to start. Unopened returns are accepted except on personal care items like brushes. **Checks, M/C, VISA**

Personal Care

NORTHWEST HAIRLINES
Bellevue: 14100 NE 20th (647-6306)
Lynnwood: 6501 196th SW (771-3733)
Hours: M-F 8-5:30; Sat. 9-3 (both stores)

You can purchase alongside the beauticians here, but you may not buy perms, hair colorings or chemical processing items. You can buy sculptured nail kits. They stock concentrates in bulk sizes as well as the smaller retail packs. Savings are always the most dramatic on the larger quantities and concentrates.

Checks, M/C, VISA

P. J.'S BEAUTY SUPPLY
Lynnwood: 18700 33rd W. (774-1999)
Hours: M-Sat. 10-6; Sun. 12-5

P. J. stocks a little of everything for everyone in the personal care lines, all are beauticians' products. What caught our eye were the sculptured nail kits. A student kit costs about $30, complete with instructions and more than one set of nails. The equivalent in having them done elsewhere would run around $100. It's time to get together with a friend and do your own!

Checks, M/C, VISA

VAAR-M BEAUTY SUPPLY
Seattle: 4517 California SW (937-9224)
Kirkland: Totem Lake (821-4488)
Federal Way: Sea-Tac Plaza (941-6363)
Hours: *California SW & Sea-Tac* **M-F 10-6; Sat. 10-5;** *Totem Lake* **M-F 10-9; Sat. 10-6; Sun. 12-5**

Vaar-M sells everything you normally see in use in a beauty shop (cosmetics, hand-held dryers, scissors, hair products, etc.), and prices are very good. The trained staff is most helpful in giving guidance in the selection and use of these professional-line products. They can also point out the best buys—such as shampoos and other products in concentrate form. We were impressed with the prices of scissors, accessories and cosmetics as compared to beauty shops and boutique departments.

Checks, M/C, VISA

SPORTING GOODS

AANNEX RENTS, INC.
Seattle: 12554 Lake City Way NE (362-5547)
Hours: M-Sat. 9-6; Sun. 9-5

We took advantage of their Year End Summer Fun Sale to buy a tent used only a few times, and saved 40%. Campers and backpackers should put this one on their calendars. Shortly after Labor Day 80% of the camping and backpacking gear and ⅓ of the camping equipment used the previous year goes on sale with many bargains in the 50% off category. The sale stock generally includes tents, backpacks, air mattresses, flotation vests and more, and these are still on sale until mid-October. Ski equipment goes on sale in April—an excellent time to shop anywhere for these items. Used medical equipment is a good buy. Once in a while used items from their many other categories are offered for sale. Inquire if you have something in mind. Returns within 48 hours. **Checks, M/C, VISA**

BACKWOODS SUPPLY CO.
Tacoma: 711 S. 48th (48th & Park) (473-4095)
Hours: M-Sat. 10-6

Backwoods sells camping and backpacking equipment and lightweight boats. We stopped by to put our names on the list for the annual sale of display models and rentals (in late August) and came out with a 2-man, rainproof, dome tent on sale for 30% less than we'd priced it elsewhere. Such is the luck of the bargain shopper! This is a small, out-of-the way store, but worthy of an outdoors person's attention—and don't miss the sale! Returns are usually allowed, and definitely if there is a defect in the item.
Checks, M/C, VISA

B & I SPORTS SHOP
Tacoma: 8210 S. Tacoma Way (584-3207)
Hours: M-F 9-9; Sat., Sun. & Holidays 10-6

Call the manager to find out when the next used equipment sale will occur, or keep your eye on the *Tacoma News Tribune* for an ad. Used camping equipment is reduced by 50% or more when it is out of style, starting to wear or no longer being stocked as a rental. Many items are Coleman appliances. Sales occur 3-4 times a year. The major one is often in early June. **Checks, M/C, VISA**

Sporting Goods

BASE CAMP SUPPLY
Tacoma: 3730 S. Pine (472-4402)
Hours: M-F 10-7; Sat. 9-5

Hikers and backpackers consign equipment at Base Camp Supply. Tents, boots, packs and other gear may be found here. Sometimes there's a large consignment grouping, sometimes not. Used European (German) wool army pants for hiking are an excellent value. **Checks, M/C, VISA**

CITY ELECTRIC SERVICE SHOP
Seattle: 2125 2nd (622-1437)
Hours: M-F 8-5; Sat. 9-1

Coleman camping fans will be happy to hear that this shop sells "factory seconds," which have been repaired or were scratched, at wholesale prices. They may have on hand lanterns, stoves, heaters, coolers, jugs and some propane items. Everything is guaranteed for a full year. **Checks**

EDDIE BAUER
Seattle: 1330 5th, Rainier Sq. (622-2766)
Hours: M-Sat. 9:30-6; F 9:30-8

Rather than describe the Eddie Bauer store's stock, we recommend that sport and outdoor enthusiasts pick up a catalog. Samples, seconds and discontinued catalog items are sent from the various factories and stores to The Loft in the basement. In addition, items which were not cleared during a seasonal sale may be offered in The Loft at even greater reductions. Savings vary. Most items are marked 30-60% off. Flaws are marked at the factory, but the tape indicators can get lost; so study all items carefully before making your purchase. Dressing room. Loft merchandise may not be returned but may be exchanged for other items from The Loft. **Checks, M/C, VISA, Amer. Exp.**

EVERGREEN SPORTING GOODS & SURPLUS
Renton: 818 S. 3rd (226-5700)
Hours: M-Sat. 9:30-5:30

"Surplus" is somewhat of a misnomer here. The merchandise is nearly all new. The stock is geared to outdoor activities such as camping, hiking, boating, etc. Kingdome tents were priced $30-$40 cheaper than "uptown"; a prominent-label sweatshirt was $9 less than regular retail, and similar savings were available on Hollofil sleeping bags and day packs. The owner intends to stock the big names at good discounts. Full refunds are accepted with your receipt. **Checks**

Sporting Goods 149

GOLFLAND DISCOUNT PRO SHOP
Tacoma: 4701½ Center (564-7155)
Hours: M-Sun. 7-7

Looking for golfing equipment and supplies? You might want to start here and then do some cross checking. Golf sets were marked 20% below suggested retail; single clubs were marked down 10%. Sporting apparel was also 10% off regular retail—some more than that. Exchanges are allowed.

Checks, M/C, VISA

HARRIS CONLEY DISCOUNT GOLF SHOPS
Seattle: 1123 1st (624-8361); 17900 Southcenter Pkwy. (Pavilion) (575-8536)
Bellevue: 1440 156th NE (747-2585)
Tacoma: Cascade Plaza on 38th (624-8057)
Hours: *Seattle* **M-Sat. 9:30-6;** *Pavilion* **M-F 10-9; Sat. 10-6; Sun. 11-5;** *Bellevue* **M-Sat. 10-10; Sun. 10-9;** *Tacoma* **M-F 10-9; Sat. 10-6**

Some other locations to check for golfing equipment of all sorts. They advertise as "one of the Northwest's largest discount golf suppliers," and run good competitive prices on golf sets, clubs, balls, apparel.

Checks, M/C, VISA

JERRY'S SURPLUS (DUFFLE BAG, INC.)
Everett: 2031 Broadway (252-1176)
Hours: M-F 9-9; Sat. 9-6; Sun. 11-5

We visited Jerry's to take advantage of the savings on repaired Coleman camping equipment. On the way to the upstairs loft, we noted many good buys on outdoor recreational items and clothing. When Jerry runs a special, it's *special!* You can expect to save up to 50% on the repaired Coleman items. Jerry's restores them to full working condition, and they are guaranteed. Returns are not given on used items, but are accepted on new merchandise.

Checks, M/C, VISA

JOBE FACTORY OUTLET
Redmond: 15320 NE 92nd (882-1177)
Hours: M-F 9-6

What a find! And just in time to make our deadline. Plus, we've been hoping for and searching for a place like this. For those of you looking for water skis, ski vests, wet suits—start here! At the beginning of the summer, we bought top-quality ski vests to use for skiing and sailing, for $19.95 and $21.95. You'd pay twice that amount most everywhere else. In fact, a man visiting the outlet that particular day said he'd paid $40 for vests that weren't as good. You'll also discover great prices on water skis, shorts (trunks), water ski bindings, ski tows, etc. Give them a call to see what's on hand. For winter, they'll be stocking snow skis and boots. If you're into these sports, you can't lose looking here. All sales final. **Checks, M/C, VISA**

NESLIN'S FACTORY OUTLET
Bellevue: 14230 NE 20th (643-7477)
Lynnwood: 19400 36th Ave. W. (775-3703)
Tacoma: 1112 Pacific Ave. S., Parkland (535-2979)
Hours: M-Sat. 10-6 (all stores)

Neslin's offers a large selection of men's, women's and children's outerwear with savings averaging around 30%. You'll find down and polyester parkas, ski bibs, vests, raincoats, rain suits, coats during the winter months. During summer, lighter weight outerwear, rainwear and swimwear are available. Along with clothing, Neslin's also stocks down and quallofil quilts and pillows. We've also discovered at various visits items such as socks, leg warmers, nylon wallets. Anyway, it's always worth stopping by. The owners gladly accept exchanges but no cash refunds.
Checks, M/C, VISA

THE NORTH FACE
Seattle: 1st & Spring (622-4111); 47th & University Way NE (633-4431)
Hours: M, Th, F 9:30-8; T, W, Sat. 9:30-6; Sun. 12-5

Twice annually (March and Oct.) North Face holds sales to clear out any of their rental equipment which is 3 years old, plus discontinued models, out-of-season and clearance items. You will find camping and backpacking gear in the fall and ski things in the spring. They do have a mailing list, although this does not guarantee advance notice of these sales.
Checks, M/C, VISA, Amer. Exp.

OSBORN AND ULLAND
Seattle: 1123 2nd (624-6954)
Hours: M-F 10-5:30; Sat. 10-5

Osborn and Ulland have combined their former Shoe Inn and Sports Annex at one location. The stock consists of active sports apparel and a small version of Nordstrom's Shoe Rack. (You ask for the size shoe you need from a sampling of styles.) The policy is to consolidate odds-and-ends from the O & U stores into a single location, plus manufacturers' closeouts, last year's models and whatever other bargains turn up. For example, clothing left over from Sniagrab ends up here and for the same prices. The bargains run from good to fabulous. Prices range from 25-70% off regular retail. All sales final. **Checks, M/C, VISA, Amer. Exp.**

OUTDOOR EMPORIUM
Seattle: 420 Pontius N. (624-6550)
Hours: M-Sat. 8-5

Don't overlook this spot when you're checking on outdoor sporting goods. We found their prices on all types of outdoor clothing, especially wool, (name brands, no seconds) to be excellent. Depth-finders are also good buys as well as other marine items, such as flotation devices and downriggers. Hollofil sleeping bags, coolers and chests, boots of all sorts, fishing lures, camping equipment and other related items were all well-priced.
Checks, M/C, VISA

PEAK EXPERIENCE
Bellevue: 1405 132nd NE (453-8041)
Hours: M-F 10-9; Sat. 10-6; Sun. 11-5 (closed Sundays in summer)

Peak Experience sells new as well as secondhand sporting equipment, hiking, backpacking and camping gear. Stock changes seasonally. You will find an excellent stock of ski equipment and clothing for men, women and children. Their prices on ski tune-ups are also quite a bit less than at other shops around town. Consignments are taken during hours that the shop is open. Sellers are paid 50% of the selling price in cash or 80% credit toward other equipment. If you have sporting equipment your family has outgrown, here's the place to take it. Inquire about reduced lift tickets.
Checks, M/C, VISA

PRO GOLF DISCOUNT
Tukwila: 17344 Southcenter Pkwy. (575-3633)
Lynnwood: 18700 33rd Ave. W. (525-5518)
Hours: M-F 10-9; Sat. 10-6; Sun. 12-5 (both stores)

What McDonald's is to hamburgers, Pro Golf is to golf. Pro Golf is the largest buyer of golfing equipment in the world. They guarantee to beat the price of anyone else in town on clubs. If you find them on sale cheaper, they'll verify the price and beat it. In addition, if you buy a set of woods or irons, you get a Buyer's Discount Card good for one year which entitles you to a 10% discount on everything in the store with the exception of sets of clubs and balls. They carry Bargain Balls and X-outs (that's a "second" in golfer's talk). They feature club repair and supply a practice cage so you can see how that new club will perform. The two stores carry a complete line of golfing accessories and clothing. Take your teenagers and challenge them to a tee-grabbing contest. Tees are $1.49 per handful. Refunds are given with a receipt.
Checks, M/C, VISA

Sporting Goods

PUETZ
Seattle: 11762 Aurora N. (362-2272)
Hours: M-Sat. 10-10; Sun. 10-8

Puetz advertises as one of the West's largest golfing stores. They stock everything a golfer could possibly want or need. Rather than quoting prices or percentages, we feel you should check them out and compare to the other golf listings.
Checks, M/C, VISA

R.E.I. CO-OP (RECREATIONAL EQUIPMENT, INC.)
Seattle: 1525 11th (323-8333)
Hours: M, T 9:30-6; W, Th, F 9:30-9; Sat. 9-6; Sun. 12-5 (summer and Christmas only)

Anyone can belong to R.E.I. upon written application and payment of a $5 membership fee, but you don't have to be a member to shop R.E.I. To stay an active member, one must purchase at least $5 worth of merchandise each year. Active members receive dividends in March based on their total purchases. R.E.I. carries top-quality, name-brand sporting goods. These are not inexpensive and cannot be called bargains. However, two annual sales are held, fall and spring, where some things are discounted up to 30% off. Prices at R.E.I. may be comparable to other stores, but taking the rebate into account, you're saving money! In addition, R.E.I. will accept your old hiking boots, packs and skis in trade for new ones—offer is good for men, women and children. Used items are resold in the store. Ask a salesperson what is available. At least 2 free color catalogs are published each year.
Checks, M/C, VISA

SECOND WIND
Seattle: 300 Queen Anne N. (284-4979)
Hours: M-F 11-7; Th 11-9; Sat. 9:30-6

An outlet for Early Winters, you'll find topnotch sporting goods at this location—sleeping bags, biking gear, cross country skis, sweaters, jackets, etc. These are not inexpensive items but top quality. Last spring, hiking boots were priced at $73 (originally $119). Sales are run often, and then you'll find items selling for up to 50% off. All sales final.
Checks, M/C, VISA

SKI RACK SPORTS
Seattle: 2118 8th (623-7318)
Hours: M-F 10-5:30; Th 10-9; Sat. 10-5; (Sun. during winter)

The Ski Rack gears itself toward being a family-oriented sporting goods store. We found them to be a great source for consigned ski boots and skis—all in excellent condition. They also will accept some top-quality, serviceable children's ski clothing. There's a 30% charge for consigning your goods. Prices are determined by the owner and you. The store offers a good, viable low-priced children's all-day ski school, which you may want to check out. **Checks, M/C, VISA**

SKI STORE
Bellevue: 2105 140th NE (746-2054)
Hours: M-F 10-9; Sat. 10-6; Sun. 12-5

A great place to buy used ski equipment for the entire family. You can also consign or trade your own used ski gear. Check with the store! **Checks, M/C, VISA**

SNIAGRAB—See Index

SPORTS OUTLET
Auburn: 136 E. Main (833-9683)
Hours: M-F 10-6; Sat. 10-5

The store policy is to keep prices a liberal 20% off regular retail. You will find backpacks, tents, camping equipment and accessories, athletic supplies and school equipment. They aim to stay under the big name stores in their lines, so it's certainly worth giving them a call to cost compare equipment.
Checks, M/C, VISA

SPORTS REPLAY
Lynnwood: 19500 36th W. (775-4088)
Hours: T-Sat. 10-5:30

We can now add another place to find consigned sporting goods—quality used skis, soccer shoes, balls, golf items, etc. You'll discover things for the whole family. They also stock some new daypacks and bags which are seconds that sell for approximately 50% off regular retail. **Checks**

THE STRAPPED JOCK
Seattle: 410 Elliott W. (283-1179)
Tukwila: Pavilion, 17900 Southcenter Pkwy. (575-4400)
Tacoma: S. 38th & G (473-6763)
Hours: M-F 9-7; Sat. 9-6; Sun. 12-6

Strapped jocks, jockesses and jockettes will love shopping at these low-overhead sports clothing and shoe outlets. Merchandise includes seconds (clearly marked), some manufacturers' closeouts and some clearance from the parent retailer. Brand-name shoes, shirts, shorts, joggers, etc. at 30-50% off draw cheers from the fans. **Checks, M/C, VISA**

ANNUAL SALES EVENTS

A variety of public and private institutions and charity organizations in the Puget Sound area hold once a year auctions, garage sales or special sample sales. Most are preceded by advertising of some sort, so keep your eye out for ads and posters and put your name on mailing lists. The bargains at annual sales are generally outstanding.

We've noticed that many small manufacturers have also been holding yearly sales because they are not large enough to open or staff year-round factory outlets. We cannot list all of these because the annual sale date and place is never certain. However, the fantastic bargains make it worth your while to watch for the large advertising campaigns which always announce these clearance sales.

Watch ads for warehouse sales too. J.C. Penney and Jafco both use this method for clearing overstocks. See's Candies adds a twist to this theme by opening a holiday candy shop which sells only bulk candy. Furniture stores are especially fond of once-a-year cleanups. Floor samples, one-of-a-kinds and seasonally dated merchandise are usually the biggest bargains at these sales. Both Scan/Design and Ken's Suburban are among our favorites.

AANNEX RENTS, INC.—See Index

BEL-BOUTIQUE
Tacoma: 2300 S. Washington (752-7701)

The Bellarmine High School Mothers' Club raises funds for scholarships and special improvements via their 4 yearly sales of all new, famous label, men's, juniors' and women's clothing. The events are Spring, Holiday, Summer and Back-to-School. Giftwear, jewelry, children's coats and sometimes lingerie can turn up at one of the sales. Each year has brought more clothing and new additions. The clothes are sold at cost plus 10%. Get yourself on the mailing list so you won't miss the next one!

BRUCE HOUGHTON & ASSOCIATES
Bainbridge Island: 3378 Point White Dr. NE (842-5489)
Hours: 10-5 during the sale

Call Bruce and ask to be added to the mailing list for his sample sales. Baskets, housewares, antiques, etc. are priced at or below wholesale. This popular Bainbridge Island event has repeatedly drawn requests for an encore.

CITY OF HOPE SECONDHAND ROSE THRIFT SHOP
Seattle: 6421 32nd NW (784-0298)
Hours: M-Sat. 10-5

A very unique "Brand X" sale is held once a year. First-quality merchandise is donated by a famous maker and sold at wholesale prices. Check to see when it takes place. Notification of the sale is published in the chapter bulletin. Only City of Hope members can shop the first day, then the sale is open to the public. Stock from other manufacturers' sales representatives is also available. To become a member, send your name, address and phone number along with $10 to: City of Hope, 8852 SE 39th, Mercer Island, WA 98040.

KUSAK CUT GLASS WORKS—See Index

SEATTLE REPERTORY THEATRE: ELEGANT ELEPHANT SALE
For Information: 447-2210

The REP holds its annual fund-raiser in May. Your donations must be valued $10 or more, and you receive a tax receipt. The costumes, props, and odds and ends of scenery from past performances add a unique note to this event.

SEATTLE SCHOOL DISTRICT
Seattle: 587-3440

The Seattle Public School District holds an annual auction (usually July or August). You can call to put your name on the mailing list.

SKI BONKERS

An excellent annual ski sale held during early September for one weekend, Fri.-Sun., at the Seattle Trade Center. You'll find a large assortment and a choice of top-quality, name-brand clothing, boots, poles and accessories for the entire family. The savings here are terrific. We were impressed by the organization and manner in which the sale was conducted. All sales final.
Checks, M/C, VISA

SNIAGRAB
Seattle: Seattle Center (624-6954)

Sniagrab (bargains spelled backwards), organized by Osborn and Ulland, is a once-a-year bargain festival at the Seattle Center held on a Fri., Sat. and Sun. in late summer. Almost everything for sale is new, though the majority of items are the previous year's models, styles, etc. You may find some "demo" boots or skis if you arrive early. All types of ski paraphernalia are on sale. Prices range from 30-70% off retail, with most items going at 50% off. All sales final. **Checks, M/C, VISA, Amer. Exp.**

SPEAKERLAB
For info call: 633-5020

When SpeakerLab runs a warehouse sale, expect to stand in line to get in. We know people who have come out of the warehouse at 735 N. Northlake Way with some incredible buys. There is no mailing list, and even the stores don't always have the information much in advance of these sales. Usually they wait until they have accumulated enough merchandise to clear it out, sometimes annually, sometimes semiannually. You can call the office number for information or watch closely for the ads.

TACOMA SCHOOL DISTRICT
Tacoma: 593-6800

The Tacoma School District holds surplus equipment auctions at least once and sometimes twice a year—commonly in May and August. Watch for the ads in the paper, or call to have your name added to their mailing list.

WORLD WIDE DISTRIBUTORS, INC.
Kent: 8211 S. 194th (872-8746)

Watch for ads announcing World Wide Distributor's Annual Warehouse Sale—normally in December. Call after November 15 to check the date. You'll find a wide range of items: toys, clothing, shoes, luggage, garden furniture, sporting goods—all at just above wholesale prices. Put this one on your calendar!
Checks, M/C, VISA

BOOKSTORES

USED BOOKS

We decided a book about bargain buys and savings would not be complete without a few words on used books. For those of you who love and enjoy books as much as we do, used bookstores can be a tremendous cost-cutting factor in your lives. We were not able to visit every single used bookstore, but we've tried to obtain valid information on each one we've listed—to let you know whether they stock hardbacks, paperbacks or comics, and whether they buy or exchange, etc. Secondhand stores usually stock used books, so check these out as well—we've not included them.

ANYTHING GROWS
Seattle: 2112 SW 152nd (243-7095)
Hours: M-Sat. 9-5

Inventory of about 4,000 books—primarily adults', few children's. The owner trades (2 for 1) and sells. **Cash only**

BAUER BOOKS/CREATIVE AWARENESS BOOK EXCHANGE
Seattle: 2241 Eastlake E. (322-1575); 714 N. 34th (547-2665)
Hours: M-F 12-7; Sat. 12:30-6:30

New and pre-read books sold here. You can get discounts on used books by receiving credit points on books you bring in. **Checks, M/C, VISA**

BEATTY BOOK STORE
Seattle: 1925 3rd (624-2366)
Hours: M-Sat. 10-5

This store carries a general stock of used books, specializing in rare books and first editions. The owner will purchase rare copies. **Checks**

BEAUTY AND THE BOOKS
Seattle: 4213 University Way NE (632-8510)
Hours: M-F, Sun. 10-11; Sat. 10-12

Lots of used hardbacks and paperbacks, plus magazines, maps, posters, records, prints—all selling for good prices. You'll find a great selection in a large-sized location, and you can browse for hours, as the store stays open late. **Checks, M/C, VISA**

BEST CELLARS
Seattle: 1910 Post Alley (624-8289)
Hours: M-Sat. 11-4

A delightful, clean, spacious, comfy, homey bookstore carrying a nice selection of mainly used hardbacks and some used paperbacks. There are couches so you can sit, relax and browse through possible purchases. The owner buys and/or trades clean, previously owned books. She specializes in women's studies and offers a book search service. Ask about the buy-back credit on books purchased there. **Checks**

BIBELOTS AND BOOKS
Seattle: 112 E. Lynn (329-6676)
Hours: M-Sat. 12-6

A small store specializing in detective fiction and children's books—mainly hardcovers, a few paperbacks. **Cash only**

BLOOMSBURY BOOKS
Seattle: 3200 Harvard E. (323-6300)
Hours: T-F 11-6:30; Sat. 11-5:30

A nice, smaller-sized bookstore well worth visiting: features literature in used hardbacks and paperbacks all in excellent condition. The owner also sells baseball cards. He will buy, sell and trade on books. **Checks**

THE BOOK EXCHANGE
Marysville: 101 State (659-5626)
Hours: T-F 9:30-4; Sat. 12-5

Approximately 30,000 used paperbacks and hardbacks—all types, including children's. There are 2 rooms: one for fiction, one for nonfiction. Everything is categorized. The owner buys, sells and trades 2 for 1 on paperbacks. If you'd like some older books appraised, drop by the shop during its opening hour when things are quiet. The owner will gladly take a look at them.
Cash only

A BOOK GALLERY
Tacoma: Villa Plaza Shopping Center (588-2503)
Hours: M-F 10-7:30; Sat. 10-5; Sun. 12-5

The shop stocks all types of used paperbacks, and they will trade, depending upon the book's condition. The owner will buy used hardbacks, but only if he feels they will sell. **Checks**

BOOK LOFT
Seattle: 4160 California (935-7325)

Hours: M-Sat. 10-5; Sun. 11-3

Good variety of over 10,000 used books, primarily paperbacks. The store buys, sells, exchanges. **Checks**

THE BOOK NOOK
Everett: 3301½ Rucker (252-4242)
Hours: M-Sat. 10-5

Don't expect to find rare books here. However, you'll enjoy their nice selection of used paperbacks (all types, including children's), as well as used stereo records, tapes and magazines. Have fun browsing. **Cash only**

THE BOOK RACK
Lynnwood: 19720 44th W. (771-0825)
Hours: M, W, F 10-6; T, Th. 10-8; Sat. 10-5

At least 10,000 used paperbacks can be found here. You may exchange books that are in the same category—romance for romance, science fiction for science fiction—as long as they're in good condition. New books are also available, and all of them for 20% off regular retail. Better check it out. **Checks**

BOOKCYCLERS
Renton: 327 Williams S. (226-2711)
Hours: M-F 10-5:30; Sat. 10-3

At Bookcyclers they buy, sell and swap paperbacks, hardbacks, magazines and comics. You'll find something for everyone—kids to collectors. Their present inventory: about 15,000 paperbacks, 2,000 nonfiction and classic hardbacks. **Checks**

THE BOOKENDS
Bellevue: 10245 Main (453-0993)
Hours: M-Sat. 10-6

Relatively small store stocking mainly used paperbacks, which sell for about 30-50% off regular price. You can exchange paperback books for credit. Owner very willing to call people if a book they want comes in **Cash only**

BOOKWORLD
Kent: 24811 Pacific Hwy. S. (839-9399)
Hours: M-Sat. 10-7; Sun. 10-6

Stop here when looking for used books. Bookworld stocks a large variety covering all categories. There's also a good selection of comics, and the salespeople can give aid to any of you who have questions concerning collectors' comics. The owner buys, sells and trades. **Checks**

THE BOOKWORM
Tacoma: 1005½ S. 11th (627-4912)
Hours: M-F 9-6

The inventory at The Bookworm consists of about 80% used paperbacks covering all categories. You'll also find a good selection of back issues of old magazines—all types. The owner sells and trades. **Checks**

BROADWAY BOOKS
Everett: 607 Everett Mall Way SE (347-3343)
Hours: M-F 10-6; Sat. 10-5; Sun. 12-5

A fairly good-sized store with a nice variety of used paperbacks. The shop will exchange your books toward a purchase but will not buy outright. **Checks**

CANYON PARK STAMP, COIN AND BOOK EXCHANGE
Bothell: 22627 Bothell-Everett Hwy. (481-3364)
Hours: M-F 10-7; Sat. 10-6; Sun. 12-6

Probably 10,000 used paperbacks stocked here with a good collection of all types. The owner trades 2 for 1. You'll also find a good selection of collectors' comics. **Checks, M/C, VISA**

CARL'S BOOKS
Tacoma: 741 St. Helens (272-8827)
Hours: M-F 9:30-5:30; Sat. 9:30-4:30

This spot carries used paperbacks and hardbacks, as well as antiquarian and out-of-print books. A search service is provided, so if you've something special in mind, give Carl's Books a call. **Checks**

CATCHPENNY
Seattle: 9101 Roosevelt Way NE (527-4530)
Hours: M-Sat. 10-6; Sun. 1-5

Browse through an inventory of 18,000 used paperbacks, covering all categories, including comics. The owner buys, sells and trades. **Checks**

COLLECTOR'S NOOK
Tacoma: 213 N. I (272-9828)
Hours: M-Sat. 1-9

Truly a delightful find for those of you interested in old magazines, comics, paperbacks and phonograph records! Don't let the general clutter get you down, for the surprises you'll unearth are worth it—magazines dating back to the 1800s, records of all sorts from earliest recordings, stamps, knickknacks and old radios similar to those in the early Norman Rockwell paintings. Children will love the stacks and stacks of comic books (comic area closes at 8). The owners buy, sell and trade. **Checks**

COMSTOCK'S BINDERY AND BOOKSHOP
Seattle: 7903 Rainier S. (725-9531)
Hours: M-F 10-6; Sun. 12-5

Comstock's buys and sells books and whole libraries: Americana, arts and crafts, first editions, juveniles, limited editions, etc. This store has a special interest in buying and selling magazines: American West, astronomy, radio control, boating and sailing (pre-1935), *Playboy* (pre-1967). Paperbacks are 50% off with an equivalent trade. **Checks**

CRUCIBLE BOOKSHOP
Seattle: 5525 University Way NE (525-3737)
Hours: T-Sun. 11-7

Used and rare books are bought and sold at this store, which stocks books of all types. You'll also find prints and records. **Checks**

A DIFFERENT DRUMMER
Seattle: 420 Broadway E. (324-0525)
Hours: M-Th 10-10; F, Sat. 10-11; Sun. 12-6

A general stock of used hardbacks and paperbacks. They buy, sell and trade. You may find out-of-print books, as they buy libraries. Browsers and mail orders are welcome. **Checks**

DONNALLY-HAYES BOOKS
Seattle: 85 Yesler Way (622-7669)
Hours: M-Sat. 11-5

This shop specializes in used books on literature and the arts. They also have vintage photographs. **Checks**

FILLIPI BOOK AND RECORD SHOP
Seattle: 1351 E. Olive Way (682-4266)
Hours: T-Sat. 10-5

You'll find a general stock of hardback books here in very good condition, including first editions and rare books. Fillipi's also carries used phonograph records, ranging from the beginning of recording up to modern day. Used books and records both bought and sold. **Checks**

FOLIO BOOK SHOP
Seattle: 1523 Queen Anne N. (282-6987)
Hours: M-Sat. 12-6:30

Folio's shelves overflow with used books, mostly hardbound with some paperbacks. The owner specializes in rare NW Americana, signed first editions, illustrated items. He buys and sells. **Checks, M/C, VISA**

FOX BOOK CO.
Tacoma: 1140 Broadway (627-2223)
Hours: M-Sat. 9:30-5:30

An extensive stock of used hardbacks and paperbacks selling for good prices (i.e., paperbacks 30¢, 4/$1). The owners buy and sell used books but do not trade. **Checks**

GEMINI BOOK EXCHANGE
White Center: 9614 16th SW (762-5543)
Hours: M-Sat. 10-6

No dusty bins or rickety shelves here! This used bookstore is a spacious, modern, clean shop stocking 40,000-45,000 used paperbacks and 20,00 comics—gothics, mysteries, westerns, science fiction, children's, etc. The owner exchanges on a 1-to-1 basis for equivalent trade, sometimes 2 for 1 plus 10¢, depending on the condition of the books. **Checks**

GLOBE BOOKS
Seattle: 5220 University Way NE (527-2480)
Hours: M-Sat. 11-5:30

Used books specializing in fiction, literature, western philosophy and poetry fill this store—along with used classical and jazz records. **Checks**

GOLDEN AGE COLLECTABLES
Seattle: 1501 Pike Place Market (622-9799)
Hours: M-Sat. 10-5:30

Comic books and movie posters are the specialty of this store with 50% off each, both old and new. They also have old radio programs on cassettes and 5,000 movie stills. The store buys, sells and trades. **Checks**

GOODWILL SHOPPING CENTER—See Index

HENDERSON BOOKS
Seattle: 1928 2nd (343-7498)
Hours: M-Sat. 12-5

A small shop literally filled from floor to ceiling, every available space, with used paperbacks and hardbacks. You'll find an excellent selection of paperback fiction in good, clean condition. The owner buys, sells and trades. **Checks**

HORIZON BOOKS
Seattle: 425 15th E. (329-3586)
Renton: 901 S. 3rd (277-0542)
Hours: *Seattle* **M-F 10:30-10; Sat. 10-8; Sun. 10-6;** *Renton* **T-Sat. 11-5:30**

Horizon Books carries used books in all fields, as well as old records and some comics. You might ask for rare books here. You'll find 7 rooms for your browsing pleasure. The shops buy, sell, trade and exchange. **Checks**

JANE'S BOOKS
Seattle: 12348 Lake City Way NE (362-1766)
Hours: M-Sat. 11-4

Used paperbacks comprise half of the inventory of this bookstore. Hardbacks include children's books, NW books and specialty books, especially used cookbooks. The owner buys books outright, but only if she can use them. **Checks**

JERRY'S DOWNTOWN STAMP AND COIN AND NOVELTIES
Puyallup: 112 S. Meridian (848-5032)
Hours: M-F 10-6; Sat. 10-5

Jerry's stocks stamps, coins, novelties and collectibles such as cards, matches and comics. We're including him for his large stock of used books—an inventory of around 110,000 and most selling for 19¢ (except for science fiction). You'll never get the kids out of this spot. The owner buys and sells. **Checks**

JOURNEY
Seattle: 211 Pine (623-7220)
Hours: M-Sat. 11-6

Clean and quiet, this used bookstore stocks mainly hardbacks, but some paperbacks and used records are also available. You might discover a few rare and/or special editions. **Checks**

LARSON BOOKS
Everett: 1513 23rd (252-6866)
Hours: M-Sat. 12-6:30

Around 6,000 titles, mainly used paperbacks with some hardbacks. The shop does trade books. **Checks**

MAGUS BOOKSTORE
Seattle: 1408 NE 42nd (633-1800)
Hours: M-W 10-8; Th, F 10-10; Sat. 11-6; Sun. 1-6

Selection of used paperbacks and hardbacks, as well as new books, stocked in this shop. Proprietor told us he'd be carrying more and more used books, due to the rising prices of new ones.
Checks, M/C, VISA

MAMA'S PROSE AND STEEL
Everett: 2723 Colby (252-7780)
Hours: M-Sat. 10:30-6

You'll find a good stock of used books and comics. The owners will trade. **Checks**

McDONALD'S BOOK EXCHANGE
Bellevue: Lake Hills Shopping Center (746-0354)
Redmond: 16136 NE 87th (885-4773)
Hours: *Lake Hills* **M-Sat. 9:30-9; Sun. 11-5;** *NE 87th* **M, T, Sat. 9:30-6; W, Th, F 9:30-9; Sun. 12-5**

An excellent way to get rid of all those old paperbacks and receive something in return. Hardbacks, comics, magazines and newspapers can also be exchanged. Cash is given for books, comics or magazines—but it is never as much as is allowed for credit. Credit slips are interchangeable at the 2 shops. Cash or book credit is given for each vertical foot of bundled newspapers.
Checks

MONOHON'S PAPERBACKS
Tacoma: 1314 E. 72nd (537-8971); 3916 100th SW (584-8830); 6611 S. 12th (564-3157)
Federal Way: 1414 S. 324th (941-4770)
Lacey: 5815 Lacey Blvd. (459-1187)
Hours: M-F 10-8; Sat. 10-6; Sun. 12-5 (all stores)

Monohon's stocks used paperbacks only, but they cover a large variety and a great many subjects. A very pleasant person helped us out and will likely do the same for you. The store buys, sells and trades 2 for 1. **Cash**

THE MUSQUAW
Renton: 919 Harrington NE (226-6590)
Hours: M-F 9:30-9; Sat. 9:30-6

Varied selection of several thousand used paperbacks, along with new books found here. The owner buys, sells, exchanges 2 for 1, 25¢ each, 5/$1. **Checks, M/C, VISA**

OLD SEATTLE PAPERWORKS
Seattle: 1501 Pike Place Market (623-2870)
Hours: Generally 11-4

Old Seattle Paperworks specializes in old magazines, posters, postcards, photos, graphics—an absolutely fascinating collection to browse through! The owner tells us his hours are sketchy, so it's worth calling before you visit to see if and when the shop is open.
Checks

O'LEARY'S BOOKS
Tacoma: 4021 100th SW (588-2503)
Hours: M-F 10-7:30; Sat. 10-5; Sun. 12-5

You'll find quite a large variety of books covering a broad scope: a third of inventory is new and used comics; a third, used hardbacks; and a third, used paperbacks. It considers itself primarily a "used and out-of-print" bookstore specializing in military history of NW Americana. Paperbacks are exchanged 2 for 1. **Checks, M/C, VISA**

PAGE ONE BOOK EXCHANGE
Bellevue: 14220 NE 20th (747-6165)
Hours: M-Sat. 11-5

Page One has more than doubled its inventory in the past year, with an excellent selection of romances, westerns, science fiction, nonfiction, mysteries. Especially worthwhile is the bargain shelf: books selling 6/$1. **Checks**

PAPER BACKS AND THINGS
Tacoma: 1314 E. 72nd (537-8971)
Hours: M-F 10-8; Sat. 10-6; Sun. 12-5

An inventory of approximately 10,000 clean, used paperbacks (all types) stocked here. You'll also find some children's paperbacks. The owner buys, sells and trades. **Cash only**

THE PAPERBACK EXCHANGE
Seattle: 209 Union (624-7250)
Hours: M-Sat. 10-6

The Paperback Exchange carries a large selection of paperbacks of all varieties, selling for 50% off or 10¢ each with 2 trades (in the same price group). Good selection of comics also stocked.
Checks

PEGASUS
Seattle: 4832 California SW (937-5410)
Hours: M-Sat. 10-6; Sun. 12-4

At the time of our visit, the store housed an inventory of about 20,000 used paperbacks—no hardbacks—lots of science fiction. The owner buys, sells and trades (2 for 1 of equal value and comparable material).
Checks

QUIET COMPANION BOOKS
Tacoma: 21 Tacoma N. (627-8948)
Hours: M-Sat. 10-6

This bookstore carries only used hardbacks, and the owner does not trade.
Checks

R. A. MEZOFF BOOKSELLER
Seattle: 5519 University Way NE (522-0577)
Hours: T-Sat. 11-5; Sun. 12-4

Used and rare books (20,000-30,000 of general stock), as well as a few collector comics line the shelves, 70% are hardbacks. The owner specializes in Jewish studies (history) and literature. The owner buys (will buy libraries) and does some trading.
Checks, M/C, VISA

RAINY DAY BOOKS
Seattle: 8329 15th NW (783-3383)
Hours: M-Sat. 10-6

All types of popular reading arranged by category and author. The shop buys, sells and trades most types of reading material: science fiction, westerns, classics, mysteries, best sellers, etc. You'll also find a good comic section and a few rare books.
Checks

RAYMER'S OLD BOOK STORE
Seattle: 920 3rd (622-0357)
Hours: M-F 11-5:30

Fascinating 95-year-old store literally full from floor to ceiling and wall to wall with a wide assortment of used hardbacks. The owner specializes in printed material on the metaphysical.
Checks

RITA DYKE'S BOOKS AND RECORDS
Seattle: 432 Pike Place Market (622-6681)
Hours: M-Sat. 10-6

A general stock of books can be found here. First editions, rare copies, out-of-print books and older, more expensive children's books (e.g., *Tarzan* series) are sold. Trade 2 for 1, or 1 for 1 plus 25¢. The shop occasionally buys libraries and old copies of books.
Checks

SEATTLE BOOK CENTER
Seattle: 2231 2nd (625-1533)
Hours: M-Sat. 9:30-6; Sun. 12-5

When we went to press, this unique book center was not completely finished. However, you'll be able to find 9-10 booksellers under one roof, 2 full floors. It's a cooperative effort of several Seattle bookshop owners. Each should have fine-quality used books—little junk—and each will have a specialty: Africa, Western Americana, mysteries, science fiction, to name a few. They'll also be looking for used books to purchase.

Checks, M/C, VISA

SHAKESPEARE AND MARTIN
Seattle: 1914 2nd (622-9370)
Hours: M-Sat. 11-5:30

Books from 25¢ and up here. The shop specializes in first editions of science fiction, poetry, literature and Western Americana. It also has excellent children's illustrated books as well as books on architecture. You'll find mainly hardbacks and very few paperbacks.

Checks

SHOREY BOOK STORES
Seattle: 110 Union (624-0221); 119 S. Jackson (622-8720)
Hours: M-Sat. 9-6 (both stores)

Advertised as the "world's largest antiquarian book dealer," Shorey's stocks over 1½ million volumes of new, used and rare books in any category you care to name. It's an ideal spot for buying used encyclopedias for your children. Browsers are welcomed. The stores also stock maps, charts, paperbacks, journals and comics.

Checks, M/C, VISA

SUNSHINE ANYTIME BOOKSTORE
Seattle: 15203 Military Rd. S. (241-0629)
Hours: M-F 11-7; Sat. 10-4:30

This shop handles a general variety of used paperbacks and hardbacks. The owner buys, sells and trades, and is looking for military history books.

Checks, M/C, VISA

SWAN'S COMIC AND MAGAZINE MART
Tacoma: 1335 Commerce (627-3028)
Hours: T-Sat. 2-5

Paperbacks found here for 50% off. Trades made; comics also sold.

Checks

TIME TRAVELERS
Seattle: 1511 2nd (624-7806)
Hours: M-Sat. 11-6

Attention comic book fans and collectors! This shop is brimming over with comic books—new, used and rare editions. If you're looking for something in particular, they'll try to get it for you. You'll also discover comic-related items and film collectibles here. The shop buys, sells and trades. **Checks**

THE UNICORN BOOKSHOP
Burien: 14900 Ambaum Blvd. SW (244-5489)
Hours: M 12-5; T-Sat. 11-5

Mainly used paperbacks. Trade 1 for 1 plus 25¢. **Cash only**

THE UPPER ROOM
Auburn: 707 Auburn Way N. (939-0005)
Hours: T-Sat. 10-6

A relatively small store (1 room) which carries primarily used books (300-400). These are not general stock but used Christian books and Bibles. The shop does not trade but will buy outright.
Checks

WALLY'S BOOK AND COMIC EXCHANGE
Kirkland: 128 Park Lane (822-7333)
Hours: M, T 10-6; W-F 10-9; Sat. 9:30-5:30; Sun. 11-5

Hardbacks, comics, paperbacks, magazines and newspapers can be exchanged here. Cash or book credit is given for each vertical foot of dry, bundled newspapers. You'll discover a large and varied stock of books here. The selection of children's books is excellent, ranging from picture books and easy readers to teenage choices. Of particular interest at Wally's is the enormous selection of comics, ranging from very old to brand new—some quite valuable. **Checks**

WINDHAVEN BOOKS
Seattle: 7502 35th NE (525-6508)
Hours: M-Sat. 10-6

A general variety of hardbacks and paperbacks—classics to fiction to science fiction. The shop emphasizes serious fiction. Windhaven will buy, sell and trade. **Checks**

NEW BOOKS

Many bookstores now feature a "bargain table" where markdowns prevail. The Elliott Bay Book Co., for example, devotes a goodly portion of their basement to reduced price books. The University Bookstore features tables of "special price" books. Walden Books and B. Dalton Bookseller operate bargain books departments offering remainders. Remainders are not used or secondhand books. Neither are they the only items stocked in discount bookstore chains like Tower Books.

DISCOUNT BOOKS BY MAIL
Seattle: P.O. Box 22011, 98122 (323-5962)

Discount Books By Mail carries an up-to-date selection of best sellers and the latest books by popular authors. Both adult and children's books are available. The books are top quality—not seconds. All are priced at 20% below suggested list price. This is not a book club but a catalog outlet. If you're interested in a catalog, give them a call. No unwanted selections will ever be sent. You will be charged for mailing ($2.25 for an unlimited number of books). **Checks, M/C, VISA**

THE LITERARY CAT
524-2957

The Literary Cat offers over 45,000 new books for sale at a 25% discount. The owner does not carry an inventory and works on a pre-order basis, passing savings directly on to the consumer. There is no minimum order. To order, call Connie Huffines with the following information: exact title, publisher, hardback or paperback, retail price if possible. She will call you when your order is ready to pick up. Allow 5-10 days. Payment is due when you pick up your order. We've ordered several books for our Book Discussion Group, and it's worked out great. Connie is very accommodating. This would be an excellent service to use when buying books as gifts. No membership fees required. **Checks**

NORTHWEST READERS' GUILD
Seattle: c/o Fifth Avenue Books, 1410 5th Ave. (Arcade level) (624-9398)
Hours: M-F 10:30-5:30; Sat. 10:30-2:30

All current paperback and hard cover best sellers are discounted 30%. Other current books and calendars, plus computer software and video games, are discounted 15-25% (including most special orders). For a flat charge of $1.35 per order, books will be sent anywhere in the United States. Membership fee is $7.50 per year. Call for a brochure and more information.

Fifth Avenue Books offers a similar discount (10-20%) to non-members. The general public is invited to come in and browse. **Checks, M/C, VISA**

RECORDINGS

The best bargain in recordings is a good used copy of a record or tape. The selection, however, is limited. One nice thing about used records, as well as their being bargains, is that you can listen to them before you buy. You'll find the best deals on new records at the time of release when good discounts can be had. Otherwise, check the bargain bins for overstocks and discontinued recordings

BACKTRACK RECORDS AND BOOKS
Seattle: 5339 25th NE (524-0529)
Hours: M-Sat. 11-5:30

Used records and paperbacks are bought outright. You can trade paperbacks 2 for 1, depending on the subject matter and the condition of the book. The proprietors will happily appraise record collections. **Checks**

BOP STREET RECORDS AND BOOKS
Seattle: 8524 Greenwood N. (784-4631)
Hours: M-Sat. 10-7; Sun. 12-6

This store buys, sells and trades paperbacks and records depending upon the quality of the item. The owner specializes in 50's and 60's. If this is your "era," be sure to stop by and see what's in stock. **Checks**

BROADWAY RECORD CENTER
THE RECORD LIBRARY
Seattle: 112 Broadway E. (Broadway Arcade) (325-9804)
Hours: *Broadway Center* **M-Sat. 12-8; Sun. 12-6;** *Record Library* **M-Sat. 11-9; Sun. 12-6**

Broadway Record Center sells new and used records. Refresh your old collection; trade it in for cash or trade toward a new record. All must be in excellent condition. We found a large, varied selection selling for very good prices. The Record Library rents records for nominal fees. You must be a member to rent ($7.50 for a 6-month membership, $10 for an annual one). Pick up a member's manual to learn all the logistics. Their used record rentals end up for sale at the Broadway Record Center. **Checks**

BUBBLE RECORDS AND TICKETS
Kent: 10451 SE 240th (854-7788)
Hours: M-F 12-8; Sat. 12-6; Sun. 1-5

Bubble Records carries a large selection of used records of all types. They also discount new records. The amount of the discount depends upon the label, etc. You can trade in your used records or sell them outright, but it's to your advantage to trade. Call to see when the person who handles trade-ins is in the store.
Checks

BUDGET TAPES AND RECORDS
Seattle: 15823 1st S. (243-4398); 539 NE Northgate Way (363-4920)
Federal Way: 30819 Pacific Hwy. S. (941-4092)
Bellevue: 203 Bellevue Way NE (455-5755)
Renton: 534 Rainier S. (228-8298)
Everett: 1130 SE Everett Mall W., Unit #11 (353-0788)
Marysville: 1371 State (653-1266)
Tacoma: 5915 6th (565-0363)
Hours: Call local store for exact hours

Good cutouts (albums no longer being made) with overstocked and discontinued recordings here. You'll find a large selection and low prices.
Checks

CELLOPHANE SQUARE
Seattle: 1315 NE 42nd (634-2280)
Hours: M-Sat. 10-12; Sun. 12-10

Rare 45's and 78's available here as well as new and used albums. Some of the used albums priced as low as 99¢. The owner buys, sells and trades recordings and used stereo equipment. Exchanges on defective items only.
Checks

CLASSIC WAX
Seattle: 3004 NE 125th (365-6820)
Hours: M-Sat. 11-9

All types of records—most are used and out of print. They will help locate things you might be looking for, and they do buy, sell and trade. You'll find classical to rock, sound tracks and vocalists.
Checks

DANDYLION RECORDS AND TAPES
Seattle: 212 N. 85th (784-3784)
Hours: M-Sun. 11-8

This record store carries new and used records: rock, folk, imports. They will try to help locate odd items for those of you who are record collectors. They buy, sell and trade records. They also sell musical equipment and electronic instruments. Some of these items are on consignment.
Checks

DRASTIC PLASTIC RECORDS
Tacoma: 2703 6th (272-2886)
Hours: M-Sat. 1-6

Approximately 1,000 used albums, cassettes and LP's can be found here. They sell for approximately 50% less than a comparable new record. The owner is strict about what he takes, so you'll not find anything badly scratched. High quality control is exercised. All sales final, unless you arrange an overnight approval agreement with the owner. **Checks**

EASY STREET RECORDS
Bellevue: 15251 NE Bellevue-Redmond Rd. (643-1433)
Hours: M-F 10-8; Sat., Sun. 12-6

We found an excellent selection and large variety of used records, including a used Glenn Miller recording—paid $5, comparable $10 new—which we couldn't resist. The store specializes in "heavy metal" for those of you who are into this type of music. It also stocks some new records and tapes. They buy, sell and trade. **Checks**

FIFTH AVENUE RECORD SHOP
Seattle: 1301 5th (624-6507)
Hours: M-Sat. 9:30-6

A large selection from jazz to children's and imported recordings. This is the spot if you're looking for new or used recordings of classical music. You'll find many from which to choose. If they don't have what you want, they'll order and even mail it. **Checks, M/C, VISA**

FILLIPI'S BOOK AND RECORD SHOP—See Index.

GOLDEN OLDIES RECORD EXCHANGE
Seattle: 4538 Roosevelt Way NE (634-0322)
Hours: M-Sun. 10-5

This store only deals in 45 RPM records. They have 800,000 "oldies" in stock and offer free finder service on rarer hard-to-find records. They also appraise and buy 45 RPM record collections. **Checks, M/C, VISA**

GOLDEN OLDIES RECORDS
Everett: 1904½ Hewitt (252-0707)
Hours: M-Sun. 10-5

A marvelous spot for those into used recordings. You'll find a good selection of 45's, 78's, albums, out-of-print records. Appraisals are made and the owner buys, trades and sells. Ask about mail orders. **Checks, M/C, VISA**

Recordings 173

PENNY LANE RECORDS AND TAPES
Seattle: 4537 California SW (932-5693)
Hours: M-F 10-9; Sat. 10-6; Sun. 12-5

You'll find some used records here—mainly rock. However, most of their inventory is new. The store buys, sells and trades.

Checks, M/C, VISA

ROXY
Seattle: 4208 University Way NE (632-1695)
Hours: M-Th 9:30-11; F, Sat. 9:30-12; Sun. 11:30-7:30

Roxy buys and sells used records, 45's, tapes, stereos, musical gear, as well as new recordings. You'll find an excellent selection of import singles and albums. No cash refunds, but exchanges accepted if item is defective and returned within 48 hours with receipt.
Checks, M/C, VISA

RUBATO'S
Bellevue: 10672 108th (455-9417)
Hours: M-F 11-9; Sat. 11-6; Sun. 12-5

You'll find Rubato's one of the best spots for used classical, rock, jazz and soul records. The store also carries some new records and will special order at a very good cost-saving price.
Checks

SECOND TIME AROUND RECORDS
Seattle: 4144 University Way NE (632-1698)
Hours: M-Th 9:30-9; F, Sat., Sun. 9:30-10

Second Time Around buys, sells and trades records, tapes, songbooks, stereos, musical gear and comics. Used comics were priced 20¢ each or 6/$1.00—nice prices! Collectible comics were priced $1 up. No cash refunds; exchanges on defective item if returned within 48 hours along with receipt.

Checks, M/C, VISA

TOWER RECORDS
Seattle: 500 Mercer (283-4456); 4321 University Way NE (632-1187)
Tacoma: 2941 S. 38th (475-9222)
Hours: M-Sun. 9 a.m.-midnight (all stores)

Tower Records carries a large selection of new records and tapes at good prices—$2.99 for cutouts, $5.99 for single albums on sale. Note the unique closing time—you'll be surprised how many people shop that late!
Checks, M/C, VISA

THE UNDERGROUND
Tacoma: 311½ S. 11th (383-2041)
Hours: M-F 10-5:30

Used record albums—mostly jazz, a little classical, a little rock 'n roll! The owners love the business—feel they have a giant record collection of their own. **Checks**

URBAN RENEWAL RECORDS
Seattle: 4548 University Way NE (634-1775)
Hours: M-F 11-9; Sat. 10-6; Sun. 12-5

This shop has a small inventory of good-quality used records tucked way in the back of the store. They specialize in new wave, folk, reggae, old classics, imports. They buy, sell and trade.
Checks

THE WHEREHOUSE
Seattle: 858 Southcenter Shopping Center (433-9856)
Bellevue: 1100 Bellevue Way NE (454-8847)
Lynnwood: 3000 348th SW (771-9944)
Hours: *Seattle, Lynnwood* **M-F 10-9; Sat. 10-6; Sun. 11-5;** *Bellevue* **M-Sat. 10-8; Sun. 12-5**

Good prices on new records and tapes, and their sales offer even better savings. Comparison shop with other record stores in your area. No cash refunds. **Checks, M/C, VISA**

YESTERDAY AND TODAY RECORDS
Seattle: 4307 University Way NE (632-1693)
Hours: M-Th 9:30-11; F, Sat. 9:30-midnight; Sun. 11:30-7:30

Selection of used records (33¢-$5) and tapes found here. The owner buys, sells and trades. New records are also sold.
Checks, M/C, VISA

OFFICE FURNITURE

ACME OFFICE FURNITURE
Seattle: 1230 1st S. (682-6565)
Hours: M-F 9-5

A small selection of used office furniture selling for about 25% off. If you don't see what you want, ask for it. The manager may be able to get it for you. **Checks**

AMERICAN OFFICE INTERIORS, INC.
Seattle: 1601 2nd (382-9810)
Hours: M-F 8-5:30; Sat. 12-4

Don't look upstairs, but in the basement arcade! You'll find a small selection of budget desks, chairs, files—many used. We also saw some office supplies on sale for good prices.
Checks, M/C, VISA

AMERICAN OFFICE INTERIORS WAREHOUSE
Seattle: 210 3rd S. (223-1652)
Hours: M-F 8-4

American Office Interiors Warehouse stocks a large selection of budget line and used office furniture—desks, chairs, etc. The used pieces of furniture are trade-ins from various offices which have bought new furniture from A.O.I. Other pieces are bought outright. **Checks, M/C, VISA**

BODEN AND GILMAN
Seattle: 2751 4th S. (682-2387)
Hours: M-F 8-5

The general styling and prices of office furniture and furnishings are middle-line. A back room and upstairs for used items consisted primarily of desks and chairs when we visited. You can buy new office furniture at 10% discount if you pay cash and pick it up yourself. No returns. **Checks**

Office Furniture

BUDGET OFFICE PRODUCTS
Tacoma: 915 Center (272-7644)
Hours: M-F 8-4:30

This is the low-overhead warehouse outlet for 3 big office furniture retailers. Much of the merchandise is left over from huge commercial orders, although they do get some used pieces and they have in-stock lines on standard items. Desks start at $65 with a good selection in the under-$200 price range. We liked the Danish fold-up home office at $289. Files start at $29 and carry a 12-year guarantee. Chairs start at $29. One model carries a lifetime frame guarantee. In fact, they guarantee all merchandise with the same generous provisions as in their regular, full-price stores. They will even take returns. The stock is generally good-to-high quality and the overall design "look" of the merchandise is excellent. If you are buying several pieces or more, they will dicker on prices. **Checks, M/C, VISA**

BUSINESS FURNITURE LIQUIDATORS
Bellevue: 13407 NE 20th (643-9988)
Hours: M-F 9-5; Sat. 10-2

What a find for the Eastside! Our own business furniture liquidator! No need to go to Seattle to get great buys on office furniture of all sorts: chairs, desks, files, office partitions—you name it. The store carries a large, varied selection from the less expensive to top quality. The day we were there, many items were discounted up to 30%. The salespeople are extremely helpful and will do their best to get you what you need.
Checks, M/C, VISA

BUSINESS OFFICE FURNITURE, INC.
Everett: 7600 Evergreen Way (625-1604; 355-5616)
Hours: M-F 8:30-5

The showroom is plush, but don't hesitate to ask about their used office furniture which is stored in the back room. Although the supply is limited, there are some super buys there—if you doubt it, check against new prices up front! Another possibility for saving money is in the occasional new but "over-ordered" items. Their specialty is "project" ordering but they treat small buyers respectfully if you are a serious shopper. All sales final on used merchandise. **Checks, M/C, VISA**

JACK FOWLD'S STATIONERY CO.
Everett: 2719 Colby (252-1201)
Hours: M-F 9:30-5 (see below)

Used office furniture is warehoused and shown by appointment only. **Checks, Store charge**

THE MART (DISCOUNT OFFICE FURNITURE MART)
Seattle: 3825 1st S. (682-6811)
Hours: M-F 8:30-5:30; Sat. 10-4

Every time we priced something at The Mart, it was on sale. Maybe we were just lucky, but they do seem to run many special sales. They claim prices are low because they are an outlet for their own company (Cascade Commercial) and ship via their own trucks. Be sure to check the room of "used, damaged, discontinued" furniture where the stock changes often. Returns accepted on new merchandise only. **Checks, M/C, VISA**

OFFICE EMPORIUM
Seattle: 1715 E. Olive Way (328-1703)
Hours: M-F 9-5:30; Sat. 10-3

Office Emporium is somewhat different from our other office furniture listings. It offers top-quality, expensive pieces (desks, chairs, etc.) at a discount of 20-30% off. Do not expect to find chairs selling for $80-$100. The ones we priced were $219.95 (suggested list price $293.27). A desk was priced $796.80 (suggested list price $1,062.40). However, these are absolutely gorgeous pieces of furniture and of the very best quality.
Checks, M/C, VISA

OFFICE FURNITURE LIQUIDATORS
Tacoma: 1732 Pacific Ave. (383-4505)
Hours: M-F 8:30-5; Sat. 10-4

We predict you'll find some of the cheapest prices in the area here—and there's plenty to choose from. The sales floor contains low- and top-end merchandise, new and used, and there are 4 floors of stock warehoused above you. If you don't see what you need, *ask*. Their merchandise turns over constantly and runs the gamut from generic items (a desk, a file, a chair) to designer lines. Average price savings on new pieces runs 40%; used, 60% and greater. They are an outlet for a noted Seattle/Tacoma quality office furniture dealer, so they receive the liquidations, consignments, overstocks, samples, freebies, etc. which fall out from the parent company's business. Expect friendly service. To give you an example, when we asked about a return policy, the reply was a cheery, "We're easy!" **Checks, M/C, VISA**

OFFICE WORLD DISCOUNT OFFICE FURNITURE
Seattle: 133 Westlake N. (682-3000)
Hours: M-F 8:30-5:30; Sat. 10-4

A large selection of desks, chairs, files, architectural drawing boards, etc. are offered for good prices. It's worth doing some comparison shopping here. Take into consideration that all merchandise is priced "cash and carry." You can exchange on most items, but not on sale items. **Checks, M/C, VISA**

R AND S SALES
Seattle: 1221 E. Pike (323-5966)
Hours: M-F 8-5; Sat. 9-1

R and S carries new and used office furniture. They can also save you money on new, top-quality furniture for your home. This stock is not carried in the store but is obtained via the Design Center. Mr. Sample, the owner, is very knowledgeable in the office furniture field and makes every attempt to offer a good price. An upstairs room is well stocked with merchandise. Save cash by picking up your selections. **Checks**

SEATTLE OFFICE FURNITURE MART
Seattle: 3035 1st (624-5710)
THE WAREHOUSE 222
Seattle: 222 Westlake N. (623-9222)
Hours: *Main store* **M-F 9-5;** *Warehouse* **M-F 9-5; Sat. 10-2**

Seattle Office Furniture sells new furniture on the main level. Catalog prices are discounted around 30%. Used furniture—primarily desks, files and other office hardware—resides in the basement. Factory seconds and freight-damaged files are usually available at good prices.

Warehouse 222 stocks essentially the same sort of merchandise. **Checks, M/C, VISA**

WINTERS OFFICE FURNITURE
Seattle: 6169 4th S. (763-2677)
Hours: M-F 9-5; Sat. 11-4

The used and damaged stock in the warehouse varies, but we've noted some good buys here. Before buying new or used office furniture, shop around and make your own cost vs. quality comparisons. Returns accepted. **Checks, M/C, VISA**

THE WOLFSTONE CO.
Seattle: 3230 1st S. (622-7000)
Hours: M-F 8:30-5

Crank up your imagination as you browse through aisles of used store fixtures. You'll find display racks of all descriptions, chairs, desks, counters, old glass shelves, etc. We saw kindergarten chairs ($5) and a piece that could become a great bar. A word of advice: For standard items such as bookshelves, price them elsewhere first to enable you to make comparisons. Esoteric items (circular clothes racks) are not as easy to price elsewhere!
Checks on approval

AUTOMOTIVE

TIRES

We called around in an attempt to locate a large group of tire dealers where you could be assured of savings. Often the best prices are at distributors who occasionally sell to drop-in retail customers, but normally they don't want publicity. We suggest that you check the Yellow Pages under "Tire Distributors and Manufacturers" and make a few calls in your area to your preferred brand's distributor. Be sure to ask whether you will need mounting and balancing done elsewhere, as these should be added to your costs. In addition, you might call the following dealers. Given the expense involved, it's well worth the research time.

CAPITOL TIRE SALES WAREHOUSES, INC.
Seattle: 422 S. Forest (624-8970)
Bellevue: 13216 NE Bellevue-Redmond Rd. (453-0422)

1ST TIRE AND WHEEL CENTERS
Bellevue: 10419 NE 4th (454-9552)
Hours: M-F 8-6; Sat. 8-5

Although they are only one among many tire dealers who sell used tires, 1st Tire is one of the few who advertise the fact. Used tires run $10-$20 and are usually available in the most common sizes. **Checks, M/C, VISA**

NELSON'S CAR CARE CENTERS
Bothell: 17210 Bothell Way NE (486-0738)
Kirkland: Totem Lake Shopping Center (821-9009)
Lynnwood: 4028 196th SW (774-3533)

Nelson's sells (among other name brands) an unadvertised Japanese tire called Sumitomo. They're supposed to be comparable to Michelin radial steel-belted tires and nearly 30% cheaper. They carry better road hazard and mileage warranties. Apparently Sumitomo, from one of Japan's largest and oldest corporations, doesn't believe in passing the high cost of advertising on to their customers. Nelson's will rotate and rebalance your tires *free* every 5,000 miles or before a major trip.

Checks, M/C, VISA

TBA WHOLESALERS, INC.
Kent: 730 S. Central (852-4032)

T & T TIRE CENTER
Tacoma: 3711 S. Tacoma Way (475-6777)

VERN'S TIRE SERVICE
Seattle: By appointment only (525-8231)

Vern has a van from which he sells new and used tires to car dealers. If you call and tell him what you want, he will get a price for you. If the price is right (and note he has minimal overhead costs), he will mount and balance your tires from his van at his home (unless you have several jobs lined up for him on location). **Cash preferred**

WORLD TIRE WAREHOUSE
Tacoma: 224 Puyallup Ave. (572-6333)

AUTO BATTERIES

BUDGET BATTERIES
For locations nearest you, call 763-1225
Hours: M-F 9-6; Sat. 9-5 (all stores)

These specialty garages are outlets for the parent wholesaler. They retail and install batteries, alternators, solenoids and starters. Guaranteed "factory seconds" batteries are half the cost of new, although demand often exceeds supply. If seconds aren't in stock, be sure to compare their new prices before you buy elsewhere. **Checks**

TACOMA BATTERY SUPPLY
Tacoma: 4548 S. Washington (474-3502)
Hours: Call first, especially in summer

During the winter months you can usually buy used (repaired if necessary) batteries for $15 or pick up a working factory second for $20. Only the older batteries can be repaired; new ones, with plastic components, either work or must be junked altogether. **Checks**

MISCELLANEOUS

RENT-A-BAY
Seattle: 115 S. 108th (241-6507)
Hours: M-Sat. 9-6

Is your car in need of a paint job? Here is a rental spray booth you can use for $25 a day. They have spray guns available for $5. You bring your own paint, tape and labor, and for $30 you could give your car a face lift. **Cash only**

TOOLS & BUILDING EQUIPMENT

NEW TOOLS

Companies listed here are not necessarily alternatives to your local hardware store. They sell mainly to contractors, carpenters and other tradespeople. Homeowners involved in major do-it-yourself projects or repairs might upgrade their tool purchases to industrial quality. Our advice —determine first if you really need long-lasting, high-quality tools or if you can live with a lower-price consumer model. Compare prices for light-weight industrial tools if you prefer higher quality.

AMERICAN TOOL & SUPPLY CO.
Edmonds: 22912 Hwy. 99 (775-7361)
Hours: M-F 7-5; Sat. 9-2

If you're setting up a home workshop or adding to an existing one, take the advice offered on American Tool's products and manufacturers list: "Call for a Quote." This industrial and construction supply company carries an immense inventory from abrasives to wheelbarrows. What they don't stock, they can usually order. You'll recognize names like Makita and Milwaukee and Bosch, as well as dozens of others. The salespeople at American are helpful and well-versed in their trade. Company policy allows refunds with receipts. **Checks, M/C, VISA**

ARONSON INDUSTRIAL SUPPLY
Seattle: 5300 Denver S. (762-0700)
Hours: M-F 8-5

Tools here run to the hefty range, as you will note on the showroom floor. If you operate a machine shop in your garage, you will find lightweight industrial tools and saw blades in their catalog. Note the marked showroom specials if you're bargain hunting. Returns accepted on unused tools. **Checks, M/C, VISA**

Tools & Building Equipment

CAMPBELL INDUSTRIAL SUPPLY CO.
Seattle: 1705 4th S. (447-7165)
Tacoma: 2316 Jefferson S. (383-2431)
Hours: M-F 8-5 (both stores)

Campbell carries a large stock of tools and parts intended for the industrial trades. This is not the place to buy an occasional nut and bolt or a cheap drill. Campbell's showroom is pleasant; the salespeople are friendly and helpful. They do run specials, which provide excellent bargains. Call before going in if you are looking for a single, specific item. Returns on unused tools with receipt. Although the Tacoma store is not as large as the Seattle one, they can order anything you need from Seattle. **Checks, M/C, VISA**

CENTER TOOL CO.
Tacoma: S. 30th & S. M (383-4416)
Hours: M-F 8-5

New contractor-quality tools represent good buys for serious do-it-yourselfers when you factor in replacement and repair costs of the less-durable models. Center sells the well-known Makita and Milwaukee lines. Check out the on-the-floor specials. Once in a while they also have used tools on hand (i.e., on consignment from a shop that is closing its doors). Ask if you are interested. We buy an excellent hand-cleaning soap with pumice for $3.98 for 32 oz., and it removes just about anything including glue, pitch and bubble gum. Work gloves and other hardware items are well priced. **Checks, M/C, VISA**

COAST LIQUIDATORS
Seattle: 8926 Roosevelt Way NE (523-7466)
Hours: M-F 8:30-5:30; Sat. 9-2

The owners guarantee that nothing is sold at full price at Coast Liquidators. This store is part of a West Coast chain that buys in sufficient volume to enable them to offer low prices on tools. They carry a full line of Makita electric power tools; other names are also represented. Coast sells hand tools (wrenches, sockets, vise-grips, clamps, etc.) and the toolboxes in which to store them. Check out their prices on tapes of all types during your visit. They will quote prices over the phone and honor all company warranties. Returns are welcome on unused items. **Checks, M/C, VISA**

GREENSHIELD'S INDUSTRIAL SUPPLY
Everett: 710 Hwy. 99 N. (259-0111)
Hours: M-F 8-5; Sat. 8-12

Generally Greenshield's sells industrial lines, but some light-duty tools are also stocked. Automotive lines are not kept on the

shelves but can be ordered. Stop by for catalogs and price lists if you're price-comparing before buying new tools. The more you buy or the more expensive the item, the better the savings (i.e., a $10 or better order nets a 10% discount; 30% off on Proto tools for a minimum amount, etc.). Returns with receipts are accepted.
Checks, M/C, VISA

MURRAY PACIFIC INDUSTRIAL SUPPLY—See Index

SEAPORT INDUSTRIAL SUPPLY CO.
Seattle: 920 NW Leary Way (784-9030)
Hours: M-F 8-5

Seaport's catalog of industrial supplies, tools, abrasives and gauges covers 700 pages. Before you take one home, look through it and check prices in your area of interest. The last section includes smaller-scale power saws, drills, bench vises, hand files and small hand tools. From our check on several items, prices appeared good. Returns are accepted on unused items with a receipt and within a reasonable period. There is a minimum purchase of $10. **Checks**

STERLING PACIFIC TOOL CO.
Seattle: 4202 6th S. (623-6891)
Hours: M-F 7:30-5

Sterling carries several lines of tools. They use manufacturers' catalogs but send out their own monthly special flyers. Their closeout section constantly changes, while specials out in the showroom appear to be good buys. Returns and exchanges on unused tools within a reasonable time period. **Checks**

TOOL TOWN
Seattle: 11522 Lake City Way (367-5151); 23639 Pacific Hwy S. (878-1148)
Lynnwood: 19809 Hwy. 99 (774-3214)
Everett: 4824 Evergreen Way (259-2590)
Puyallup: 620 Meridian N. (845-7748)
Hours: M-F 10-6:30; Sat. 10-4

Tool Town's buying philosophy is to get the best goods at the best price. We talked to several customers who are in the trades and learned that they definitely respect the prices at Tool Town. However, they cautioned us that much of the stock is imported from the Orient, hence it's hard to pin down quality: could be high, can be low. Tool Town's intent is to get their merchandise at a good price so they can pass on the savings. You should check out tolerance capabilities to be sure the larger equipment can per-

form to your specs. You should compare prices elsewhere, but put this one on your list when you're shopping for your workshop. Returns vary with the tool, from 90 days to a lifetime.
Checks, M/C, VISA

YOUR TOOL HOUSE, INC.
Renton: 155 Rainier S. (255-1216)
Hours: M-Sat. 8:30-5:30

This wholesale/retail distributor of light industrial tools stocks everything the home mechanic and machinist could use. They specialize in items used at Boeing. They also try to offer price cuts on most lines by eliminating the middleperson. Boeing employees have a special credit plan. Exchanges only.
Checks, M/C, VISA

REBUILT & USED TOOLS

BLACK AND DECKER MANUFACTURING CO.
Seattle: 701 3rd N. (282-6432)
Tacoma: 2602 S. 38th (473-6040)
Hours: M-F 8-5:30; Sat. 10-3 (both stores)

Black and Decker fans can purchase rebuilt tools here for 20-25% off new list prices. All rebuilts carry the same guarantee as new tools. Or buy replacement parts for Black and Decker tools and service them yourself. No new tools sold here. Returns on reconditioned tools allowed. **Checks, M/C, VISA (over $5)**

HARDWICK'S SWAP SHOP
Seattle: 4214 Roosevelt Way NE (632-1203)
Hours: T-Sat. 9-6

We took a husband along to scout out this one. His assessment? A great place to look for hand tools! The shop stocks a tremendous selection and variety of tools for the handyperson, both new and used. Not many places carry an assortment like this, and the prices are good (below normal retail) on both name-brands and off-brands. If you're going to buy something used, be sure to check what you're getting. Located with the tools are all the other "fixins" you might need: nuts, bolts, hinges, sinks, etc. Beside tools, Hardwick's carries a conglomeration of glassware, cookware, furniture, etc. Some merchandise is new, some used. Use your comparative buying instincts! They buy or trade on used items. **Checks, M/C, VISA**

PORTER-CABLE
Renton: 268 SW 43rd (251-6680)
Hours: M-F 8-5

Planning to start a home project or some carpentry work? If so, this spot sells reconditioned tools (contractors' models, as well as some you might find in local hardware stores). Rockwell's portable line is now manufactured under the Porter-Cable name. These are very good reconditioned tools, selling at a savings and they carry a 90-day warranty. You'll also find extremely good prices on some new, overstocked items. Exchanges are allowed.

Checks, M/C, VISA

SKIL CORP.
Seattle: 2424 4th (622-4404)
Tacoma: 1610 Center (572-7107)
Hours: M-F 8-5 (both stores)

This is a repair shop for Skil tools where rebuilts can save you money. Savings over new tools can range from 10-40% during a clean-up sale. All rebuilt Skil tools carry the same guarantee as new ones. The quantity and variety of tools fluctuates. When available, you can also rent industrial power tools.

Checks, M/C, VISA

TOOL & EQUIPMENT DISTRIBUTORS
Lynnwood: 18800 Hwy. 99, Bldg. A (771-7288)
Hours: M-F 8-5

Great buys on used and rebuilt tools can be found here. All tools are guaranteed for 90 days. This shop's main business is the repair of all types of tools, hence the reason for such a variety. A compressor business shares the space, so ask, if you are looking for a used compressor. Both shops sometimes can work out a trade deal with you.

Checks, M/C, VISA

TOOL PROS
Seattle: 5521 University Way NE (525-6448)
Hours: M-F 8-5

A small store selling some used, reconstructed power tools (drills, etc.). You'll find a limited supply and stock. Call first to see what's available. The reconditioned tools carry a 90-day guarantee, except for the very inexpensive ones. All sales final. **Checks**

BUILDING SUPPLIES

DOORS & WINDOWS

CHINOOK DOOR
Tacoma: 1515 S. Tacoma Way (472-9614)
Hours: M-F 8-5

Buy a prehung door direct from the factory floor and save middleman costs. *Note*: Their scrap wood is the best kindling buy in town! **Checks**

CUSTOM BIFOLDS
Tacoma: 3210 Ward Rd. E. (922-6986)
Hours: M-Sat. 8-8; Sun. 8:30-5

While pricing louvered doors, we discovered this little shop. For our standard-measure set, we saved compared to the Sears catalog and a local builder's outlet prices. If you can use a common width (12″, 15″, 18″), a second-grade set reduces costs further. Custom Bifolds also makes shutters, cafe doors, accordion-folding doors and house doors. An extra bonus for customers—take home free a variety of wood leftovers to keep small carpenters happy for weeks. **Checks**
(1/3 down, balance on pick up)

TIMBER WINDOWS
Everett: South complex of Paine Field, Bldg. #121 (745-9665)
Hours: M-F 8-4:30 (some Sat.)

You can save 60% on glass *if* you can use the misordered or "customer changed their minds" stock they have on hand. You may find a few woodframed windows as well. All glass carries a guarantee. Since the stock is limited, you may want to call ahead if you are not in the area. **Checks**

WEATHER MASTER OF WASHINGTON, INC.
Everett: 1200 Norton (745-1839; Seattle 621-9329,
or 1-800-562-0322)
Hours: M-F 8-4:30

There are several ways to save money on home construction projects at Weather Master's Everett location. (1) Raw glass (3/16-in. which is either left over from other cuts or possibly scratched is $2.50/sq. ft. (2) "Salvage" glass door panels which carry a 10-year seal guarantee are $30 apiece. There are stock sizes, but there's no guarantee they'll have something on hand when you need it. It's wise to call first. **Checks**

WILL-WOOD PREFIT, INC.
Tacoma: 2319 S. Tacoma Way (473-6673)
Hours: M-F 8-5

You will save by going directly to this bona fide door factory. You can select A-grade or B-grade doors. They will also machine your old door to an exact fit if you have such a need. "Rejected" doors are available (with holes or flaws) at great savings. They have prefinished and unfinished doors, lock sets and millwork. There's no fancy showroom—in fact, no showroom at all.
Checks

ELECTRICAL SUPPLIES

BELLCO ELECTRIC & SUPPLY, INC.
Federal Way: 1720 341st Pl. (952-3131)
Hours: M-F 8-5; Sat. 9-1

Do-it-yourself electricians can save on contractors' electrical tools, equipment and supplies at Bellco. They stock wire, conduit, panel gear, electric heat supplies, etc. and sell all merchandise to all buyers at one price. **Checks, M/C, VISA**

R. L. COOK SALES AND SUPPLY
Seattle: 222 S. Holden (763-8777)
Hours: M-F 8-5

188 Building Supplies

Here is a place to find a complete line of new and used industrial electrical supplies. Many of these items would be appropriate for a home builder or remodeler. You'll find such things as circuit breakers,lighting equipment and electrical wire. Items could be used or surplus new that sell for less. **Checks**

LUMBER, HARDWARE & OTHER MATERIALS

GREEN RIVER SAWMILL, INC.
Maple Valley: 28620 Maple Valley-Black Diamond Rd. SE (432-4446)
Hours: M-F 9-4:30; Sat. 10-3

You may be able to save on building costs by buying cedar, hemlock and fir lumber and fencing direct from this sawmill. They will quote prices over the phone. If you drive out, take a truck and bring home a load of firewood. Short lumber ends cost $20 a truckload. Five- to 10-ft. slab wood edging is $10 per truckload. **Checks**

INTERPACE
Seattle, Kirkland, Kent, Everett: For info call 282-5100

MUTUAL MATERIALS CO.
Bellevue, Auburn, Everett, Kenmore, Tacoma: For info call 455-2869

These 2 companies manufacture their own brick and clay products and sell directly from their many retail outlets. They also sell to other retailers. You can save some middleman costs by shopping for masonry materials here. Both companies stock all the tools and equipment necessary for the do-it-yourselfer to complete the project.

McLENDON HARDWARE, INC.
Renton: 710 S. 2nd (235-3555)
Sumner: 1111 Fryar Ave. (863-2264)
Hours: M-Sat. 8-6; Sun. 10-5

After many price checks, we strongly recommend McLendon's to the do-it-yourselfer. We base our recommendation on several things: (1) The stores carry a vast variety and selection and therefore will probably have what you need: building supplies, electrical fixtures and supplies, garden items, hardware, housewares, fireplace accessories, paint, lighting fixtures, plumbing supplies, tile and floor coverings, hand and electric tools. (2) In most price checks, McLendon's was lower than or close to other sources. (3) Helpful clerks roam the aisles and offer advice in a friendly manner. Checking out is quick. (4) When you pay cash, you automatically receive a 10% discount except for special sale items marked "net."   **Checks, M/C, VISA**

REBOUND—BUILDING MATERIALS SALVAGE
Seattle: 1517 12th (324-0802)
Hours: Th-Sat. 10-5

Why waste money? Try Rebound! Rebound is a new concept in the recycling of building materials. It receives donations (tax deductible) of leftover paint, lumber, windows, doors, toilet fixtures, etc. from construction jobs as well as damaged but usable materials that contractors return to distributors. Rebound sells damaged goods at 30-50% of retail cost and used materials for even less. The outlet is a great alternative for homeowners to beat the high cost of new materials. Rebound is a project of CAMP (Central Area Motivation Project). Profits are used to cover the cost of running the operation (rent) and providing funds for a tool-lending library, home-improvement classes and other activities of the Inner City Self-Help Program. Before you start your building projects, check out Rebound. We feel you'll be extremely pleased with their inventory and prices. For those of you who are contractors/remodelers, they can use your tax deductible donation!   **Checks**

SURPLUS, SALVAGE & LIQUIDATIONS

A.A.A. LIQUIDATING AND AUCTION
Des Moines: 22340 Marine View Dr. (824-3686)
Normandy Park: 19945 1st S. (824-3033)
Hours: T-Sat. 9-6 (both stores)

It's rather hard to list everything A.A.A. stocks, as the goods they acquire change continually. Sharp shoppers check out the store often to see what bargains are available from week to week. General merchandise of all sorts is sold: tools, bikes, yard items, hardware, housewares, sporting goods, stereos, small appliances. These are closeouts and overstocks as well as unclaimed freight. Most sell at bargain-saving prices, others do not! Watch your prices and check the quality of the merchandise closely and carefully. If you think something is overpriced, ask the manager about it. Exchanges or refunds. **Checks, M/C, VISA**

ABC SALES
Seattle: 2202 1st S. (623-5766)
Hours: M-F 10:30-4:30

The selection is limited, but the prices are great. ABC "wholesales" liquidated and salvaged goods to other dealers who sell it to you in "retail" outlets for this type of merchandise. ABC has a few items available in the office area by the piece or by the case, usually for at least 50% off. Nonperishable food items and a little clothing are most common, but you could discover just about anything. **Checks**

APE
Phone: 242-4059

If you are into a remodeling project that could benefit from materials salvaged from demolition jobs, you might call this company to see what they have on hand, or what they anticipate acquiring in the near future. They also deal with surplus (new and used) electrical and electronic equipment, such as starters, electric motors, air compressors, aircraft parts, tools and even computers.

ART'S
Seattle: 1115 S. Elizabeth (no phone)
Hours: M-Sat. 9:30-6:30

This place can't be described. They are salvage/liquidators, and the items crammed into this store in helter-skelter order defy enumeration. The phone isn't listed because they are too busy to answer questions about their current stock. Groceries and non-edibles sit side by side. You get the impression merchandise was opened and shelved wherever a free space could be found. We spotted many excellent bargains in many categories (hardware, paints, clothing, a few toys, fabrics, a few pieces of furniture), but be prepared for some dusty browsing. Nothing is overpriced, but quality varies. Regulars at Art's stock up on 50-lb. packages of flour, sugar and dog food. Nearly everything except food is sold 50% off retail. Our food purchases checked out as excellent savings over a discount market, but avoid items which do not represent above-average savings. No returns except for spoiled grocery items. Art's is near the northwest corner of Boeing Field. **Checks**

ATLAS BUILDING WRECKERS
Seattle: 10900 27th S. (246-6336)
Hours: M-Sat. 8-5

Atlas occupies 17 acres on a dead-end road behind Boeing Field. You will find used timbers, lumber and bricks at salvage prices, but the stock on hand varies widely. Call first if you need something in particular. **Checks**

BOEING SURPLUS
Kent: 20651 84th S. (773-9084)
Hours: T-F 11-6; Sat. 9-4

Over 35,000 items surplused by The Boeing Company are available at varied prices. The pricing system is based upon original cost, depreciation and other factors. Because the stock varies tremendously, the following only suggests the range of items: electric typewriters, adding machines and office furniture; nuts, bolts, drill bits and hand tools; aluminum, sheet-metal, plastics and rubber; electronic test equipment and parts; automobiles; laboratory test equipment, etc. Visit it yourself for a better understanding of the stock. Allow plenty of time for browsing. There is a variety of surplus wood products—boxes, skids, salvage lumber and plywood in the outside sales yard. The variety and quantity is somewhat overwhelming. Don't miss this section. If it's primarily lumber you are after, be sure to go early because the lumber sells fast. If you are into saving money on a building project or have a creative youngster, this is the place to start. No returns.

Surplus, Salvage & Liquidations

Don't forget, Boeing employees and Boeing retirees get a 20% discount if ID is shown before sale is rung up.

Directions: North of Kent on E. Valley Hwy. at 84th Ave. S. and S. 208th St. **Checks**

CAPTAIN SAM'S LOFT
Seattle: 2702 1st S. (624-1478)
Hours: M-Sat. 10-6

This company salvages and sells vintage doors, windows, sinks, columns, mantles, spindles, railings, iron works, bathtubs and more. If something isn't marked, you're free to dicker on the price. In fact you're free to dicker even if is IS marked. The owners want this to be a place in which to enjoy yourself as well as a spot where you can cut costs. They'll search with you if you're looking for an item you can incorporate into your building or remodeling plans. If it isn't on the premises, they'll try to get it for you. Captain Sam's boasts a complete line of reproductions—hardware, plumbing and lighting fixtures, all discounted. You may take most items home on approval—ask about this policy.
Checks, M/C, VISA

FLOYD TYSON'S MERCHANDISE
Auburn: 743 Auburn Way N. (839-6282)
Hours: M-F 10-6; Sat. 10-5

This is where you can purchase kitchen cabinets, Formica, carpeting, hardwood flooring, furniture, hardware, wallpaper, window coverings and anything else that the owner can obtain at a good price. Nearly everything is new and acquired via closeouts and other special deals. There is no used merchandise, and only a small percentage of the stock is freight-damaged goods. Give the owner a call to see if he has or can get what you want at a good price.
Checks, M/C, VISA

HILLSTEAD'S SURPLUS
Seattle: 14121 Pacific Hwy. S. (241-0303)
Tacoma: 6234 S. Tacoma Way (474-7945)
Hours: M-Sun. 10-6

We found some fantastic bargains at this spot. It stocks a little of everything: tennis shoes, paper products, hardware, some clothes, toys, housewares, tools, variety, pet supplies—and all selling for 50% off the original ticket price. We picked up a pair of canvas tennis shoes for $3.50. Merchandise turns over rapidly, and there are always things arriving. You'll usually find top-quality toilet tissue and paper towels selling at "loss leader" prices. Another pleasant surprise is the neatness and cleanliness of this liquidator as compared to many others. **Checks, M/C, VISA**

JAMES M. GLASS CONSTRUCTION CO.
Seattle: 316½ 2nd S. (622-7133)
Hours: M-Sun. 9-5

The company crest reads, "In Salvage We Trust." Evidence of this is found in the basement. Glass Construction salvages big jobs, entire buildings and often historic ones. Hence the enormous supply of windows (both stained glass and leaded) and solid brass hardware. A multitude of other items can be found, such as bathtubs, light fixtures, marble, etc. The phrase they use is "nostalgic building materials," although recessed lighting fixtures and other modern pieces are also on display. **Checks**

JB'S DISCOUNT CITY
Burien: Payless Mall (244-8888)
Hours: M-F 9:30-7:30; Sat. 9:30-6; Sun. 11-5

A small spot selling liquidated and freight-damaged items: cosmetics, candy, some housewares, a few tools. The store also has a good stock of used books which they buy, sell and trade.
Checks

KNOX NORTH HOMES SERVICES
Phone: 362-6906

If you are into a remodeling project that could benefit from materials salvaged from demolition jobs, you might call this company to see what they have on hand or what they anticipate acquiring in the near future.

THE LIQUIDATOR
Bellevue: 12005 NE 12th, Suite 10 (454-5888)
Hours: Th-Sat. 10-5:30

You'll find a conglomeration of things here and an ever-changing inventory. Tools, from hammers to drill presses, are a big seller. Camping and hiking gear (backpacks, stoves, sleeping bags, dehydrated foods), jewelry, TV's, stereos and gift items sell for 30-50% off regular retail. Wholesale jobbers welcome. There are no seconds or damaged merchandise. Returns? Willingly with receipt. The store stands behind both quality and price.
Checks, M/C, VISA

MERCHANTS PLUS
Lynnwood: 5421 196th SW (775-6792)
Hours: M-Th 10-5; F 10-9; Sat. 10-5

While you're checking out the Goodwill Store next door, stop in at Merchant's Plus for liquidated merchandise specials. The stock is primarily housewares and related goods. Also some tools and toys and trinkets. Prices can be very good or so-so depending

on the item and your local discount store specials. Liquidators always challenge our ability to recall prices elsewhere, but if you're good at it, you'll find bargains every time. They take full returns with a receipt.
Checks, M/C, VISA

MOLIN AND OFFER
Seattle: 1770 4th S. (682-6740)
Hours: M-Sat. 9-6

A large sign outside tells you that this building contains "Merchandise Damaged in Shipping." It also contains market samples, factory-defective items and overstocks. Outside the grocery section (see Food listing), you may encounter furniture for the home and office, toys, clothing, china odds and ends, cosmetics, luggage, marble sinks (with cracks), refrigerators and other appliances, cleaning items and who knows what else. It's not a glamorous place to shop, but the bargain hunter with a sharp eye can find excellent buys. Be familiar with quality and price or check out big-ticket items against "uptown" prices. A fair return policy; ask first if you are contemplating a home trial period.
Checks, M/C, VISA

MURRAY PACIFIC INDUSTRIAL SUPPLY
Seattle: 2960 4th S. (767-8240)
Hours: M-F 8-5; Sat. 9-3

Brisk business here thanks to their abundance of salvage. Much of the stock is industrial (salvaged pipe, fittings, wiring, scrap metal, plastics, scrap and mechanical oddments). We noted ropes of all kinds, small anchors, large sheets of Plexiglas, rubber hose, marine supplies, pipe, wire, nuts and bolts, etc. They will cut metal to size. New stock includes hand tools, machine tools, battery chargers, electrical cord, trouble lights, welding supplies, tool boxes, Styrofoam and lubricants.
Checks, M/C, VISA

NORTH END STEEL OUTLET
Seattle: 105th Aurora N. (no phone)
Hours: M-Sat. 9-5

This open-air salvage yard stocks steel and aluminum pipe and steel sheets in many sizes. Other items pop up like 4 ×4 cedar posts.
Checks

NORTHWEST TRADER
Kent: 1315 W. Meeker (Meeker Mall) (852-3200)
Seattle: 20226 Ballinger Way NE (362-6886)
Hours: *Kent* **M-F 10-8; Sat. 10-6;** *Seattle* **M-F 11:30-7; Sat. 10-6**

Surplus, Salvage & Liquidation 195

These are good bargain-browser stores. Northwest Trader buys liquidations or whatever else he can get at a good price. You will find many items at 50% off, some at "good" sale prices. They carry a regular stock of stereos and tools which they buy in quantity to keep the prices down. The merchandise includes paintings, dry goods, drugstore sundries, camping gear and anything else in the general household line they can get (like tennis shoes and sunglasses). The Kent store carries a larger and more varied stock. Exchanges only. Refunds on defective merchandise within 90 days only. **Checks, M/C, VISA**

THE OLD HOBBY SHOP
Lynnwood: 17707 Hwy. 99 (743-1003)
Hours: T-Sat. 9:30-5:30

A junk store junkie's delight! Also a heck of a place to buy windows. That's incongruous, but they are *the* major outlet for local window dealers who need to dispose of unclaimed or mismeasured stock. The price of an item depends on what they paid for it, and except for the windows, much of it is "distressed merchandise" like their sign says. **Checks**

PACIFIC IRON & METAL'S BROWSVILLE
Seattle: 2230 4th S. (628-6256)
Hours: M-F 8-5:30; Sat. 9-5:30; Sun. 10-3

As the name indicates, if you have time, you will find all sorts of odds and ends here. This is Pacific Iron's outlet for salvage, overstocks, freight-damaged, etc. Pacific Iron still buys and sells scrap, but the Browsville sales slip lists building materials, fiberglass, doors, windows, tools, metals, hardware and many items for general home use. We found some great specials, but as in any store of this type, it pays to know quality and prices before you shop. **Checks, M/C, VISA**

THE SALVAGE BROKER
Lynnwood: 19801-E. Lynnwood Shopping Center (771-3233)
Hours: M-Sat. 10-5

If you know your prices, you'll quickly find the best bargains here. As with many salvage outlets and liquidators, the discount runs 30-50% off retail, *but* you need to know if the suggested retail price is realistic. Watch quality closely. The great buys lie alongside the so-so ones, so take time to browse through bric-a-brac, furniture, greeting cards, games, toys, clothing (some queen size), sporting goods, shoes, etc. etc. etc. When the mood takes him, the owner announces a 50%-off sale, and everything in the store is "One-half regular retail." The return policy varies with the merchandise. Check first. **Checks, M/C, VISA**

Surplus, Salvage & Liquidations

S & H SALVAGE
Seattle: 10426 16th SW (241-5518)
Hours: M-F 10-6; Sat. 12-4

This is a humdinger of a spot for shoppers who can pick out a great buy no matter where they run across it. The surroundings are strictly salvage warehouse, but a careful gleaning can uncover some top brands at terrific prices. Some merchandise has been damaged or soiled. We've been fortunate in finding that most soilage can be easily removed. S & H is in the insurance salvage business, so they are likely to end up with just about anything from ice cream to a 5-piece set of Lane furniture. We found jewelry, rainwear, cosmetics, clothes of all sorts and sizes, ski equipment, carpeting, groceries, books, etc. Keep an eye out for ads which they run when they have an especially large offering of an item (such as a famous-maker ladies' sportswear gathering which included Pendleton, Jantzen and Ship 'N Shore). They do not normally take returns. **Checks**

SEATTLE BUILDING SALVAGE, INC.
Seattle: 704 N. 34th
Hours: M-F 10:30-6; Sat. 11-5

If you are restoring a vintage house, this is a good spot to check for doors, sinks, light fixtures, toilets, faucets, etc. If you want to remodel and get the highest quality for your dollar, you might check this outlet also. It is the philosophy of the owner that "using salvage for remodeling a place doesn't cost you any less, but you end up with a lot better quality for the same price." The same door you buy from him for $25 may retail at several hundred dollars for the same quality and workmanship. We like the fact that the measurements are given on a tag on the side of every door. There are no refunds, but exchanges may be made on all items except "as is" sales. **Checks**

SESSIONS SURPLUS
Seattle: 9125 10th S. (762-5454)
Renton: 2826 Sunset Lane NE (271-5555); 809 S. 4th (271-5255)
Hours: M-F 10-5; Sat. 10-3 (all stores)

These 3 stores, which carry damaged-in-transit merchandise, are a pleasure to shop. Merchandise is clean and neatly displayed. The Seattle store is a warehouse and contains the larger items such as mattresses, wood paneling and appliances. However, you can find just about anything at each location with 30-50% reductions. We saw toys, furniture, groceries, housewares, greeting cards, cosmetics, dog food and laundry soap to start the list. Returns sometimes; check before buying. **Checks**

Surplus, Salvage & Liquidation

SHERMAN SUPPLY
Seattle: 2456 1st S. (624-0061)
Hours: M-Sat. 8-5

This is not a "browse until you uncover a neat item" style salvage yard. You will find mainly industrial plumbing but also home plumbing salvage and an assortment of other building salvage stock. Be willing to search for yourself. Regular customers do very well here, judging from the purchases made during our visit. **Checks, M/C, VISA**

SOUTH ACRES BUILDING DEMOLITION
Puyallup: 4103 Meridian N. (927-0405)
Hours: Call first; by appointment only

You may luck out and find they have what you need as the result of a recent demolition job: used brick, lumber, windows and doors are all possibilities. Evenings are the best time to call. **Checks**

TACOMA SCREW PRODUCTS ANNEX
Tacoma: 2001 Center (572-3444)
Hours: M-F 8-5; Sat. 9-1

Here's an experiment that started in November of 1982 and quickly took hold. The Annex contains general surplus goods from Los Angeles importers plus occasional closeouts from the parent company next door. Tools, work gloves, various hardware items and great specials abound. We bought a hammock and some sterile-packed first aid equipment. Returns are accepted with the receipt. **Checks, M/C, VISA**

TYSON'S GENERAL STORE
Auburn: 743 Auburn Way N. (839-6282)
Hours: M-F 10-6; Sat. 10-5

Tyson's sells furniture, building materials, groceries and general household merchandise of all types. Nearly everything is new and acquired via closeouts and other special deals. Less than 20% of the stock is freight damaged, but be sure to check everything carefully. There is no used merchandise. Give the owner a call to see if he has or can get what you want at a good price. Refunds and exchanges on most items, but check with the manager first. **Checks, M/C, VISA**

W & S SALES
Kent: 1315 W. Meeker (852-3200)
Hours: M-F 10-8; Sat. 10-6

Surplus, Salvage & Liquidations

This liquidator's shop advertises that they "buy and sell new merchandise—anything and everything." That's a good description of the stock which includes stereos, gift items, tools, sporting goods, toys, etc. As always with stock of this nature, there are super buys and so-so buys depending on many variables, so it is always worth your while to rummage through the aisles in search of the best bargains. Exchanges, no refunds.

Checks, M/C, VISA

WASHINGTON LIQUIDATORS
Seattle: 5828 Airport Way S. (762-4284)
Hours: M-Sat. 9-5:30

Hardware, small parts, pipe, wire, electrical parts, CB supplies and equipment, plumbing fixtures, nuts, bolts, metal shapes— and whatever. Washington Liquidators contains big and little parts of almost anything you could imagine—a crated roller coaster seat, for example—things you must see to believe. It's wise to check out your selection carefully for damage or irregularity, but the prices are right. A veteran browser can consistently come up with a find he or she did not expect. We found bright boating flags for 50¢, Mickey Mouse school bags for 98¢ and a flower-sized brandy snifter for 25¢. Typewriters and office machines as well as unusual office filing materials, graph paper of odd rulings and adding machine tapes can be found. Price savings as much as 95% off! No returns unless you obtain an agreement before purchasing.

Checks

WESTERN NUT AND BOLT
Seattle: 4797 1st S. (762-4603)
Hours: M-F 10-5; Sat. 10-4

Electronic surplus and wire are among the best bargains here, although good buys can be found anywhere among the hardware and equipment of this large store. They have a large selection of radio, TV and CRT tubes.

Checks, M/C, VISA

WESTERN SALVAGE
Seattle: 6901 E. Marginal Way (763-2340)
Hours: M-F 8:30-6; Sat. 9-4

Government and industrial salvage constitutes 90-95% of the stock at Western Salvage. Much of this is too large for the average consumer's use, but our visit turned up a good buy on a file cabinet. Browsers will encounter hammers and nails, chain, bolts, pencils and tablets, tape, gun holsters and helmets, electrical wiring and fixtures, paint, etc. Obviously a scavenger's delight!

Checks

ODDMENTS

AMUSEMENT DEVICES

AMERICAN GAMES
Seattle: 3rd and Wall (682-4492)
Hours: M-F 9-5:30; Sat. 9-5

American Games sells reconditioned games and machines: pinball, jukeboxes, pool tables, foosball, bumper pool, video games, etc. Price examples are: pinball $200 and up; video games $500 and up. They offer a 30-day guarantee. **M/C, VISA**

APOLLO
525-3585 (shop: 363-3225)
Hours: call first

Apollo offers new and used jukeboxes and games. You can buy reconditioned used games as well as "as is" machines to tinker with at home if you are clever at that sort of thing. "As is" models start at $250 and reconditioned machines at $600.

AURORA COIN DISTRIBUTING, INC.
Snohomish: 20924 76th Dr. SE (481-1360; Seattle 823-5848)
Hours: Call first

All Aurora's games are reconditioned. They have video and pinball machines for $595 and offer a 30-day guarantee. They will deliver.

MUSIC VEND DISTRIBUTING CO.
Seattle: 1550 4th S. (682-5700)
Hours: M-F 8:45-5:30

If your game room isn't quite complete, how about a new or used pinball machine or foosball game? Reconditioned games start at $245. Used pinballs carry a 30-day warranty; complete reconditioned foosballs are sold "as is" at 40-60% savings.

Checks, M/C, VISA

PINBALL
Seattle: 7319 Greenwood N. (782-1167)
Hours: M-F 3-7; Sat., Sun. 12-10

Pinball sells full-size used pinball and video games for use at home. Modern pinballs average $350; those from the 1930's average $500. We learned that video games depreciate fast: from a new price tag of $3,000 to $600 or less in a year, and there isn't much that can go wrong with these harbingers of the computer age.

Checks, M/C, VISA

VIDEOSYNCRASY
Bellevue: 10680 NE 8th (362-0520)
Hours: M-Sun. 11-11

Videosyncrasy sells reconditioned video and pinball machines starting at $300 with a 90-day guarantee. They also rent machines delivered and picked up at the following rates for 24 hours: 1 machine/$125; 2 machines/$150; 3 machines/$200.

CONSIGNMENT—GENERAL MERCHANDISE
See also CLOTHING—Consignment

JOANNE'S TREASURE CHEST
Lynnwood: 7300 196th SW (771-4608)
Hours: M-F 9-4; Sat. 9-2

You can consign just about anything at Joanne's, including dried prunes from your aunt's farm. The clothing racks are not as well stocked as the shelves of "garage-sale" type treasures.

Cash only

MACHIAS RUMMAGE & THRIFT
Everett: 2931 Broadway (252-6209)
Hours: T-Sat. 10-5

Over 600 consignors "own" the goods in this crowded storefront treasure-box. The dedicated bargain browser will enjoy this garage-sale potpourri: in fact, the store had its humble beginning as a multi-family garage sale in Machias. All sales final. **Checks**

PACKRATS DELIGHT
Tacoma: 3111 6th (752-1445)
Hours: M-Sat. 10-6

We were extremely impressed with this unique consignment store, because it sells odds and ends of furniture, appliances, household items, kitchen gadgets, toys, baby equipment. It will not accept objects under $1 in value, clothes or junk. The other consignment shops we've ventured into have been primarily interested in clothing.

The store will help you price the things you wish to consign. The object will remain at full price for 2 weeks, then is reduced 10% each week thereafter. No charge if you reclaim it. Consignments are taken any time the store is open for business. Returns must be made within 3 days. **Checks, M/C, VISA**

QUEEN ANNE CONSIGNMENT SHOP
Seattle: 8 Boston St. (282-5996)
Hours: M-Sat. 10:30-5:30

This consignment store falls under the "general" category. Its shelves are filled with collectibles, glassware, household items, porcelain, some antiques. You'll also find one or 2 pieces of furniture. We discovered some fun gift ideas. Items left longer than 4 months and not picked up are donated to Children's Orthopedic Hospital. **Checks**

CRAFTS

TREASURE HOUSE IMPORTS, INC.
Seattle: 8135 1st S. (762-0900)
Hours: M-Sat. 9-5:30

It will take you a few moments to adjust to the quantity of merchandise available at this huge importer's warehouse. Most wholesalers of this kind are not open to the general public. There are more craft supplies, party goods, novelties, baskets, decorative items, etc. in this one room than we've ever seen gathered under one roof. And Treasure House knows no seasons: items for Christmas and Valentine's Day, spring and Halloween are fully stocked at all times. Their pricing requires explanation—some items are much cheaper in sets or groups. They are quite accommodating about explaining their system and pointing out good buys. Plan to spend plenty of time browsing and checking prices. **Checks, M/C, VISA**

WASHINGTON CRAFT AND NOVELTY
Kent: 313 S. Washington (852-7927)
Hours: M-Sat. 9:30-9; Sun. 10-5

This is a popular stop for the Buffy Bus. The inventory of craft supplies and related items is staggering, and some of the prices are very good. Bulk gift wrap (you roll your own off their rolls) at 12¢/ft. is about 50% off regular retail. If you know this type of merchandise, you can determine which prices merit return visits. They also sell wholesale to those with a tax number. Returns with the receipt and within 14 days. **Checks, M/C, VISA**

DRUGS

APEX WHOLESALE
Seattle: 521-A 1st N. (285-2639; 285-3034)
Hours: M-F 8-3

This wholesaler of drug store merchandise offers considerable savings to organized buyers. Their $100 minimum is flexible, but meant to discourage small purchases. Ask for a price sheet and familiarize yourself with the rules (certain discounts for certain categories). You collect the merchandise from the shelves. Everything is cash and carry. (Shoppers note: stores running 2-for-1 specials can sometimes beat even wholesale prices.) *Directions:* In an alley behind Dick's Drive-in, parallel to Queen Anne Blvd. **Checks**

COST PLUS Rx
Tacoma: 204 N. I (572-6473)
Hours: M-F 10-6; Sat. 10-3

We heartily support the philosophy of pharmacies such as Cost Plus which are willing to keep costs down and reduce their markup. They'll quote prices over the phone. They will also call your physician to get generic prescriptions if you ask them. Although they offer free prescription delivery, it's worth a trip into this small pharmacy to compare savings on their extensive line of generic over-the-counter health products. Cost Plus stocks generics next to brand names, so it's quickly evident that you can save almost 50% by buying generic. Look for the brands that begin with "gen..." and are chemical copies of popular drugs. The great advantage with these products is that you can easily compare the chemical components thanks to the FDA's labeling requirements. **Checks**

Shopper's note: The private labels at stores like Pay 'n Save and Fred Meyer offer price advantages similar to the "generics." If you feel squeamish about taking advantage of these bargains, ask your pharmacist or check with the Food and Drug Administration for information on drugs and drug labeling. There truly is no need to pay for the brand names' advertising costs—unless you own stock in the company.

DRUG EMPORIUM
Seattle: 17348 Southcenter Pkwy. (575-3103)
Hours: M-F 10-10; Sat. 10-8; Sun. 10-6

Wow, what a find! We can't rave enough about this one. Drug Emporium sells everything you'd expect from a drugstore: cosmetics, paper goods, drugs, sundries, etc., and it is very well stocked with a large variety. Prices are comparable to good sale prices at other drugstores. We figure we saved approximately 40% on most of our purchases; 70% compared to the drugstores that price on the higher side. Cards, giftwrap and stationery were around 40% off. According to a friend the savings on prescription drugs is also great, and they will keep a record for you. The only thing Drug Emporium does not beat is a "loss leader" running somewhere else. **Checks, M/C, VISA**

THE MEDICINE MAN
Seattle: 1752 NW Market (789-6804); 323 N. 85th (789-0800)
Hours: M-F 10-6; Sat. 10-4 (both stores)

We'll simply quote one of their ads in case you haven't seen them: "We will undersell any and all locally advertised prices on RX or OTC medications. We state unequivocally that we will undersell these so-called discount chains, such as Pay 'N Save, Fred Meyer, Payless, Bartells, etc. Just bring in the advertisement in which the item appears and we will undersell from that price or charge you our everyday low price—whichever is lower." The Medicine Man advertises drug prices and will assist you in obtaining generic in place of brand-name drugs. *Money* magazine found a 406% difference in the cost of one drug in the same city, so if you are currently spending heavily for prescriptions, it is worth your while to consult this pharmacist. **Checks, M/C, VISA**

THE RUBBER TREE
Seattle: 4426 Burke N. (633-4750)
Hours: M-F 12-8; Sat. 12-7

Winner of our first prize for original names. This is a nonprofit shop which sells nonprescription contraceptives, the only one of its kind in the country. They endeavor to keep their prices 10-40% below regular outlets, and they also provide free (or donation) literature. If you have doubts about the responsible function of this small shop, a quick glance at the names on its Board of Directors and Advisory Committee should reassure you. **Checks**

EYEGLASS FRAMES

For those of you who've been spending *many* dollars on eyeglasses during the past few years, we feel we have an answer. Hopefully, this is the start of healthy competition in the optical business. The following stores consistently offer good savings. We were *stunned* at the prices. Don't forget to cross-price-check here when you're in the market for new frames.

ECONOLINE OPTICAL, INC.
Bremerton: 4181 Wheaton Way (373-9595)
Federal Way: 32700 Pacific Hwy. S. (838-8250)
Tacoma: Highland Hill Shopping Center (565-7040);
  4620 Pacific Ave. (473-3443)
Puyallup: 14910 Meridian S. (848-0377)
Hours: M-F 9-6; Sat. 9-3

Good prices on all frames. Over 1,500 fashion frames to choose from. **Checks, M/C, VISA**

EYES RITE OPTICAL
Seattle: 1120 4th (622-9598)
Bellevue: 14701 NE 20th (641-7309)
Burien: 501 SW 148th (244-2700)
Hours: *Seattle* **M-F 10-6; Sat. 10-2;** *Bellevue* **M-F 9:30-5:30; Sat. 10-3;** *Burien* **M-F 9:30-6; Sat. 9-4**

FUR & WOOL SCRAPS

AUSSIE WOOLIE IMPORTS
Seattle: 12608 Interurban S. (248-3584)
Hours: M-F 1-5:30; Sat. 11-3

Aussie Woolie sells bags of sheep wool scraps. These are left from different sheepskin items they make and sell for approximately $5.50/half bag, $10/whole bag. **Checks**

KLEMZ
Seattle: 9720 Holman Rd. NW (782-8022)
Hours: M-F 10-4; Sat. 10-1

Ideal spot for fly-tying hobbyists! Klemz has been in the fur business for 55 years and has all types of fur scraps on hand at different times depending on what's been made. The scraps are priced according to size and availability. Call first to see what they have. **Checks**

SALVATOR P. TRIPPY FURS
Seattle: 609 Union (624-0481)

May have fur scraps available. Give them a call before going by.

NEWSPRINT FROM NEWSPAPERS

For those of you interested in some inexpensive paper for your children's art work, some local newspapers sell roll ends of newsprint. These roll ends are either free or sold for a small fee. Although many are now recycling the leftover paper, we've listed the ones in the Puget Sound area that have sold roll ends in the past. Please call before hand to see if any rolls are on hand.

THE EVERETT HERALD
Everett: Grand & California (339-3000)

THE JOURNAL AMERICAN
Bellevue: 1701 132nd NE (453-4281)

THE SEATTLE TIMES
Seattle: Fairview N. & John (464-2483)

THE SNOHOMISH COUNTY TRIBUNE
Snohomish: 114 Ave. C (568-4121)

TACOMA NEWS TRIBUNE
Tacoma: 1950 S. State (597-8711)

PAPER PRODUCTS & OFFICE SUPPLIES

ARVEY PAPER AND SUPPLIES CO.
Seattle: 2930 1st S. (622-9232)
Bellevue: 1910 132nd NE (643-4333)
Hours: M-F 8:30-5:30; Sat. 9-1

Their sign reads, "Envelopes—All Sizes—All Kinds—Office Supplies—Paper—Disc. Prices." Expect 10-50% off compared to retail when you buy envelopes in boxes of 500 and paper by the ream. The selection is very large and the staff knowledgeable. You'll like Arvey's for consistently saving you money on paper goods. **Checks**

DISCOUNT PAPER PRODUCTS
Lynnwood: 6815 SW 196th, Suite G (771-2944)
Hours: M-F 9-5; Sat. 10-4

Get out your pad and pencil and get ready to compare prices, so you can determine the best buys among the many party and stationery store items in this shop. Plastic wrap and aluminum foil come in 1,000-plus-ft. rolls, curling ribbon was $3.49 for 500 yards, "banker" storage boxes were a good buy at $3, and there was a nice special on a stationery closeout at $1.99/ream. Plastic tumblers, scratch pads, gift boxes, industrial pack toilet paper by the roll or by the case, streamers, plastic baby bibs (15¢) all should be priced well below the usual store outlets, but it's a good idea to check first if you plan to buy in any quantity. Returns (with a receipt) only on factory-packaged goods. **Checks, M/C, VISA**

EVERETT WHOLESALE PAPER COMPANY
Everett: 2914 McDougall (252-2105)
Hours: M-F 8-4:30

This wholesaler to industry and the food service trade will sell to individuals—generally on a medium-quantity basis. You might visit them before a clan gathering or to stock up for a while on paper and plastic items (cups, tubs, trays, napkins, foil wrap, straws, etc.). Some stationery supply items are available. Large spools of ribbon and giftwrap may be purchased in bulk rolls. Since this is not a retail outlet, it's a good idea to defer to their regular trade clients when shopping. **Checks**

IRWIN BRENNER PAPER CO.
Seattle: 416 Bell (624-2320)
Hours: M-F 8:30-4:45

You can order cutter boxes (100 ft. long, 24 in. wide) of giftwrap in many patterns and grades priced from $11.50 to $15. There is a one-month waiting period, sometimes longer. Plan ahead if you have Christmas wrap in mind. Kraft paper and curling ribbon are also available. You will also save plenty on bathroom tissue, kitchen towels and light bulbs. **Checks**

MR. OFFICE SUPPLY, INC.
Everett: 6829 Evergreen Way (347-2001)
Hours: M-F 8:30-7; Sat. 9-5

Mr. Office Supply discounts all items: office supplies, furniture, equipment, computer paper, etc. Most goods show the regular retail price and the discounted Mr. Office price.
Checks, M/C, VISA

PAPER FACTORY OUTLET
Tacoma: 1565 Center (272-2181)
Hours: M-F 10-6; Sat. 10-5

This shop is a must for planning a wedding or a large party. On top of their discounted floor prices, you receive an additional discount for large purchases (5% for $25, 7% for $50 and 10% for $100). They stock an extraordinarily complete line of party goods: cocktail picks, 4th of July banners, balloon bouquets ($6.50 for one dozen helium-filled balloons), caterware, napkins, artificial flowers...Outstanding buys are giftwrap and ribbon. You roll your own off their bulk roll. The 26-in. shiny print we bought at 17¢/ft. was 50% off the packaged store price. Shiny ribbon was a steal during their half-price ribbon sale (1½¢/ft.). They'll take back unopened packages, but not caterware, cutlery or loose items. No store discount on sale items.

Checks, M/C, VISA

THE PAPER MERCHANT
Seattle: 2720 4th S. (622-8223, Ext. 23)
Hours: M-F 8-5

Check the prices here on paper, office and printing supplies. The savings over stationery store purchases on some items can be nearly 50%. Closeout stock from the Kaplan Paper Co. is sold at big reductions on the closeout table in the rear of the store. Buying in bulk usually offers the biggest savings. If you really use paper or can split up a case with some friends, you can obtain the case price reduction on everything else you buy that day—and the case can contain mixed stock. Exchanges only, no refunds.

Checks, M/C, VISA

THE PAPER PICK-UP
Everett: 9423 Evergreen Way (355-7703)
Seattle: 87 S. Holgate (682-8644)
Redmond: 3838 148th NE (883-0273)
Hours: M-F 8-5 (all stores)

These warehouse outlets for the West Coast Paper Company can save you money on stationery and home paper supplies. One visit should convince you that buying in quantity is well worth the extra storage space you will use. Their minimums are not high—a ream of paper (500 sheets), 100 cups, etc., but the more you buy, the better the price. Their policy is to give the case price on broken lot orders and the 5-case price on single-case orders. Check out colored artist-type papers as well as everyday items like toilet tissue and envelopes. They usually have something unexpected on special (e.g. hot chocolate packages, sheepskin seat covers, etc.).

Checks

THE PAPERWORKS
Seattle: 911 Western (682-9199)
Hours: M-F 9-5 (call first)

If you run a nursery school, have a scout troop or just need paper for craft projects for a home preschooler, here is a place to call. They often have end cuts—scrap paper—that they will give away.

WORLD WIDE DISTRIBUTORS, INC.—See Index

RAGS

Need rags for home and shop projects? The following may have them. Call to see what's available.

BABY DIAPER SERVICE
Seattle: 456 N. 36th (634-2229)
Hours: M-F 8-5

BARCO WIPER SUPPLY CO.
Seattle: 2938 16th SW (682-0822)
Hours: M-F 8-4:30

BUFFALO SANITARY WIPERS
Seattle: 99 S. Spokane (682-9900)
Hours: M-F 7:30-4

FRESH 'N READY DIAPER SERVICE
Tacoma: 1934 Market (383-5598)
Hours: M-F 9-5

STEINER CORPORATION
Tacoma: 2011 S. Tacoma Way (474-9446)
Hours: M-F 8-4:30

SUPERIOR LINEN SERVICE
Tacoma: 1012 Center (383-2636)
Hours: M-F 8-4:30

TOO DIVERSE TO CLASSIFY

AAA (AUTOMOBILE CLUB OF WASHINGTON)
Seattle (main office): 330 6th N. (292-5353)
Plus local offices throughout the Puget Sound area
Hours: M-F 8:30-5

AAA offers many excellent services, but we are listing them for the following savings which are available only to members:
1. Free maps, tourbooks and camping guides to the U.S. and abroad
2. Free traveler's checks
3. Cheap ($2), same-hour passport photos
4. No service fee for Washington state vehicle tags
5. Periodic discounts on books and other items (offered through the monthly newspaper for members)

First year membership is $36; $26 per year thereafter. If you use the free towing or startup services just once, you will probably pay for your membership and all the above items are then truly "free." Since AAA and the BCAA (British Columbia Auto Association) have a reciprocal agreement, your privileges extend into Canada, where road maps are scarce *and* expensive.

ACE NOVELTY CO.
Bellevue: 13434 NE 16th (644-1820)
Hours: M-F 8:30-5

Take your children here for a treat; what a great place to browse. However, be prepared to say, "No," to their many requests to purchase something. Ace Novelty stocks toys of all sorts and brands, party favors, crepe paper, napkins, decorations, glassware and adult jokes and games. According to our calculations, many items sell from about 25% off retail. Some of the stock requires close comparison. A big hit for parties or to fill piñatas is their party box, ranging in price from $3.50 to $20. Each box contains 100 party prizes. **Checks, M/C, VISA**

Too Diverse to Classify

ANTIQUE LIQUIDATORS
Seattle: 503 Westlake N. (623-2740)
Hours: M-Sat. 10-5:30

Antique dealers have been excluded as a general category from this book. Anyone experienced in the field understands the intricacies involved in identifying high-value-potential pieces, much less determining bargain prices. However, Antique Liquidators is included due to their high volume operation. Some items have gone from their barnlike salesfloors to higher price tags elsewhere. The stock changes constantly. Each time you browse, leave your address on a postcard, and they'll notify you of the next shipment's arrival date. All sales are final. **Checks**

BERGMAN LUGGAGE CO.
Seattle: 1930 3rd Ave. (622-2354); 146 Northgate Plaza (365-5775)
Bellevue: 15116 NE 24th (643-2344)
Federal Way: 2012 S. 320th (941-7990)
Lynnwood: Room 320, Alderwood Mall (774-9533)
Tukwila: Pavilion, 17900 Southcenter Pkwy. (575-4090)
Hours: *3rd Ave.* **M-F 9-5:30, Sat. 9-5;** *Northgate* **M-Sun. 10-9;** *Bellevue* **M, F 10-9; T-Th 10-6; Sat. 10-5;** *320th* **M-Th 10-6; F 10-9; Sat. 10-5;** *Lynnwood* **M-F 9-9; Sat. 10-6; Sun. 11-5;** *Pavilion* **M-F 10-9; Sat. 10-6; Sun. 11-5**

After searching Seattle for good bargains in luggage, we've placed Bergman's at the top of our list. Bergman's advertises as the "most complete luggage store in the USA" with the greatest selection. They've recently added a wide range of gift ideas as well. The store is 56 years old, and its recent growth attests to its popularity. It's grown from one outlet to 6 since the first *Seattle Super Shopper* came out in 1976. Bergman's offers excellent prices on an enormous selection of every imaginable variety of luggage, attaché cases, wallets, purses and other leather items. Things are discounted 20-25% off list price (30-40% on discontinued models). The overall quality is high. They sell top-quality imitation leather goods as well—many of these are indistinguishable from the leather. Returns are accepted.

Checks, M/C, VISA, Amer. Exp.

BLACK OAK FOUNDRY
Bainbridge Island: 7869 NE Day Rd. W. (842-3107)
Hours: M-F 8:30-5

This factory manufactures belt buckles for men, women and children and ships them all over the USA. The owner will sell to individuals but call first to see when he'll be there. The buckles are bronze, single-cast and come in ready-made designs or special orders. Please don't call unless you are seriously in the market for a belt buckle, as there is no retail outlet for browsing at the factory.   **Checks**

THE BUFFY BUS
Bellevue: P.O. Box 6051, 98007 (643-8929)

Named for its originator, Buffy McCune, local syndicated columnist and weekly guest on the *Northwest Today* show, these bargain hunters' tours are available to individuals and groups. Reservations are required. Nearly 5,000 shoppers have boarded the Buffy Bus since its beginning. Each tour has a specific theme (Fashion Fling, Junky Jaunt, Bon Appetit, Mistletoe Express and Take Off To Tacoma) with stops at 7 to 8 wholesalers or factory outlets. Lunch, beverages and snacks are included in the $24 tour price. All stops offer bona fide bargains. Several shops feature discounts available only to shoppers on the Buffy Bus, and some locations are closed to the general public. Here's a fun way to be introduced to bargain shopping, especially when a group of friends board the bus together.

CARTON SERVICE
Tukwila: 1141 Andover Park W., Bldg. C (575-9111)
Hours: M-F 8-4

PAYLESS CONTAINERS
Redmond: 4526 232nd NE (885-4517)
Hours: Call first

These 2 companies specialize in used or surplus boxes. They can cut your costs on moving or storage containers by as much as 50%. Call first to be sure they have a supply of what you need.

Move-it-yourselfers note: U-Haul gives away an excellent free booklet which tells you how to compute the number of cartons you need for your move as well as the size truck you will need.

CHRISTMAS TREE FARMS

Traditionalists may obtain a Christmas Tree Growers map from the Puget Sound Christmas Tree Association, c/o Bill Magelssen, 9630 27th Ave. SE, Everett, WA 98204. The map indicates varieties available at each location and the farms that would allow you to chop down your own tree.

If you've never made a family outing in search of the Perfect Tree, we guarantee it will add a dimension of love to your Tannenbaum that no precut tree can match. There are 26 farms on the map, ranging from Tacoma and Sumner to Mt. Vernon and Sumas and east to Darrington and Sultan. Whidbey Island has 3 tree farms. For a truly Northwest experience, ride a ferry to cut a Christmas tree! At a few farms you can dig your tree rather than cut it, but call first to locate these special dealers.

Additional information may be obtained from Loren Curry, County Extension Forester, 3001 Rockefeller, Everett, WA 98201 (259-9422). King County Extension Service, 312 Smith Tower, Seattle (344-2686) will have information right before Christmas, or check your local library. Hardy types should contact the National Forest Service (442-0170) for information concerning cutting trees in the National Forests. Don't forget your axe!

For a traditional holiday decoration, try the **Holly Farm** in Bellevue located on SE 34th, between 110th & 112th Ave. SE. They sell holly to drop-in customers only during the holiday season.

CHUBBY AND TUBBY STORES
Seattle: 3333 Rainier S. (723-8800); 7906 Aurora N. (524-1810)
White Center: 9456 16th SW (762-9791)
Hours: M-Sat. 9-8; Sun 10-6 (all stores)

For the past 30 years or so Chubby and Tubby Christmas trees have been one of the best bargains in town. Hopefully they will continue to offer a huge selection of trees—all at one low price. If you are patient, you can find just the tree for your house and pay a real bargain price for it. The trees usually are out the first or second week in December, and all three stores sell them.

Checks, M/C, VISA

CHURCHILL BROTHERS
Everett: 1130 Norton (259-3500)
Hours: M-F 8:30-5

This outlet on the waterfront reflects the parent company's expertise in marine repair. They stock everything you'll need for a do-it-yourself project, plus free instructions. You'll find marine hardware, fabrics and canvas products by Churchill Bros. for use on or off a boat (duffle bags and bos'n chairs, for example). Canvas roll ends are sometimes available, as well as kites and windsocks. **Checks, M/C, VISA**

DIRECT BUYING SERVICE
Seattle: 906 3rd (623-8811)
Hours: M-F 9:15-6; Sat. 9:30-4

Here is a discount house whose showroom has luggage, TVs, jewelry, small appliances, VCRs, computers, diamonds, cameras and much more, all immediately available. Direct Buying is also a catalog order house. Call or visit to place an order. Give them the brand and/or model number; keep the regular retail figure on hand for comparison. Check discounted prices against advertised specials elsewhere. Chances are Direct Buying can obtain it for you at considerable savings. "You Name It—We Get it" has been their motto for over 30 years. **Checks preferred, M/C, VISA (on small purchases)**

EVERETT ANCHOR AND CHAIN
Everett: 3126 Hill Street (258-4505)
Hours: M-F 8-4:30

Pleasure boaters can expect to find substantial savings on anchors, chain, marine hardware products, wire rope and similar items. We priced one anchor at better than 50% below a specialty boat shop. Returns are accepted. **Checks, M/C, VISA**

THE FOAM SHOP
Seattle: 5311 Roosevelt Way NE (525-2301)
Hours: M-Sat. 10-6

Be sure to price check The Foam Shop if you need a foam item whether it be quantities of shredded stuff for pillows, a mattress or a fold-out chair. Cutting is free. They carry a range in quality and can tell you more about foam density than you probably care to know, but it *will* make you more knowledgeable about future purchases. **Checks, M/C, VISA**

H. E. GOLDBERG & CO.
Seattle: 9050 Empire Way S. (722-8200)
Hours: M-F 8:30-4:30

At H. E. Goldberg you'll find furs, suedes and leathers to make into belts, clothes, etc. The day we visited, small leather scraps were selling for 75¢/lb. They are packaged in 5-lb. lots. Don't be shocked to find the door locked, just ring the bell to be admitted. Exchanges possible with sales receipt and if you *have not* cut or marked the piece of hide. **Checks, M/C, VISA**

K-9 KUSTOM MIX, INC.
Everett: 3018 79th NE (334-4843)
Hours: Generally M-F 8-6; call first on weekends

Feed Rover the stuff show-dog breeders and boarding kennels use for around 36¢/lb. You can purchase an organic natural dog food in frozen 5-lb. packages from K-9. Defrosted, it will keep 7 days in the refrigerator. The meat/oats/kelp combo contains 13% protein and 61% moisture. Feeding rule of thumb is 8 oz./20 lbs. of dog. They will sell as little as 1-lb. packages (at 40¢) if you want to see if the flavor is agreeable to your animal. **Checks**

LAST MINUTE TICKETS
Seattle: 1320 2nd (623-9068)
Hours: M-F 10:30-6; Sat., Sun. 11-5

You can now obtain same-day performance tickets to several performing arts events for 50% off plus $1.25 handling fee/ticket. Last Minute Tickets has contracted with several organizations (Act Theater, Intiman Theater, Seattle Repertory Theatre, Seattle Opera, Seattle Symphony, Pacific Northwest Ballet) to sell day-of-performance tickets. Available performances are posted in the office window. You might want to call before going in. The day we stopped by nothing was available, and the office was locked. This is an excellent way to see some of Seattle's outstanding performing arts and at quite a price break. It also helps the theaters, opera, ballet and symphony by helping to sell out the house. All sales final. **Cash only**

MacPHERSON LEATHER CO.
Seattle: 1209 2nd (622-0855)
Hours: M-F 8-5; Sat. 10-3

MacPherson's specializes in making top-quality leather and suede items. We're including them not for that reason, but because they have several bins full of leftover leather, suede and woolskin scraps. These sell for various prices depending on type and size. No returns allowed on scraps. **Checks, M/C, VISA**

MODERN PRODUCTS, INC.
Seattle: 9221 Roosevelt Way NE (525-2226)
Hours: M-F 8-4:30

Off-color rejects of plastic bottles, jars and caps are a real bargain. If you want first quality, there is no minimum purchase, and the sizes run from 6 oz. to 5 gals. They also sell boxes of scrap plastic shapes for kids' art project for very little. **Checks**

NORTHWEST MANNEQUIN
Bellevue: P.O. Box 6053, 98007 (644-2629)
Hours: (call first)

Ever wonder where you might get a good buy on spare body parts for a haunted house? We have found the place. This is no joke; you can buy parts of mannequins for very little (usually $5 and up). In fact, you can buy the whole body for $25-$30 if it's in bad shape. Northwest Mannequin repairs and refinishes mannequins. They serve small shopowners who can save at least 50% by buying used dummies instead of new ones. You can rent a body by the day, week or month. The best deal is to rent with an option to buy ($30/mo. with a 3-mo. minimum). Rental is applied to the purchase price. This plan applies to females and children only—males in good condition are in short supply. **Checks**

OPTECHS
Seattle: 1424 4th (4th and Pike Bldg.) (621-8923)
Hours: M-F 10-6; Sat. 10-4

A cameraman for one of our local TV stations suggested this place to us. You'll find top-quality used cameras and photo equipment such as lenses, etc. These are not your low line, inexpensive ones, but more middle to top line as well as professional equipment. The stock varies as to amount and type available. The owners are extremely helpful in pointing out the pros and cons of one model as compared to another. **Checks**

PACKRATS DELIGHT
Tacoma: 3111 6th (752-1445)
Hours: M-Sat. 10-6

We were extremely impressed with this unique consignment store, because it sells odds and ends of furniture, appliances, household items, kitchen gadgets, toys, baby equipment. It will not accept objects under $1 in value, clothes or junk. The other consignment shops we've ventured into have been primarily interested in clothing. Returns must be made within 3 days.
Checks, M/C, VISA

PUGET SOUND TENT AND AWNING
Seattle: 2107 3rd (622-8219)
Hours: M-F 8-4:30

Custom-made banners and big top tents are this company's specialty. We shop them for inexpensive, utilitarian, waterproof tote bags ($3.50), which they make during lulls in production and pile just inside the front door. Fabrics from the banner production are available downstairs. Canvas can also be purchased. In the case of the canvas, we advise you to call first and come with your measurements in order to minimize the use of their time, since they are not set up to be a fabric outlet. **Checks**

THE PURDY CO.
Seattle: 2929 SW Florida (Harbor Ave.) (932-0992)
Hours: M-F 8-4:15 (closed 12-12:30)

Eight-foot railroad ties are generally available at $8, cash and carry. If they don't have any, try West Waterway Lumber (935-9900). Look for additional sources of railroad ties in the classified section of newspapers. **Checks**

RADIO PRODUCTS SALES AND ELECTRONICS SUPPLY CO./ZORBRIST CO.
Seattle: 1214 1st (624-2424)
Hours: M-Sat. 9-5:30

A good spot to begin your shopping for electronic equipment, stereos, tape recorders and tapes, computers, CB equipment, antennas, marine equipment, etc. Ask if they have any used or unclaimed pieces of the merchandise you are seeking. Some prices at Radio Products are consistently dependable, such as 50% off radio and TV tubes. All the salespeople are electronic technicians, which is an advantage for those seeking advice on home repair or do-it-yourself projects. *Note:* It's *always* wise to comparison shop big ticket items. **Checks, M/C, VISA**

READ PRODUCTS, INC.
Seattle: 3615 15th W. (283-2510)
Hours: M-F 8-5

You'll discover lamps, TVs, stereos, radios, major appliances, furniture, carpets, etc. at Read Products. The owner does not quote any set percentage discount—it varies depending on the item. A friend of ours saved $50 on a stove. No other store offered as low a price on the particular model she wanted. We cross-checked prices on 2 different portable color TVs, and Read's was a bargain. If they don't have what you want on the sales floor, ask if they can get it for you. **Checks**

RUMMAGE SALE
Tacoma: 1503 Commerce (no phone)
Hours: M-Sat. 10-4 (usually)

Where do rummage sale junkies go? To the corner of 15th and Commerce. Handmade signs in the windows will tell you which group is raising money by renting this space. For nearly 30 years this historic Tacoma building has been used for rummage sales. The fee is $20/day (you must have the appropriate but not expensive licenses from City Hall). The building is often booked a year in advance by charity groups who hold annual sales. It's rare for a week to go by without a sale a day. Most groups rent for 1-3 days. If your group wants to get in on the action, call the Riley-Griffin Co. at 272-3848 from 8:30-5 on weekdays.

TACOMA LUGGAGE COMPANY
Tacoma: 913 Pacific (572-4532)
Hours: M-F 10-5:30; Sat. 11-4

We drooled over the elegant $400 top-of-the-line pieces and cross checked prices on some sturdy, good-looking but *far* less expensive bags. Our suggestion is that you give Tacoma Luggage a call. It may well be worth a trip to Tacoma if what you want is on special. They'll quote prices over the phone. Tacoma Luggage stocks current, popular colors as well as discontinued colors and styles. Wallets, travel kits and other leather and synthetic items are well priced. Keep your eye out for special clearance and sale tags scattered around the store. Returns are welcome on unused luggage with saleslip. **Checks, M/C, VISA**

VALLEY SUPPLY CO-OP
Seattle: (622-5766)
Auburn: (833-7220)
Tacoma: (924-0564)

Valley Supply Co-op is a nonprofit corporation which supplies home delivery of heating oil and gasoline, as well as complete burner service. As in any co-op, you join and share the benefits. Goods and services are provided to the members at cost—the original selling price less patronage refund. Patronage refunds are paid to members yearly on participating purchases. Patronage is paid 20% in cash with the remaining 80% retained in the form of stock (owner equity) as operating capital. Ownership equity can be withdrawn upon retirement age (65) or when moving out of the trade area. Heating oil service is available to Puget Sound area residents, with per gal. prices in the middle to low range. Cennex gas stations in Auburn, Spanaway and Tacoma are only part of the other services offered to members.

VALLEY SUPPLY STORES offer discounts to members on farm hardware, feed and fertilizer via the same "patronage" system outlined above. For store locations and hours, call any of the numbers listed.

LAST MINUTE DISCOVERIES

THE DOWN & OUTER
Seattle: 13555 Aurora Ave. N. (362-2641)
Hours: M-F 10-8; Sat. 10-6; Sun. 12-5

Name Brand outdoor/activewear from 30%-70% off.
Checks, M/C, VISA

HAL'S OF LAKE CITY
Seattle: 14001 Lake City Way NE (363-4377)
Hours: M-Th 10-5; F 10-6; Sat. 10-4

This restaurant supplier can save you 20%-40% on meats, seafood, cheeses and other food items.
Checks

RAINIER LABS, INC.
Seattle: 8730 Rainier Ave. S. (722-2646)
Hours: M-F 10-6; Sat. 10-3

Film (all major brands), photographic paper and chemicals at 10% over wholesale. A price list is available.
Checks

SEAPORT CHEMICALS, INC.
Seattle: 1215 E. Columbia (329-1200)
Hours: M-F 8-5

Seaport manufactures paint strippers, solvents and cleaning products. You can save approximately 50% by buying in gallon sizes.
Cash only

SOFTWARE CITY
Bellevue: 1100 Bellevue Way (451-1141)
Hours: M-Sat. 10-6; Th 10-8

You'll discover software for most home computers at this store. Percentage off depends upon the amount you purchase.
Checks, M/C, VISA

STUSSER & SWEENEY
Seattle: 1930 1st Ave. at Virginia (624-3003)
Hours: M-Sat. 9:30-5:30

Salesman's samples and factory overruns in men's, women's, children's and toddlers' sizes in clothing and shoes. Merchandise is priced at or very slightly above wholesale costs.

INDEX

A

A-1 Beauty Supply, 144
A & R Cutlery Service, 127
AAA (Automobile Club of
  Washington), 209
A.A.A. Liquidating and Auction, 190
AAA New and Used Restaurant
  Equipment, 125
Aannex Rents, Inc., 147
ABC Sales, 190
ABCO Supply Co., 16
Ace Novelty Co., 209
Accent on Fashion, 55
ACME Office Furniture, 175
Act II, Inc., 55
Aetna Marketing, Inc., 2
AFCO Furniture Rentals, Inc., 109
Ajax Electric, Inc., 95
Al's Potato Service, 21
Alfalfa Patch, 27
All City Vacuum & Janitorial, 122
Alley Cat, 55
Allied Restaurant and Gourmet
  Shop, 125
Amberson Egg Farm, 14
American Drapery Factory, 102
American Games, 199
American Office Interiors, 175
American Tool & Supply Co., 181
Ander's Clothing Clearance Center,
  73, 139
Andy's Drapery Co., 102
antiques, 47, 48, 50, 52, 53, 54, 63,
  201, 210
Antique Liquidators, 210
Anything Grows, 157
APE, 190
Apex Wholesale, 202
Apparel Déja Vu, 55
appliances:
  new: 95-97, 116-118, 125-126,
    144-146, 190, 212, 216
  used: 46, 48, 51, 52, 54, 70-72, 96,
    97, 125, 126, 155, 156
Apollo, 199

Après-Vous Consignments, 56
Arctic Ice Cream Novelties, 14
Ardie's Carpets, 98
Aronson Industrial Supply, 181
Art's, 191
Arty's Custom-Built, 113
Arvey Paper and Supplies Co., 205
Aslan's, 45
Assistance League Thrift Shop, 45
Atlas Building Wreckers, 191
Aurora Coin Distributing, Inc., 199
Aussie Woolie Imports, 204
automobiles:
  batteries, 180
  services, 180, 209
  tires, 179, 180

B

B & B Upholstery, 102
B & I Sports Shop, 147
B.J.'s Closet, 56
Baby Diaper Service, 208
backpacking supplies, 147-153, 193
Backtrack Records and Books, 170
Backwoods Supply Co., 147
Bader's Dutch Biscuit Co., Inc., 2
Baker & Chantry Orchids, 128
balloons, 139, 206-207
Baltam Trading Co., 134
Barco Wiper Supply Co., 208
Bargain Boutique, 46
Bargain Fair, 46
Bargain Land, 46
Bargreen Coffee & Restaurant
  Equipment Co., 24
Bargreen-Ellison, Inc., 125
Bargreen's Restaurant Supply,
  Inc., 34
Base Camp Supply, 148
Baskin-Robbins Ice Cream Stores, 14
batting and foam products, 106, 107,
  213
Bauer Books/Creative Awareness
  Book Exchange, 157

220   Index

Bayside Supply Co., 95
Beatty Book Store, 157
Beauty and the Books, 157
beauty salons, 140
beauty supplies, 140, 143-146, 202, 203
Bedspread Warehouse, 102
Bella's Baby World, 88
Bel-Boutique, 154
Bellco Electric, 187
belt buckles, 210
Benoy's Carpet, 98
Bergman Luggage Co., 139, 210
Best Cellars, 158
Best Prepared Foods, 34
Bibelots & Books, 158
Bi Lo Clothing, 75
Black and Decker Mfg. Co., 184
Black Oak Foundry, 210
Bloomsbury Books, 158
Bob Stafford (Burien Budget Furniture), 109
Boden & Gilman, 175
Boehm's Homemade Swiss Candies, 10
Boeing Surplus, 191
Bon Shoe Rack, The, 85
Bond's Picture Frames, 115
books:
    used: 157-168
    new: 168-169, 142
Bookcyclers, 159
Bookends, The, 159
Book Exchange, The, 158
Book Gallery, A, 158
Book Loft, 158
Book Nook, The, 159
Book Rack, The, 159
Bookworld, 159
Bookworm, The, 160
Bop Street Records and Books, 170
Boss Manufacturing (George A. Johnston Co.), 65
Botanic Designs, 128
Bothell Appliance & TV, 96
Boyd Coffee Co., 34
Branam, 103
Bread Garden, The, 2

Broadway Books, 160
Broadway Record Center, 170
Brown & Haley, 10
Brown's Quality Foods, 27
Bruce Houghton & Associates, 155
Bubble Records and Tickets, 170
Buddy Squirrel's Nut & Candy Shops, 11
Budget Batteries, 180
Budget Boutique, 56
Budget Furniture Rentals, 110
Budget Office Products, 176
Budget Tapes and Records, 171
Buffalo Sanitary Wipers, 208
Buffy Bus, The, 211
Button and Bows, 88
building materials, 97, 186-189
Bulk Commodities Exchange, 28
Bur-Bank Domestics, Inc., 103
Burien Budget Furniture, (see Bob Stafford)
Burien Thrift Center, 46
Business Furniture Liquidators, 176
Business Office Furniture, Inc., 176
Butterfly, The, 47
buttons, 107

C

C. Rhyne & Associates, 133
cabinets, 97
Cacallori Marble Co., 127
Cal-ga-Crete Northwest Inc. (The Tile Factory), 98
Calico Corners, 103
Camelot Thrift Center, 47
cameras, 212, 215
Campbell Industrial Supply Co., 182
camping equipment, 147-153
candles, 135
Can D Man, 11, 28
candy, 10-14, 28, 142
canned and bottled foods:
    fish, 40
    full-line, 12, 29, 34, 35, 37, 43, 190-192, 194, 196
Canned Food Store, 35
canvas and canvas products, 104, 108, 109, 212, 215

Index   221

Canyon Park Stamp, Coin and Book Exchange, 160
Capitol Tire Sales Warehouses, Inc., 179
Captain Sam's Loft, 192
Carabee Food Products, 11
Carl's Books, 160
Carpet Exchange, The, 98
Carpet Warehouse, 99
carpeting:
   new: 97-102, 119, 120, 216
   used: 100-102
carob products, 11, 25
Carousel Children's Consignment Shop, 88
Carroll & Associates, 132
Carter's Factory Outlet, 89
Carton Service, 211
cartons, 211
Cascade Co., 104
Cascadian Sportswear, 65
catalog sales, 212
Catchpenny, 160
Cellophane Square, 171
Center Tool Co., 182
Central Co-op, 42
cheese, 15, 16, 25, 26, 28-31, 38, 43, 218
cheesecake, 2, 33
Cheese Factory Store, 15
Cheryl's Interiors in Green, 128
Chickabiddy Trading Co., 89
Children's Orthopedic Corner Cupboard, 47
Children's Orthopedic Thrift Shop, 47
Chinook Door, 186
Chris Loken & Co., 122
Christmas trees, 211, 212
Chubby & Tubby Stores, 212
Churchill Brothers, 212
Cider Shed, 9
Cinderella's Closet, 56
Circle Seafoods, 39
City Electric Service Shop, 148
City of Hope Secondhand Rose Thrift Shop, 47, 155
City Produce Co., 21

Classic Wax, 171
Clay Art Center, 130
Clothes Club, The, 75
Clothes Out, 80, 140
Clothes Encounter, 56
Clothes Menagerie, 56
clothing:
   new: 65-70, 73-85, 87-94, 116-118, 139-143, 154-156, 218
   used: 45-64, 70-72, 87-94, 200, 216, 218
Cloud 9, 48
Coast Brush Co., 122
Coast Liquidators, 182
Coast Oyster Co., 39
Coast Wide Supply, 123
Coat Outlet Northwest, 65
Coats Galore, Inc., 76
coffee, tea, 24, 34, 37, 43, 44
Cold Mountain Juice Co., 9
collectibles, 54-64, 88-94, 151-153, 163-165, 200, 201
Collector's Nook, 160
comics, 159, 160, 162-168
Company Store, The, 65
computers and supplies, 212, 215-216, 218
Comstock's Bindery & Bookshop, 161
Consignment Closet, 57
Consignment Shop, 57
consignment shops, 54-64, 88-94, 129, 151-153, 200-201
Consolidated Carpet Warehouse, 99
Continental Furniture, 110
contraceptives, 203
Contract Floors, Inc., 99
Cookie Conspiracy, 3
cookies, pies and cakes, 2-8, 20, 29
Cornplanter Co., 21
cosmetics, 140, 143-146
Cost Plus Rx, 202
Council Thrift Shop, 48
Cracker Barrel, The, 57
craft supplies, 136, 201, 202, 204, 205, 207, 213, 214
Cram's Interiors, 104
Crozier Fine Foods, Inc., 35
Crucible Bookshop, 161

crystal, china, glassware, 125, 126, 132, 134, 136, 137, 139, 140
Custom Bifolds, 186
Custom Made Foods, 24
cutlery, 125-127

D

dairy products, 10, 14, 15, 25, 26, 29, 31, 42, 43
Dalton Carpets, 99
Dandylion Records and Tapes, 171
Danny's Milk Barn, 21
Dark Horse, The, 57
DeeDee's Kloset, 80
Deli Products, Inc., 28
Deseret Industries Thrift Store, 70
Dick Wynne Floor Covering, 100
Different Drummer, A, 161
Dilettante Chocolate, Inc., 11
Direct Buying Service, 212
Direct Carpet Sales, 100
Discount Books By Mail, 169
Discount Paper Products, 205
Dollar's Worth, A, 89
Donnally-Hayes Books, 161
Don's Tacoma Carpet Sales and Cleaning, 100
Down Factory, The, (Don Shingler, Inc.), 66
Down and Outer, The, 218
Draperies, Inc., 104
Drastic Plastic Records, 172
Drug Emporium, 203
drugs and sundries, 202-203
Dutton's, 35

E

E.C.A. Thrift Shop, 48
Eastside Cheese Co., 15
Eastside Mattress Co., 115
Easy Street Records, 172
Econoline Optical, 204
Eddie Bauer, 148
Eidem's Custom Upholstery, 104
electric and electronic equipment and supplies, 187-191, 194, 197, 198, 215, 216
Elfie's Consignment Boutique, 57

Emmy's Attic, 49
Encore Boutique, 58
Encore Consignments, 58
Encore Fashions, 58
Ener-G Foods, 36
Everett Anchor and Chain, 213
Everett Cash and Carry Beauty Supply, 144
Everett Tent and Awning Co., 104
Everett Wholesale Paper Co., 206
Evergreen Fruit and Produce, 22
Evergreen Sporting Goods and Surplus, 148
Everrest Mattress, 113
eyeglass frames, 143, 204
Eyes Rite Optical, 204

F

1st Tire and Wheel Centers, 179
F. and L. Foods, Inc., 39
fabrics, 102-109, 140
Fabrik, 13
Factory Direct Draperies Budget Shop, 105
Factory Fallouts, 66
Family Closet, The, 58
Fanta Sal, 22
Farbest Eggs, 15
Far Fetched, 58
farm supplies, 217
Farwest Garments, 66
Fashion Club, 76
Fell & Co., 73
Fifth Avenue Record Shop, 172
Figleaf, The, 59
Fillipi Book & Record Shop, 161, 172
Findery, The, 59
Finnegan, C.B. & Co., 81
First Stop, 81
floor coverings, 97-102, 119, 120
Floor Shoppe, 101
Floyd Tyson's Merchandise, 192
Foam Shop, The, 213
Folio Bookshop, 162
Food Bag Co-op, The, 42
Food Cupboard, The, 24
Fox Book Co., 162

Foxy Lady Anonymous, 59
frames, picture, 115, 116
Fran's Carpets and Interiors, 101
Frank's Red Carpet Stores, 101
Frankie Boy Produce Co., 22
Fresh 'N Ready Diaper Service, 208
Frugallily's, 49
Frugalman's, 77
fruits:
  fresh: 21-23, 30, 31, 43
  frozen: 16, 35
furniture:
  infants & children's: 88-94, 201
  office: 175-178, 191
  new: 109-112, 114, 116-118, 127, 136, 216
  used: 109-111, 45-54, 70-72, 210
Furniture Warehouse Sales Center (The Bon), 116
furs, 74-75
Fuzzy Wuzzy Rug Co., 101

G

Gaffney Supplies, Inc., 15
Gagnon Supply Co., 122
Gai's Seattle French Baking Co., Inc., 3
games (pinball, jukebox, video), 199-200
Gemini Book Exchange, 162
gems, 132, 133
Gena's Resale Fashions, 59
General Store, 59
Generic Make-up, 144
gift items, 127, 128, 131-137, 139-143, 155, 210, 216
giftwrap, 136, 137, 201, 202, 205-207
Glacier Bay Foods, 39
Glad Rags and Great Things, 77
Glavin's Sample Shop, 81
Globe Books, 162
Gloria's Budget Boutique, 59
Gold, Silver and Gem Exchange, 132
Golden Age Collectibles, 162
Golden American, 36
Golden Giraffe, 89
Golden Oldies Records, 172
Golden Pheasant Noodle Co., 17

golf equipment and clothing, 149, 151, 153
Golfland Discount Pro Shop, 149
Goodwill Industries, 70
Goodwill Shopping Center, 71, 162
Gordon's Shoe Land, 85
gourmet foods, 30, 31, 35
grains, 23-26, 31, 42, 43
Grain Grinder, The, 25
Grand Mattress Co., 113
Grand Central Mercantile, 127
Grandmother's House, 90
Granny's Attic, 49
Grantree Furniture Rental, 110
Great American Cheese & Dairy Co., 29
Great Clothes, 78, 140
Great Northwest Baking Co., 3
Green River Cheese and Dairy Products Corp., 16
Green River Sawmill Inc., 188
Green River Sportswear, Inc., 67
Greenshield's Industrial Supply, 182
greeting cards, 136, 137, 139, 195
Grocer's Assoc. Inc., 29
Growing Green Gardens, 129
gumballs, 13

H

H.E. Goldberg & Co., 213
Hadassah—Nearly New Store, 49
Hal's of Lake City, 218
Hallis Produce, 29
Han Boo Oriental Mfg., 17
Hancock Fabrics, 105
hardware, 119, 120, 181-185, 187-198
Hardwick's Swap Shop, 184
Harlan-Fairbanks Co., 36
Harris Conley Discount Golf Shops, 149
Hazel's Candy, 11
health foods, 23, 25, 26, 31, 36, 43, 44
Henderson's Books, 162
herbs, spices and seasonings, 22, 25, 36, 43, 44
High Hopes Thrift Shop, 50
High Hopes Two, 50

224   Index

Hillstead's Surplus, 192
Holly Farm, 212
honey, 24-26, 43
Horizon Books, 163
hors d'oeuvres, 1, 6
hot fudge, 34
House of Pies, 4
household chemicals and supplies, 122-126, 218
housewares:
   new: 116-118, 125-127, 136, 137, 139-143, 190-198
   used: 44-54, 56, 59, 61, 63, 70-72, 95-97, 155, 200, 201, 216
Hoven Food Co., 17
Hubbard's Bargain Basement, 105
hunting and fishing equipment, 151, 194
Hyde's Northwest Candy, Inc., 12

I

ice-cream novelties, 14
Ikeda & Co., 29
Imperial Mattress Co., 113
Interior Plant Design, 129
Interpace, 188
Irwin Brenner Paper Co., 206
Italian foods, 16, 17, 19, 27, 33
Italian Specialty Foods, 17
Item House, see Coat Outlet Northwest

J

JB's Discount City, 193
JFK Attic, The, 50
Jack Fowld's Stationery Co., 176
Jack Murray Co., 106
Jafco's Round the Corner Store, 117
James M. Glass Construction Co., 193
Jana Imports, 67, 140
Jane's Books, 163
Jay Jacob's Warehouse, 78
Jeans 'N Stuff, 74
Jeans To Go, 74
Jen-cel-lite Corp., 106
Jensen Draperies, 106
Jerry's Downtown Stamp and Coin and Novelties, 163
Jerry's Surplus (Duffle Bag, Inc.), 149
jewelry:
   new: 75, 132, 133, 136, 140, 142, 212
   second-hand: 45-64, 70-72
Jim's Quality Bakery, 4
Joanne's Treasure Chest, 200
Jobe Factory Outlet, 149
Johnson Candy Co., 12
Journey, 163
Just for You, 90

K

K9 Kustom Mix, 213
K & J Distributors, 129
K and K Co., 134
K's Beauty Supply, 145
Kalberer Restaurant Equipment, 126
Karin's Beauty Supplies, Inc., 145
Kathy's Kloset, 60
Kathy's Other Place, 60
Katy Did, The, 67
Kay's Sample Shoppe, 82
Keeg's Discovery Room, 127
Ken's Suburban Clearance Center, 110
Kid's Closet, The, 90
Kid's Exchange, 90
Kid's Kloset, 91
Kid's Korner, 91
Kid's Korral, 91
Kid's Stuff, 91
King Chung Lung Import & Export, 18
Kirkland Custom Cannery, 40
Kleenco, Inc., 23
Klemz, 204
knick-knacks, 45-64, 70-72
Knox North Homes Services, 193
Kokesh Cut Glass Co., 134
Korean Food Production, 18
Kuppenheimer Factory Store, 78
Kusak Cut Glass Works, 134

L

L. A. Frames, 115
La Baquette, 4
Lake City Forest Products, 116

Index

Lampaert Meats, 32
La Mexicana, 18
Langendorf Bakeries, 4
Larry's Nursery, Inc., 129
Larson Books, 163
Last Minute Tickets, 214
Lawson Mfg., 68
leather goods, 74, 139-142, 210, 213, 214, 216
Leather Palace, 74
Lee's Food Sales, Inc., 30
Les Boulangers Associés, Inc. (LBA), 5
Liberty's Consignment Clothing and Collectibles, 60
linens, 102-104, 106, 107, 116-118, 127, 131, 134, 135, 137, 141
Liquidator, The, 194
Literary Cat, The, 169
Little Bread Co., The, 5
Liz's Pantry, 5
Loehmann's, 82
louvered doors, 186
luggage, 139, 156, 210, 212, 216
lumber:
  new: 188
  used: 189, 190, 191, 193, 197

M

Machias Rummage and Thrift, 200
MacPherson Leather Co., 214
Magus Bookstore, 164
Major Brands, 119
Mama's Prose and Steel, 164
mannequins, 214
marble, 127
Marci Jewelry, 133
marine supplies, 149, 212, 213, 215-216
Market Spice, 37
Marquis Beauty Products, 145
Mart, The (Discount Office Furniture Mart), 177
Mary's Pop Ins, 60
Marysville Home Bakery, 6
maternity clothes, 79, 88-94, 141
Maternity Factory, 79

mattresses, 46, 70, 112-115
Mattress and Maple Shop, 114
McCarthy & Co., Merchants, 9
McDonald's Book Exchange, 164
McLendon's Hardware, Inc., 188
Meat Distributors Inc., 32
meats, fish, poultry, 25, 32, 33, 38-41, 218
Medicine Man, The, 203
Mekong Market, 19
Me 'N Mom's, 91
Merchants Plus, 193
Merlino, Attilio A., & Associates, Inc., 17
Merlino's, 19
Mexican foods, 18, 19
Mexican Grocery, The, 19
Miller's Interiors, 101
Modern Products Inc., 214
Molin and Offer, 37, 194
Mondo's World, 9
Monohon's Paperbacks, 164
Monte-Vista Distributor's Bulk Warehouse Sales, 25
Montgomery Ward and Co., 117
Moss Bay Mercantile, 82
Mountain Products, 68, 141
Mountain States Restaurant and Bar, 126
Mouse Closet, 92
Mr. Office Supply Inc., 206
Murray Pacific Industrial Supply, 194
Murtough Supply Co., Inc., 123
Music Vend Distributing Co., 200
musical equipment, 171, 173
Musquaw, The, 164
Mutual Materials Co., 188

N

NW Shoe Outlet, 86
Nandy's Bridal, 60
National Foods, 16
National Furniture Rentals & Sales, Inc., 111
Natural Foods Warehouse/Manna Milling, 25
Nearly New Shop, 61
Nelson's Car Care Centers, 179

Index

Neslin's Factory Outlet, 150
newsprint, 205
Nicest Things, The, 128
Noel Produce, 30
Nordstrom's Clothes Rack, 79
Nordstrom's Shoe Rack, 86
North Coast Chemical Co., Inc., 123
North Coast Importing Co., 30
North End Steel Outlet, 194
North Face, The, 150
Northern Fish Products Co., 40
Northgate Egg Farm, 16
Northwest Distributors, 12
Northwest Ground Covers and Nursery, 129
Northwest Hairlines, 146
Northwest Mannequin, 214
Northwest Reader's Guild, 169
Northwest Trader's, 194
nuts, seeds, 13, 14, 23, 25, 26, 31, 38, 39, 42-44

O

Oberto Sausage Co., 33
Odds & Ends of Friends, 50
Off Center Furniture Warehouse, 111
Office Emporium, 177
Office Furniture Liquidators, 177
Office World Discount Office Furniture, 177
office equipment and supplies, 175-178, 191, 198, 205-207
oil, heating and gasoline, 217
Old Hobby Shop, The, 195
Old Seattle Paperworks, 165
Old Town Potters, 131
O'Leary's Books, 165
One More Time, 61
Optechs, 215
organic foods, *see* health foods
oriental products, 17-20, 29-31
Oroweat Baker's, Inc., 6
Osborn & Ulland, 150
Otto's Enterprises, Inc., 6
Outdoor Emporium, 151
Overlake Service League Thrift Shop, 50

P

P.J.'s Beauty Supply, 146
Pacific Food Importers, 30
Pacific Fruit & Produce Co., 31
Pacific Iron & Metal's Brownsville, 195
Pacific Linen Outlet, 106, 141
Pacific Rim, 31
Pacific Trail Sportswear, 68
Packrat's Delight, 201
Page One Book Exchange, 165
paint products, 121, 218
Pambihira Oriental Food Mart, 19
Pandora's Box, 61
Pandora's Castle, 61
Paperbacks and Things, 165
Paperback Exchange, The, 165
Paper Factory Outlet, 206
Paper Merchant, 207
Paper Pick-up, 207
paper products, 29, 30, 37, 125, 126, 136, 137, 139, 191, 192, 194, 196, 201-203, 205-209
Paperworks, The, 207
party goods, 135, 136, 139, 201, 202, 205-207, 209
pasta and noodle products, 17-19, 20, 31, 33
Patrick-Hart Inc., 126
Pavillion Outlet Center, 138-143
Payless Containers, 211
Peak Experience, 151
Pegasus, 165
Penny Lane Records and Tapes, 173
Perfect Fit/McDonald Co., 107
pet foods, 37, 213
Peterson Fruit Co., 22
Peterson's (Floyd Peterson Co.), 31
petite sizes, 141
Phase Two, 61
Philco Imports, 135
Phinney Street Co-op, 43
photo equipment and supplies, 215, 218
Pic-A-Dilly, 83, 142
plants, 128-130, 142
Plants and Planting Greenhouses, 130
plastic containers, 214

Plaza del Sol Jeans Warehouse, 83
Plenty of Textiles, 107
popcorn, 36, 37
Popcorn Plus, 37
Port Chatham Packing Co., 40
Porter-Cable, 185
Post Office Grocery, 39
Post Wall Covering Distributors, 120
potatoes, processed, 25
pottery, 127, 129-131
Powder River, Inc., 69
Prasad's, 135
pretzels, 38
Primo's Sales, 12
produce:
   fresh: 20-22, 24, 26, 28-31, 34, 43, 44
   frozen: 16, 24, 28, 30, 31, 35
Pro Golf Discount, 151
Puetz, 152
Puget Consumers Co-op, (Seattle, Eastside and Fremont), 43
Puget Sound Pretzel Co., 38
Puget Sound Tent & Awning, 215
Punch & Judy, 92
Purdy Co., The, 215

Q

Queen Anne Consignment Shop, 201
queen size fashions, 79, 139
Quiet Companion Books, 166

R

R.A. Mezoff Bookseller, 166
R.E.I. Co-op (Recreational Equipment Inc.), 152
R E and P, Inc., 87
R.L. Cook Sales and Supply, 187
R and S Sales, 178
Radio Products Sales and Electronics Supply Co./Zorbrist Co., 215-216
rags, 208
Rags 'N Riches, 50
Rags To Riches, 62
Raff's Shoes, 86
railroad ties, 215
Rainbow's End, Fashion Outlet for Children, 92

Rainier Labs, Inc., 218
rainwear, 65, 69, 76, 148, 150, 152
Rainy Day, 69
Rainy Day Books, 166
Rascal's Glad Rags, 93
Raymer's Old Book Store, 166
Read Products, Inc., 216
Rebound Building Materials Salvage, 189
Record Library, The, 170
records and tapes, 160, 162, 170-174
Redi-Vend (Tom's Snacks), 13
Redress, 62
Remco, 96
Remington Shaver Factory Service, 96
Rent-A-Bay, 180
Restaurant Equipment Brokers, 126
Restaurant Mart, 126
restaurants, 7, 36
restaurant supplies and equipment, 34, 125-127
Restmore Mattress & Furniture Co., 114
Rewear Apparel, 62
rice, 18-19, 20, 23, 25, 29-30
Rindler Display, 135
Rising Sun Farms & Produce, 26
Rita Dyke's Books & Records, 166
Ritz Emporium, 136
Roger's Candy Co., 13
Roos Market, 6
Rosebud Shop, 93
Roxy, 173
R Shoppe, 51
Rubato's, 173
Rubber Tree, The, 203
Rug Barn, The, 102
Rummage Sale, 216

S

S & H Salvage, 196
S.T. Produce, 22
SV Chemicals, 124
St. Vincent de Paul, 71
Safeway Stores, 1, 38
Saints Alive, 51
salvage:
   industrial, 189, 190, 193-198

228 Index

plumbing, 189, 192, 196, 197
salvaged and liquidated goods, 187, 189-198
Salvage Broker, The, 195
Salvation Army Thrift Store, 72
Salvator P. Trippy Furs, 205
Sam Heller Men's Clothing, 142
Sample Mart, 111
Sample Savings Co., (see K.C. and Friends, Co.), 81
Sample Shop, The, 83
Sample Shop, 84
Sample Shoppe, Etc., 84
SARCO, 96
sausage and deli meats, 15-17, 28, 31-33
Saks Off Fifth Avenue, 62
Scan Import Furniture, 111
Schoenfeld's, 112
seafood, 39-41
Seaport Chemicals Inc., 218
Seaport Industrial Supply Co., 183
Sears Bargain Basement Store, 117
Sears Burien Surplus Store, 117
Sears Retail Outlet, 118
Sears Surplus Store, 117
Seattle Better Bedding Co., 115
Seattle Book Center, 167
Seattle Building Salvage, Inc., 196
Seattle Card Mart, Inc., 136
Seattle Design stores, 116
Seattle Furniture Factory, 112
Seattle Office Furniture Mart, 178
Seattle Repertory Theater, 155
Seattle School District, 155
Second Avenue, 62
Second Closet, 51
Second Edition, 62
2nd Time Around, 63
Second Time Around Records, 173
Second Time Around Shoppe, 63
Second Wind, 152
Secret Garden Children's Bookshop, The, 93
senior citizens, 36
Service Wholesalers, Inc., 13
Sessions Surplus, 196
Sexton, John, & Co., 30

Shakespeare and Martin, 167
Shamek's Button Shop, 107
Shaver Center, The, 97
Sherman Supply, 197
Ship Ahoy Seafood, 41
shoes, new, 85-87, 139, 142, 143, 148-153
Shoe Factory, The, 86
Shop 'N Save Thrift Store, 51
shopping tours, 211
Shorey Book Stores, 167
Show and Sell, 52
silver, gold and precious gems, 132, 133
Silver Bow Honey Co., 26
Ski Bonkers, 155
ski equipment and clothing, 65-69, 147-153, 155, 156
Ski Rack Sports, 152
Ski Store, 153
Skil Corp, 185
Slater, W.A., Co., 32
Sleep-Aire Mattress Co., 115
Slumber Ease Mattress Co., Inc., 114
snack foods, 12-14, 23, 30, 31, 33, 38, 40
Sniagrab, 156
Software City, 218
Soroptomist Cupboard, The, 52
South Acres Building Demolition, 197
South Seattle Community College (Food Services Division), 7
Sparrow, The, 52
Speakerlab, 156
Sportcaster Co., Inc., 69
sporting goods and clothing, 65-69, 140, 141, 143, 147-153, 155, 156, 190, 192-195, 198, 218
Sports Outlet, 153
Sports Replay, 153
Spring Crest Drapery Center, 108
Sprout Garden, 23
sprouts, 21, 23, 27
Squak Mountain Greenhouse, 130
Standard Brands, 120
Star Tofu Mfg, Co., 19
Steiner Corp., 208

Index

stereos, tape recorders:
  new: 143, 156, 190, 194-195, 198, 212, 215-216
  used: 171, 173
Sterling Tool Co., 183
Steuart Seafoods Market, 41
Stonefelt & Co., 38
store fixtures, used, 178, 214
Strapped Jock, 143, 153
Stusser and Sweeney, 218
Sucker Factory, 13
Sunbeam Oster Appliance Service Co., 97
Sunset Vending Co., 13
Sunshine Anytime Bookstore, 167
Superior Linen Service, 87, 208
Sutliff's Candy Co., 14
Swan's Comic and Magazine Mart, 167
Swiss Pastry Corp., 7

T

T & T Tire Center, 180
TBA Wholesalers, Inc., 179
Tacoma Battery Supply, 180
Tacoma French Bakery, 7
Tacoma Luggage Co., 216
Tacoma School District, 156
Tacoma Screw Products Annex, 197
Tacoma Tent and Awning, 108
Tacoma Thrift Center, 52
teas, see coffee
televisions, new, 116-118, 143, 190, 194-195, 198, 212, 215-216
tennis equipment and clothing, 148, 150-153
This 'N That, 52
Thistles 'N Things Thrift Shop, 52
Thrift Center, 53
Thriftco (Thrift Korner), 53
tickets, 214
tiles (ceramic, concrete), 98, 99, 188
Timber Windows, 187
Time Travelers, 168
Tool and Equipment Distributors, 185
Tool Pros, 185
Tool Town, 183

tools, 129, 181-185, 190-198
Top Drawer, 63
Torino Sausage Co., 33
Totem Food Products, 38
Touch of Class, A, 64
Tower Records, 173
toys:
  new: 93, 94, 139, 140, 156
  used: 45-54, 61, 88-94
Toys R Us, 93
Tradewinds, 136
Treasure House Imports, Inc., 201
Tree House, The, 94
Trinity Thrift Shop, 53
Trinkets & Treasures, 53
Tru Art Picture Frame Co., 116
Trudi's Backroom, 79
Truland Greeting Card Co., 137
Tsue Chong Co., 20
Turn About, 64
tuxedos, 75
Twenty-fifth Street Market, 23
Twice As Nice Boutique, 64
Tyson's General Store, 197

U

Underground, The, 174
Unicorn, The, 94
Unicorn Bookshop, The, 168
Union Gospel Mission Bargain Center, 53
Upper Room, The, 168
Urban Renewal Records, 174

V

Vaar-M Beauty Supply, 146
Valerie's, 85
Valley Harvest, 23
Valley Supply Co-op, 217
Value Village Thrift Stores, 72
Van de Kamp's Holland Dutch Bakers, 7
Verax Chemical Co., 124
Vern's Tire Service, 180
Verone McCleery Foods Inc., 33
Videosyncrasy, 200
Viet Hoa, 20
Village Craftsman, The, 94

230 Index

vitamins, 25, 26, 42, 43, 202, 203
Volume Interiors, 106
Volunteers of America Thrift Store, 54

W

W & S Sales, 197
Walia's of India, 70
Walt's Milk House, 10
Warehouse 222, The, 178
Warehouse Kitchen Sales, 97
Washington Craft and Novelty, 202
Wallpapers To Go, 120
Wally's Book and Comic Exchange, 168
Washington King Clam, 41
Washington Liquidators, 198
Washington Pottery Co., 131
Weathermaster of Washington, 187
Wellworth's, 108
Wessco, 108
West Coast Gold & Silver Exchange, 133
West Coast Fruit & Produce, 23
West Side Supply, 123
Western Fish & Oyster Co., Inc., 41
Western Nut and Bolt, 198
Western Salvage, 198
Western Soap and Sanitary Supply, 124
Wherehouse, The, 174
Wholesome Foods Corp., 26
Wigwam Tent and Awning, 109
Will-Wood Prefit, Inc., 187
Windfall, 137
Windhaven Books, 168
window coverings, 102-109, 116-118
wines and liquors, 8, 9, 44
Winter's Office Furniture, 178
Wise Penny, The, 54
Wolfstone Co., The, 178
Woll's Baking, Co., 8
Wonder Hostess Thrift Stores, 8
Workshop, The, 109
World Tire Warehouse, 150
World Wide Distributors, Inc., 156

Y

Y's Buys Thrift Shop, 54
Ye Olde Fish Market, 41
Yesterday and Today Records, 174
Yesterday's, 64
Your Tool House, Inc., 184

REGIONAL INDEX

Auburn, 50, 51, 56, 61, 67, 71, 85, 97, 135, 153, 168, 188, 192, 197, 217

Bainbridge Island, *see* Bremerton/Bainbridge Island

Bellevue, 2-4, 6, 8, 50, 52, 56-59, 61, 62, 73, 74, 77-79, 82, 83, 86, 88, 92, 98, 100, 102-106, 109-111, 115, 116, 120, 123, 126, 133, 136, 144, 146, 149-151, 153, 159, 164, 165, 170, 172-174, 176, 179, 188, 193, 200, 204, 205, 207-212, 214, 218

Bothell/Kenmore, 47, 64, 88, 96, 160, 179, 188

Bremerton/Bainbridge Island, 8, 46, 72, 83, 115, 155, 204, 210

Burien, 7, 46, 50, 57, 71, 72, 75, 83, 90, 105, 117, 120, 180, 193, 204

Des Moines, *see* Federal Way

Edmonds, 60, 62, 64, 89, 90, 104, 120, 181

Enumclaw, 13, 67

Everett, 3, 4, 6, 8, 10, 12, 14, 21-25, 41, 45, 52-54, 56, 62, 65, 67, 71, 72, 83, 87, 95, 97, 98, 104, 106, 108-110, 122, 144, 145, 149, 159, 160, 163, 164, 170, 172, 176, 182, 183, 187, 188, 200, 205-207, 211-213

Federal Way, 6, 37, 55, 63, 67, 70, 71, 80, 83, 98, 145, 146, 164, 170, 187, 190, 204, 210

Gold Bar, 65

Issaquah, 10, 45, 88, 130

Kent, 2-4, 8, 11, 16, 19, 22, 30, 34, 38, 39, 51, 52, 56, 62, 64, 67, 90, 99, 103, 109, 112, 121, 125, 156, 159, 170, 179, 188, 191, 193, 197, 202

Kirkland, 31, 40, 43, 51, 55, 77, 81, 82, 94, 101, 121, 146, 168, 179, 188

Lacey, 164

Lynnwood, 16, 26, 46, 58, 64, 70-74, 76, 83, 89, 90, 93, 98, 101, 106, 108, 110, 120, 126, 136, 145, 146, 150, 151, 153, 159, 174, 179, 183, 185, 193, 195, 200, 205, 210

Maple Valley, 188

Marysville, 16, 34, 114, 158, 170

Mercer Island, 49, 84

Milton, 5

Mt. Vernon, 72

Mountlake Terrace, 7, 25, 53, 136

Poulsbo, 39

Puyallup, 15, 22, 59, 69, 75, 130, 163, 183, 188, 197, 204

Redmond, 15, 41, 48, 59, 61, 80, 83, 94, 102, 115, 129, 149, 164, 207, 211

Renton, 23, 50, 51, 57, 67, 72, 75, 83, 90, 102, 115, 129, 145, 148, 159, 164, 170, 184, 185, 188, 196

Snohomish, 9, 24, 26, 124, 199, 205

Snoqualmie, 25

Southcenter/Tukwila, 11, 66-68, 73, 77, 80, 83, 93, 106, 111, 116, 117, 120, 121, 138-143, 151, 153, 210, 211

Stanwood, 15

Sumner, *see* Puyallup

Tacoma, 3, 4, 6-8, 10, 12, 13, 15, 17, 23, 29, 30, 33, 35, 40, 41, 42, 51-53, 56-59, 61-63, 65, 66, 70-72, 75, 78, 83, 85, 87, 89, 90, 95, 96, 98-100, 102, 104-106, 108-117, 120, 123-126, 128, 130, 131, 144, 145, 147-150, 153, 154, 156, 158, 160, 162, 164, 165-167, 170, 172-174, 176, 177, 180, 182, 184-188, 192, 197, 201, 202, 204-206, 208, 214, 216, 217

Tukwila, *see* Southcenter

Vashon Island, 49

White Center, 18, 71, 162, 212

Woodinville/Duvall, 31, 39, 98, 106, 124, 128, 129